# Mike Meyers' A+® Guide to Operating Systems Lab Manual

## Michael Meyers
## Lloyd Jeffries

McGraw-Hill Technology Education

New York  Chicago  San Francisco  Lisbon  London  Madrid  Mexico City  Milan
New Delhi  San Juan  Seoul  Singapore  Sydney  Toronto

McGraw-Hill Technology Education
1333 Burr Ridge Parkway
Burr Ridge, Illinois 60527
U.S.A.

**Mike Meyers' A+® Guide to Operating Systems Lab Manual**

For information on translations or book distributors outside the U.S.A., please see the International Contact Information page at the back of this book. Some ancillaries, including electronic and print components, may not be available to customers outside the United States.

1 2 3 4 5 6 7 8 9 0 QPD QPD 0 1 9 8 7 6 5 4

ISBN 0-07-223123-8

This book was composed with QuarkXPress 4.11 on a Macintosh G4.

www.mhteched.com

**Sponsoring Editor**
Christopher Johnson

**Developmental Editor**
Pamela Woolf

**IT Skills Consultant**
Laurie Stephan

**Project Editor**
Laurie Stewart
Happenstance Type-O-Rama

**Copy Editor**
Kim Wimpsett

**Proofreader**
Paul Medoff

**Indexer**
Jack Lewis

**Composition**
Craig Woods
Happenstance Type-O-Rama

**Series Design**
Maureen Forys
Happenstance Type-O-Rama

**Cover Series Design**
Jeff Weeks

**Cover Photograph**
Tom Collicott/Masterfile

To Sue Leanox, for teaching me how to keep the smoke in the chips.

—Mike Meyers

I dedicate this book to my wife, Raylene. She is very patient and understands my need to immerse myself in the realm of computer repair and to teach others to become excellent technicians focused on user needs. She is always there with the barley green and vitamins to keep me going.

—Lloyd Jeffries

# About the Authors

**Mike Meyers** the industry's leading authority on A+ Certification. He is the president and co-founder of Total Seminars, LLC, a provider of PC and network repair seminars, books, videos, and courseware for thousands of organizations throughout the world. Mike has been involved in the computer and network repair industry since 1977 as a technician, instructor, author, consultant, and speaker. Author of numerous popular PC books and A+ and Network+ courseware, Mike is also the Series Editor for both the highly successful *Mike Meyers' Certification Passport* series and the *Mike Meyers' Computer Skills* series, both published by McGraw-Hill/Osborne. Mike holds multiple industry certifications and considers the moniker "computer nerd" a compliment.

**Lloyd Jeffries** came to Total Seminars after 31 years of customer service with NCR Corp. While at NCR, in addition to holding various management positions, he spent 20 years as a field technician and six years as a technical trainer, becoming an accredited course developer. His CBT course on computer number systems for NCR field technicians was also sold to the general public. At Total Seminars, he teaches CompTIA certification courses and manages other instructors. Lloyd's CompTIA certifications include A+, Network+, Server+ and iNet+.

# About the Technical Editor

**Lee Cottrell** has been teaching computer programming, hardware, and networking at the Bradford School in Pittsburgh, Pennsylvania, for more than ten years. In addition to his teaching duties, Lee maintains the school's LANs and computers. He holds an MS in Information Science from the University of Pittsburgh. Lee has authored and contributed to several books from the McGraw-Hill/Osborne line.

# Contents

# Acknowledgments

This book was a highly collaborative effort, and in this case, top collaborator honors go to Total Seminars CEO, Dudley Lehmer, who labored tirelessly over virtually every aspect of the project, even taking up an editing pen, to make sure it would be a success.

David Biggs did his usual superlative graphics work on an extremely tight schedule, as well as contributing to the writing and editing process. The A+ expertise and technical writing skills of Martin Acuña and Scott Jernigan were brought to bear with great effect on almost every chapter, ensuring that the final product was accurate, up to date, and educationally sound.

Scott, Martin, and David were ably assisted in their work by Total Seminars' crack editors Cary Dier and Cindy Clayton, as well as Jeremy Conn, our "Grow Your Own Geek Authors" project guinea pig.

Special thanks go to one of Lloyd's instructors, Lida Kafka, for her creative suggestions and valuable feedback.

As always, the folks at McGraw-Hill kept the train on the tracks and our noses to the grindstone. Chris Johnson's velvet-clad fist of iron kept us moving and "near" deadline. Pamela Woolf provided her usual superlative support as the project's developmental editor, and Laurie Stewart's Happenstance Type-O-Rama team wielded its copy editor's red pen and compositor's pica ruler with great effectiveness.

# Preface

## Information Technology Skill Standards and Your Curriculum

Students in today's increasingly competitive IT career market are differentiated not only by their technical skills, but by their communication, problem solving, and teaming skills. More and more, these professional skills are the ones that guarantee career longevity and success. The National Workforce Center for Emerging Technologies (NWCET) and McGraw-Hill Technology Education have partnered in an effort to help you build technical and employability skills in the classroom.

## NWCET and McGraw-Hill in Partnership

McGraw-Hill Technology Education and the NWCET have partnered with the goal of helping IT educators by making the IT skill standards more easily available and ready to use. McGraw-Hill Technology Education and the NWCET have developed four different products that will help you address the IT skill standards in your A+ programs and courses:

- A summary crosswalk that highlights the IT skill standards addressed by the McGraw-Hill *Mike Meyers' A+ Guide to Operating Systems*.

- A detailed crosswalk listing Technical Knowledge, Employability Skills, and Performance Indicators addressed by the compliant curriculum (textbook, lab manual, and learning activities in the instructor pack CD).

- 10 skill standards–based activities with associated assessment tools.

- A training document that helps instructors understand and use the features of teaching a skill standards–aligned curriculum.

These four products give you a very solid basis on which to deliver skill standards–based curriculum to your students. They are explained in some detail here:

**Summary crosswalk**  Maps the content of the A+ textbook to the NWCET IT skill standards. The crosswalk is shown in Table 1. Each chapter is listed with the correlated key activity performed by a technical support person as these have been identified in the industry as the skill standards. For instance, Chapter 2 correlates closely to Key Activity C2—Evaluate present data and system configuration. This table will help you demonstrate to your stakeholders that your curriculum maps to industry-identified workplace skills. It will also help you focus on which workplace skills are most emphasized in your curriculum.

| Chapter | Key Activity |
| --- | --- |
| Chapter 1 | C2: Evaluate present data and system configuration |
| Chapter 2 | C2: Evaluate present data and system configuration |
| Chapter 3 | C2: Evaluate present data and system configuration |
| Chapter 4 | C5: Install, configure and test new operating and application software and software upgrades |
| Chapter 5 | C4: Install, configure, and test system hardware and peripherals |
| Chapter 6 | C5: Install, configure and test new operating and application software, and software upgrades |
| Chapter 7 | D1: Operate computer system and run system applications |
| Chapter 8 | D1: Operate computer system and run system applications |
| Chapter 9 | C5: Install, configure and test new operating and application software, and software upgrades |
| Chapter 10 | C5: Install, configure and test new operating and application software, and software upgrades |

**TABLE 1** Summary Crosswalk

**Detailed crosswalk**   Illustrates how each chapter of the textbook, the lab manual, and the NWCET-developed supplemental learning activities on the instructor CD map to the IT skill standards. An excerpt of this crosswalk is provided in Table 2. This matrix maps out all your resources and provides you with sound learning outcomes and performance assessment criteria for your curriculum. This detailed crosswalk illustrates how a skill standards–compliant curriculum emphasizes both technical and employability skills.

**Learning activities**   Mapped to the IT skill standards and include learning outcomes, student handouts, and rubrics for assessment. There are ten learning activities on the instructor CD.

**Training document**   Provides you with background information about the NWCET IT skill standards, how they're developed, and how they're used within industry and education.

# NWCET Background and Mission

In 1995, the National Science Foundation (NSF) designated and funded the NWCET as a National Center of Excellence in Advanced Technological Education. The Center was created to advance Information Technology (IT) education and improve the supply, quality, and diversity of the IT workforce.

The National Workforce Center for Emerging Technologies has since become a leader in new designs for IT education developing products, services, and best practices that provide timely, relevant, and lasting solutions to meet the needs of IT educators and the IT workforce. The NWCET translates the rapidly

| Mike Meyers' A+ Guide to Operating Systems Chapter and Instructor Pack CD Activity | Learning Outcomes (students will be able to) | NWCET IT Skill Standards (Critical Function and Key Activity) | NWCET IT Skill Standards Technical Knowledge | NWCET IT Skill Standards Employability Skills | NWCET IT Skill Standards Performance Indicators |
|---|---|---|---|---|---|
| Chapter 1: Introduction to the Personal Computer | Describe how the PC works | **Critical Work Functions:** | Ability to identify system components | Ability to examine information for relevance and accuracy | Information is effectively and correctly gathered, organized and analyzed |
| | Identify common computer hardware components | C: Perform Hardware and Software Installation, Configuration and Upgrades | Knowledge of multiple operating systems, applications and hardware | | |
| Instructor Pack CD Activity 1: Careers in Technical Support | Describe microcomputer operating systems | C2: Evaluate present data and system configuration | | Ability to understand, interpret and recognize the accuracy of information | |
| | Describe a variety of careers that require A+ certification | | | | |

**TABLE 2** An Example of the Detailed Crosswalk

changing demands of the technology workplace into programs, curricula, courseware, and assessments that prepare students for current and future IT careers.

The NWCET is perhaps best known for its IT skill standards. Skill standards provide an agreement of what is expected to be successful in a given career area. They provide a validated, industry-derived framework upon which educators can build curricula. Using industry skill standards as the foundation for curricula will result in a closer alignment between educational programs and workplace expectations, and result in a better-skilled workforce. To support new and innovative IT programs and degrees, the NWCET (www.nwcet.org) provides other professional development opportunities for high school teachers and community college and university faculty. The Educator-to-Educator Institute (E2E) (http://e2e.nwcet.org), the training branch of the NWCET, is dedicated to helping IT educators achieve excellence in IT instruction. CyberCareers (www.cybercareers.org) is a web site oriented toward middle and high school students and teachers, providing a wide variety of career education materials such as job descriptions and an IT Interest Inventory.

# Instructor and Student Web Site

For instructor and student resources, check out www.mikemeyersaplus.com or mhteched.com. You'll find all sorts of stuff that will help you learn more about troubleshooting and fixing computers.

# Additional Resources for Teachers

Resources for teachers are provided via an instructor's resource kit that maps to the organization of *Mike Meyers' A+ Guide to Operating Systems* and includes solutions to exercises in the lab manual. This instructor's resource kit includes the following:

- Answer keys to the end-of-chapter activities in the textbook and solutions in the lab manual

- ExamView® Pro testbank software that generates a wide array of paper- or network-based tests, and features automatic grading

- Thousands of questions, written by experienced IT instructors

- A wide variety of question types and difficulty levels, allowing teachers to customize each test to maximize student progress

- Engaging PowerPoint slides on the lecture topics

- WebCT and Blackboard cartridges

# Chapter 1

## Introduction to the Personal Computer

### Lab Exercises

**A** modern PC may be faster and prettier than the original IBM PC, but the basic challenges haven't changed, and neither have the fundamentals of the solutions. This includes the basic requirements for an operating system, which provides the interface between the human and the hardware, and the platform from which to run the application software that makes all the magic happen! Different operating systems meet these challenges in more or less successful ways—some provide more control, some are more intuitive, some are better at sharing, and some are better at security. As a tech, you should have a basic understanding of these issues.

The A+ exams focus on Windows, and so does this lab manual, but one way to understand how Windows meets the requirements of an OS is to look at a completely different solution, so besides investigating the different flavors of Windows, you'll also investigate a major up-and-coming Windows competitor, the open-source OS called Linux. The final lab in this chapter helps you become more familiar with information sources for the many versions of the Windows operating system.

 30 MINUTES

## Lab Exercise 1.01: Investigating Windows

Your company's computers all run Windows 98 SE, but the boss has decided it's time to consider an upgrade to Windows XP. He comes to you, his computer tech, for information and advice, because he's heard conflicting stories about the ease and advisability of switching from Windows 98 to Windows XP. All the PCs meet the minimum hardware requirements to run XP, but he wants to know whether the software he already owns will work in XP, and whether his employees risk losing data and/or personal settings during such a transition.

---

✔ **Cross-Reference**

For an overview of Windows 9x and Windows XP, check the corresponding sections of Chapter 1 of *Mike Meyers' A+ Guide to Operating Systems*.

---

## Learning Objectives

In this lab, you'll learn how to use Microsoft's support web site to find answers to Windows software compatibility and upgrading questions.

At the end of this lab, you'll be able to

- Research Windows XP software compatibility issues on Microsoft's support web site
- Research Windows XP upgrade issues on Microsoft's support web site
- Explain how to use the Windows Application Compatibility Mode

## Lab Materials and Setup

The materials you need for this lab are

- Note-taking materials
- Access to the Internet

## Getting Down to Business

Thanks to the Web, techs have a much easier time finding the information they need to answer upgrade questions like the ones in this scenario. So grab your pen and paper, fire up your web browser, and start exploring for answers with the following steps.

**Step 1** The first place to check for information on Windows is Microsoft's very excellent support web site, in particular the collection of troubleshooting and how-to articles called the Knowledge Base.

To begin, go to http://support.microsoft.com (note that there's no "www"), and click the Search the Knowledge Base link.

Select Windows XP as the product about which to search, and type **software compatibility** into the Search for field. Click Go.

Take a look at the list of files you generated. Find and read the Knowledge Base article that explains how to determine if your hardware or software is compatible with Windows XP.

What is the article number? _____295322_____

**Step 2** After you read the article, click the link under More Information that takes you to the Windows Catalog. Using the Search box in the upper-left corner of the page, determine what versions of the following software have been approved by Microsoft as compatible with (or designed for) Windows XP:

| Acrobat | Versions: | 4.05, 5, 6, |
| WordPerfect Office | Versions: | 2000, 2002, 11 |
| HomeSite | Versions: | 4.5.1, 4.5.2 |
| Norton Antivirus | Versions: | 2002, 2003, 2004, XP 7.51 |

It's good to keep in mind that computers do exactly what you say, not what you mean. Try a Windows Catalog search for **Norton Anti-Virus** (with a hyphen). How does the result differ from the search above? _____ *Sorry, No Results* _____

It's also important to realize that it sometimes takes more than one type of search to find the best information. Return to the Search the Knowledge Base page, and search for **Norton Antivirus 2001** rather than just any version. Look for a more specific answer to the Windows XP compatibility question as concerns that particular version. Notice how the program's name is spelled in the article title.

What is the article number? _____ *286601* _____

### ✔ Hint

If you try a Windows Catalog search to check for compatibility and you come up empty, that doesn't necessarily mean the software won't work. It does mean you'll need to do some further research to determine whether and to what extent the program in question will function properly in the Windows XP environment.

**Step 3** Return to the Microsoft Help and Support page (http://support.microsoft.com), and click the Search the Knowledge Base link.

Select Windows XP as the product about which to search, and type **upgrade Windows 98** into the Search For field. Click Go.

Take a look at the list of files you generated. Find and read the Knowledge Base article that explains how to restore disabled startup programs after an upgrade to Windows XP.

What is the article number? _____ *298427* _____

What utility must you use to restore the startup programs? _____ *Microsoft System Configuration Utility Msconfig.exe* _____

### ✖ Warning

At this time, do not try out any utility you are directed to use in a Knowledge Base article, especially ones that affect the Registry. You will learn more about how to use these features of Windows in future chapters, but until you know more, you risk doing very unfortunate things to your system!

**Step 4** Return to the Microsoft Help and Support page (http://support.microsoft.com), and click the Search the Knowledge Base link.

Select Windows XP as the product about which to search, and type **program compatibility** into the Search For field. Click Go.

Take a look at the list of files you generated. Find and read the Knowledge Base article that explains how to use Windows Application Compatibility Mode.

What is the article number? _____292533_____

What is the alternate name for this feature? _____ *Windows Program Compatibility mode.*

Briefly explain what it does:

_____ *It provides an environment for running*

_____ *programs that closely reflects the behavior of earlier Windows operating systems*

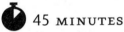 **45 MINUTES**

# Lab Exercise 1.02: Investigating Linux

Your company has just absorbed a small technology outfit, which means those employees are now part of your PC tech support responsibilities. The problem: they all run Linux on their PCs, rather than Windows. They will be forced to switch to the corporate Windows standard, but helping them with that transition will be part of your job. Your challenge is to get more familiar with Linux, in particular how it compares and contrasts with Windows, so you can help them with the transition.

---

✔ **Cross-Reference**

For a brief overview of Linux, read the "UNIX/Linux" section of Chapter 1 of *Mike Meyers' A+ Guide to Operating Systems*.

---

## Learning Objectives

In this lab, you'll learn how to explore the Web for good sources of information on alternative operating systems, using Linux as a case study. You'll gather some basic information on the differences between Linux and Windows and summarize your findings.

At the end of this lab, you'll be able to

- Research Windows alternatives such as Linux on the Web
- Explain some of the differences between Linux and Windows

## Lab Materials and Setup

The materials you need for this lab are

- Note-taking materials

- Access to the Internet

## Getting Down to Business

Linux is still pretty much David to Microsoft's Goliath, but it's definitely on the way to carving its own sustainable niche in the business computing arena. Most businesses run Windows on their PCs, but Linux and other Windows alternatives continue to thrive, and you're likely to encounter them at one time or another during your career. A good tech is at least familiar with the major players and knows how to find out more if necessary.

Once again, open your browser, grab your pen and paper, and begin the hunt!

**Step 1** The first place I go when I want to find something on the Web is the search engine Google (www.google.com). Successful Google searches are a bit of an art, but I've yet to find a better starting place. Go to Google, and start with the simplest search term: **Linux**.

The very first result should be the Linux Online site, the official "home" of Linux on the Web. Scrolling down through the first couple of pages of search results, you should also find the web sites of the major Linux versions—"distributions" in Linux lingo—such as Red Hat, SuSE, Debian, Slackware, and Mandrake. You should also find a documentation site, and the site of a magazine called *Linux Journal*. Record the URLs of these resources here:

Linux Online _____ www. linux. org

Debian GNU/Linux _____ www. debian. org .com

Mandrake Linux _____ www. linux-mandrake.com

Red Hat Linux _____ www. Redhat. Com

Slackware Linux _____ www.slackware.com

SuSE Linux _____ www. SuSE. com/us

Linux Documentation _____ www. linuxdoc. org

*Linux Journal* _____ www. linuxjournal. com

**Step 2** Go to the Linux Online site, click the General Info button, and find the answers to these questions:

Who created Linux? _____ Linux Torvalds

What other operating system is Linux based on? _____ Minix a version of Unix OS

What is the Linux mascot (a basic piece of "geek cred" info)? _____ Tux the Penguin

Linux is written and distributed under the GNU General Public License. What is the stated intention behind that licensing scheme?

*to quartee your Freedom to Share and Change Free Software — to make sure that the software is free for all to use.*

**Step 3** Go to the Debian GNU/Linux URL you conveniently recorded above, click the GNU Project link, and find the answers to the following questions:

What does GNU stand for? _____

In a sentence, what was the goal of the GNU Project?

_____

What four things do the GNU folks believe are fundamental to the concept of free software?

_____

_____

_____

_____

Return to the Debian home page and click the Read More link. Read their answer to the question, "How can you give it away?" Consider how the new employees—your PC tech "clients"—who have been part of the Linux world might feel about being required to switch to Windows. Briefly explain how understanding the Linux/GNU culture could help you work with them successfully to accomplish the changeover.

_____

_____

**Step 4** Return to the Google search page. Your next task is to search for comparative information on Linux and Windows. Start by searching for **Linux Windows compared** and see what information you can find. Then follow the alternate search suggestions for each question.

As a general rule, can you run a program written for Linux on a Windows system? _____ How about running a program written for Windows on a Linux system? _____ (Alternate search: **running program Linux Windows**)

Can Linux machines be part of a Windows network? _____ Can Windows machines be part of a Linux network? _____ (Alternate search: **Linux on a Windows network**)

What is the default file system for Linux? _____ (Alternate search: **default file system Linux**)

Of the two basic file systems (FAT32 and NTFS) used to format a Windows partition, which ones can a Linux system read? _____ Which ones can it write to? _____ (Alternate searches: **Linux NTFS read write; Linux FAT32 read write**)

The text mode interface in Windows (often referred to as a command line interface or DOS prompt) corresponds with what feature of Linux? _____ (Alternate search: **Linux command prompt**)

Are Linux text mode commands case sensitive (for example, ABC is different from abc or abC)? _____ Are Windows command line interface commands case sensitive? _____ (Alternate search: **Linux command case sensitive**)

 30 MINUTES

# Lab Exercise 1.03: Finding Answers to OS Questions

It's late in the evening, but you're still at the office, trying to solve a particularly intractable problem that seems to have afflicted the PC your client uses for billing applications. All the obvious things have failed, and you wish you had some other tech to bounce things off of—surely somebody else has encountered these symptoms before and would know what to do, if only you could find them. Ah, but you can, because the truth is out there, posted on the Internet by fellow techs, and you have a T1 line!

## Learning Objectives

In this lab, you'll locate some techie discussion boards and practice finding the answers to operating system problems.

At the end of this lab, you'll be able to

- Locate and search discussion boards for troubleshooting answers

## Lab Materials and Setup

The materials you need for this lab are

- A working computer system

- Access to the Internet

# Getting Down to Business

You can find the answers to many troubleshooting mysteries quickly and efficiently by checking to see if anyone else has encountered them before, and some of the best places to check are the online discussion boards frequented by PC techs. So run your favorite web browser and let's start looking!

---

✔ **Cross-Reference**

To review the basic functions of operating systems, check the "How the PC Works" section of Chapter 1 of *Mike Meyers' A+ Guide to Operating Systems*.

---

**Step 1** Your first stop in this lab is going to be a discussion board frequented by many A+ techs, which is sponsored by my company, Total Seminars. To get there, go to www.totalsem.com. Click the Tech Forums link at the top of the page and select Discussions. That takes you to the Total Seminars tech forums, where all manner of geeky topics are open for discussion.

---

✔ **Hint**

Whenever you come across a useful web site such as these discussion boards, bookmark it in your browser so you don't have to hunt for it next time you want it. It's helpful to organize these bookmarks into Favorites folders that match how you use them. Possible folder titles might include Hardware, Windows XP, Discussion Boards, Publications, Troubleshooting, How-to Articles—whatever makes sense to you.

---

**Step 2** To get an idea of the sort of help you can find, you're going to read some of the message threads in the Applications forum, where many OS topics are raised. Click the Applications forum link. There are pages and pages of posts, but instead of browsing, click the Search link (just above the Topic bar, between Register Your Free Account and Help).

Type in **XP**, uncheck the Case Sensitive box, and change the search selection from Subject Only to Entire Message. Click the Search button, and read through the resulting list of posts.

Now return to the search screen and using the same search parameters, type in **98.** Click the Search button and read through that set of posts.

**Step 3** Now that you've gotten a feel of a discussion board, let's check out another. This time, open this page in your browser: www.abxzone.com/forums/index.php. Scroll down to the Software Zone, and click the Windows NT, 2000, XP & 2003 link. This opens that discussion forum. Take a minute to browse through the subject headers as you scroll down the page. What sorts of topics do you see?

**Hint**

Web sites have the annoying tendency to either disappear or lose the information that was once relevant to a particular subject. If any of the links in this lab manual are no longer active or don't seem to contain information relevant to the exercise in question, please direct your browser to www.mikemeyersaplus.com to find an updated list of links or modified lab exercises.

At the bottom of the page you'll find a Search field. Let's suppose your client is complaining that it takes forever when he boots into Windows XP. Try typing **boot** in the Search field. Scroll through the first half-dozen pages of results and see if you can find useful posts. Make notes below of any useful suggestions, links, or instructions you find.

_____

_____

_____

_____

_____

# Lab Analysis Test

1. Briefly explain the four stages of the computing process.

   _____

   _____

2. Explain the difference between RAM and ROM.

   _____

   _____

3. Explain the basic function of an operating system and the role of its user interface.

   _____

   _____

4. Name at least six hardware components common to most PCs.

   _____

   _____

5. Name three ways in which Windows 98 improved upon Windows 95.

   _____

   _____

# Key Term Quiz

Use the following vocabulary terms to complete the following sentences. Not all of the terms will be used.

discussion boards

Knowledge Base

Linux

open source

operating system (OS)

Windows Application Compatibility Mode

Windows Catalog

1. Many PC techs and enthusiasts ask and answer computer troubleshooting questions by posting to online _____.

2. Microsoft provides the _____ to assist users of its operating systems in determining whether a particular version of a software program is compatible with a particular version of Windows.

3. Microsoft calls its comprehensive collection of troubleshooting and how-to articles covering all its software products the Microsoft _____.

4. If an OS is _____, it means that anyone can have access to its source code.

5. The _____ operating system includes many different distributions, such as Red Hat, Slackware, and SuSE.

# Chapter 2
## Introducing Microsoft Windows

### Lab Exercises

**E**very good PC technician should know the Windows environment inside and out. It's really pretty vital to any troubleshooting scenario. This won't happen automatically—it takes some practice and discovery on the technician's part. I don't mean you need to learn how to program but rather how to use the PC from a user's perspective. If there's anything magical about Windows, it's that there's almost always more than one way to get a desired result, and your preferred way might not be the same as your client's. As a good customer-oriented tech, you need to be flexible in your thinking, and this only comes through practice and more practice. During your studies, always look for more than one way to access the files or programs you need. Also, it's been my experience that many of the shortcuts and hot keys can be invaluable aids for a busy tech!

---

✔ **Hint**

Windows XP enables alternate-click menus for many icons. Be sure to alternate-click everything you see in Windows XP to explore the many shortcut menus and options.

---

In the field, the PC tech is perceived as the master or mistress of "All Things Technical." This might not be a fair assessment—why should a PC hardware technician need to know how to open and close the user's programs?—but that's the way it is. You need to be comfortable and confident with the Windows interface or you'll lose credibility as a PC technician. If you show up to service a PC and have trouble moving or resizing a window or locating the information you seek, this won't instill a lot of confidence in your client! There's nothing more embarrassing to a tech than having to ask the user how to find or use a Windows feature!

The creators of the A+ Certification exams understand this, so they test you on Windows user-level information, such as using power saving settings, changing the appearance of the interface, manipulating files and folders, locating information stored on drives, and using Windows' built-in OS tools. You must also know how to *navigate* to the basic Windows features—the A+ exam is big on identifying paths to features. Although you may already know much of the information about to be covered, the labs in this chapter will help you review and perhaps catch a few bits and pieces you might have missed along the way.

 30 MINUTES

# Lab Exercise 2.01: Windows XP Interface

Most new PC systems sold as of this writing have Windows XP installed, so that's where you'll start. There are two versions of Windows XP—Professional Edition and Home Edition. Microsoft is targeting Home Edition at consumers and Professional Edition at business and power users. At its most basic level, XP Home is a subset or truncated version of XP Professional. "Everything you can do in Home Edition, you can do in Pro," Microsoft says. The major advantages of Professional Edition include remote access, tighter security, and the ability to network in domains. For the purposes of these lab exercises, you'll use Windows XP Professional Edition.

## Learning Objectives

The main objective of this exercise is to familiarize you with the different "looks" of Windows XP. Because the Windows XP default theme looks different from Windows 9x, the paths to the old familiar ways of finding or configuring things such as the Desktop, Control Panel, and other options have changed.

At the end of this lab, you'll be able to

- Switch the system appearance between the new Windows XP–style (default) interface and the Windows Classic style, which looks more like Windows 98/2000
- Switch between the new Start menu mode (default) and the Classic Start menu mode
- Switch the view of the Control Panel between the Category view (default) and Classic view

## Lab Materials and Setup

The materials you need for this lab are

- A fully functioning PC with Windows XP Professional installed
- Ideally, access to other systems with Windows 2000, NT, and 98/Me installed for comparison

## Getting Down to Business

Windows XP has a new look that's more aligned with a task-oriented Web view. You'll notice changes right away when you open a window and look at the title bar and window contents. It's filled with bright colors, round edges, and big icons. Some think the new look is a great improvement and welcome it. Others really don't like it. Happily, though, if you don't like the new look, you can change it back to the familiar Windows 98/2000 Classic look.

---

✔ **Hint**

As a technician, you'll probably be working with all the flavors of Windows. Because the majority of systems installed still have the Classic look, it'll benefit you to learn Windows XP in the Classic modes and views first. Once you're comfortable with locating the configuration screens, practice again in the new Windows XP style of operating.

---

**Step 1**    To set the system theme to Classic mode, follow these steps:

a)    Alternate-click the Desktop.

b)    Select Properties.

c)    Select the Themes tab.

d)    Under Theme, use the drop-down menu to select Windows Classic (see Figure 2-1).

e)    Click Apply and then OK.

Change back and forth between the two interfaces. Each time, open other windows to observe the different looks.

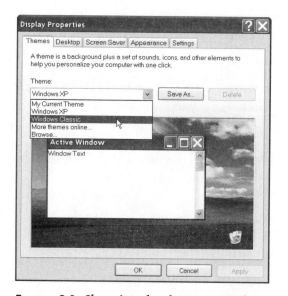

**FIGURE 2-1** Changing the theme to Windows Classic

**Step 2**   Changing the theme of your Windows XP interface doesn't change the way the Start button works, and XP's Start menu is significantly different from earlier versions of Windows. It still has the same functionality as previous Windows versions, but it has been restyled. As it does for the overall theme, Windows XP allows the user to change the Start button to Classic mode for those who prefer it that way. Before you can explore the new style of Start menu, though, you need to know which style you're working with. The following steps will ensure that your menu is set to the new Windows XP Start menu style:

a)   Alternate-click the Start button, and select Properties to display the Taskbar and Start Menu Properties window.

b)   Select the Start Menu tab.

c)   Select the Start Menu radio button (see Figure 2-2).

d)   Click Apply and then OK.

Click Start to open the Start menu. Notice that the left side of the Start menu shows the recently used applications. You can adjust the number of applications that Windows displays there. The top two applications are the default Web browser and e-mail client, which can also be modified. Follow these steps:

a)   Alternate-click the Start button, and select Properties.

b)   Select the Start Menu tab.

c)   Be sure the Start Menu radio button is selected, and click Customize.

d)   Under the General tab, decide on the following:

   •   The number of programs on the Start menu

   •   Whether to show the icons for the Internet and e-mail

   •   Which browser and e-mail client to use

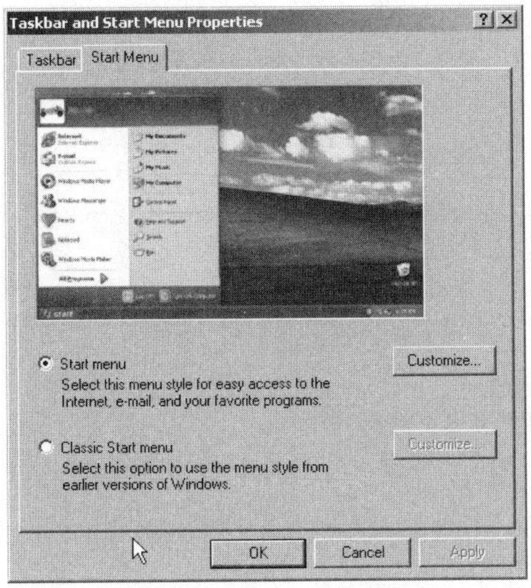

**FIGURE 2-2**  Using the Taskbar and Start Menu Properties dialog box

The Start menu's All Programs command shows a list of all programs installed on the system; it works like the Programs list in Windows 9x.

**Step 3**    The most eye-catching change for Windows XP is the presence of only the Recycle Bin icon on the Desktop. The icons for My Computer and My Documents no longer appear on the Desktop. In a default XP installation, these icons are now in the Start menu. However, you can add them to the Desktop:

a)    Click the Start button.

b)    Alternate-click My Computer or My Documents.

c)    Select Show on Desktop.

d)    Place both icons on the Desktop.

**Step 4**    For greatest compatibility with the lab exercises in upcoming chapters, you should now put your Start menu in the Classic Start menu mode.

To set the Start menu to Classic mode, follow these steps:

a)    Alternate-click the Start button.

b)    Select Properties.

c)    Choose Classic Start Menu.

d)    Click Apply and then OK.

---

**✖  Warning**

Most of the following lab exercises will assume you have the XP system in the Classic mode or are using Windows 98/2000.

---

**Step 5**    The other change that comes with Windows XP is the way you view the Control Panel. The Control Panel icon now opens by default in Category mode (see Figure 2-3).

Follow these steps:

a)    Select Start | Settings | Control Panel (Classic Start Menu).

b)    Depending how it was configured when you turned on the system, you'll see either the Category (default) or Classic view of the Control Panel.

c)    An option on the top-left sidebar in the Control Panel allows you to switch between the two modes.

d)    Set your Control Panel to the Classic view for the rest of the exercises.

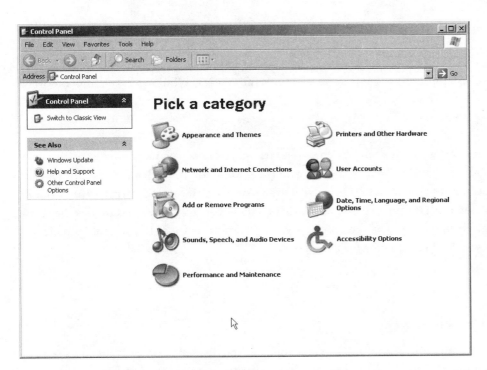

**FIGURE 2-3**  Viewing the Control Panel in Category mode

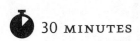 30 MINUTES

# Lab Exercise 2.02: Windows Desktop

The Windows Desktop is the starting point for all operations. It doesn't matter whether you have a new XP installation or an existing installation of Windows 98 from years ago; there's a Desktop graphical user interface (GUI) from which to get started. The purpose of this lab exercise is to help you become more familiar with the Desktop.

## Learning Objectives

In this lab, you'll work with certain features of the Windows Desktop.

At the end of this lab, you'll be able to

- Use the Windows taskbar

- Run a program from the Start menu

- Change settings for the Recycle Bin

- Change the appearance of the Desktop

## Lab Materials and Setup

The materials you need for this lab are

- A working computer running Windows 98/Me, Windows NT, Windows 2000, or Windows XP

✖ **Warning**

Because outlining every step for each Windows operating system is beyond the scope of this book, these labs are designed to be as Windows-generic as possible. If the lab exercise doesn't produce the expected results, it may be because you're using a different operating system than the lab systems used to write the exercise. I've tried to show you a variety of examples. Be flexible and look on your system for the same results via a different method. If you can't produce the results, please ask the instructor for assistance.

## Getting Down to Business

If you haven't really examined it before, take a close look at your Desktop. Everything you see has a purpose (with the possible exception of the background wallpaper—but even that has amusement value!). You have icons that start a variety of programs, such as Windows Explorer, Internet Explorer, and Outlook Express, and you have the taskbar with all of its built-in features.

✔ **Cross-Reference**

To refresh your recollection on the various parts of the Windows interface, refer to the "User Interface" section of Chapter 2 of *Mike Meyers' A+ Guide to Operating Systems*.

**Step 1**   The taskbar, by default, runs along the bottom of all Windows Desktops (although you can move it to any side: top, bottom, left, or right). The taskbar handles a number of critical jobs. Most important, it displays the Start button, probably the most frequently clicked button on all Windows systems. To find the Start button, look at the far left end of the taskbar (see Figure 2-4). Next to it is the Quick Launch toolbar. At the right end of the taskbar find the system tray—it displays the time, and small icons for system programs currently stored in RAM. In the middle of the taskbar are buttons representing the user-started programs currently running.

**FIGURE 2-4** Examining the Windows XP taskbar

**Step 2**   Microsoft says, "Everything starts with Start." Clicking the Start button opens the Start menu, where you'll find (with a few more selective clicks) the programs available on the system, the system settings (the Control Panel), and a few system tools such as Search and Help. Another useful feature is the ability to review your recent documents. Also, the Start button is where you'll find the Shut Down command (okay, that makes less sense, I agree).

Click the Start button. Move your mouse pointer slowly up to the Programs menu (remember, XP should be in Classic Start menu mode), and hesitate at each icon along the way. As the mouse moves upward through the Programs menu, notice how other submenus appear.

Look closely at the icons on the Start menu. Some icons have a small arrow pointing to the right on the edge of the menu bar. When you see an arrow, it means there's another menu beyond the one you're observing. To access the next menu, slide your mouse pointer across the highlighted Start menu icon area toward the arrow and into the next menu. This concept applies throughout Windows (see Figure 2-5). If you don't choose to click an option, you'll need to click somewhere else on the Desktop to tell Windows, "Never mind, close the Start menu."

Start again by clicking Start, sliding your mouse pointer up to Programs and then across and into the menu, and moving up to Accessories.

Move the mouse pointer across into the next menu and down to highlight the Notepad icon. If it doesn't show, you'll need to click the double arrows at the bottom of the menu to expand it further. Start the program by clicking the Notepad icon. Notepad should open in a window, and you should see a button appear on the taskbar. Most running programs show up on the taskbar in this way.

Close the Notepad program by clicking the button with the × in the upper-right corner of the Notepad window. Look again at the taskbar to see that Notepad no longer appears there.

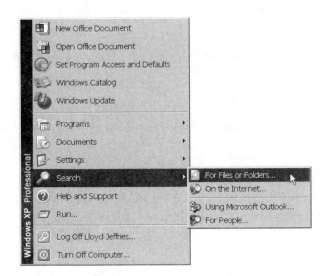

**Figure 2-5**  Exploring cascading menus

**Step 3**    Now look all the way on the right side of the taskbar. This is known as the *system tray*. Windows XP calls this area the *Notification area*.

At the least, you'll see the current time in the system tray, but on most Windows systems, you'll also see a number of small icons. These icons represent programs running in the background.

You often see icons in the system tray for network status, volume controls, and virus programs, and laptops may have additional icons for battery state and PC Card status. All kinds of icons show up there. What shows up in your system tray depends on your version of Windows, what hardware you use, and what programs you have loaded.

Click the various icons in your system tray to see what they do. Depending on the icon, you may need to use a single-click, double-click, or alternate-click and select from a menu.

**Step 4**    Now you'll look at customizing your environment a little. (Once again, if you're using XP, the Start menu should be in the Classic mode.)

Click the Start button, and select Settings | Taskbar & Start Menu. Then click the icon to run the applet. Notice this is the same configuration screen you get by alternate-clicking the Start button and selecting Properties (in Windows XP only). Yes, Windows offers many paths to each destination.

Windows 98, Me, NT, 2000, and XP each have a slightly different look, but you'll find the following three items listed in some manner on the leftmost tab of the Taskbar & Start Menu (or equivalent) dialog box in all Windows' versions:

**Show Clock**    Controls for displaying the time in the right side of the taskbar.

Turn off the Show Clock option, and click Apply. Did the time disappear from the taskbar?

_____

Select the Show Clock option, and click Apply. Does the time now show in the taskbar?

_____

**Auto Hide**    Some programs are screen hogs and require all the display area they can get. The Auto Hide feature minimizes the taskbar to allow more room on the screen.

Select Auto Hide, and click Apply. Did the taskbar disappear? _____

Move your mouse pointer toward the bottom of the screen. Does the taskbar pop up when you reach the bottom? _____

Turn Auto Hide off. Is the taskbar now on your screen? _____

**Always on Top**    This feature prevents programs from covering up the taskbar. If you observe a program using the entire screen, you know this feature is turned off, and you can't access the taskbar until you resize the program window.

**Step 5**    As you know, a file isn't actually erased from your hard drive when you delete it. When you delete a file in Windows, a copy of the file is saved in the Recycle Bin. It stays there until you empty the

Recycle Bin, until you restore the folder or file, or until the Recycle Bin grows larger than a preset size. Once you empty it, the files are permanently deleted, so make sure you're certain before you do this.

✔ **Hint**

Remember that most everything in Windows has a Properties setting, which you can generally access by alternate-clicking the object and selecting Properties. You can also access Properties by highlighting the object and pressing ALT-ENTER.

To change the Recycle Bin's properties, access the Recycle Bin settings by alternate-clicking the Recycle Bin icon on the Desktop and selecting Properties. The Recycle Bin Properties dialog box may look different because of the version of Windows you have, because you have multiple hard drives, or because of some other factor, but all versions basically work the same way (see Figure 2-6).

Note that 10 percent is the default amount of drive space to use for the Recycle Bin. Change this to 5 percent and close the Recycle Bin Properties dialog box.

✔ **Hint**

If a hard drive starts to run low on space, the Recycle Bin is one of the first places to check to see if you can free up some space.

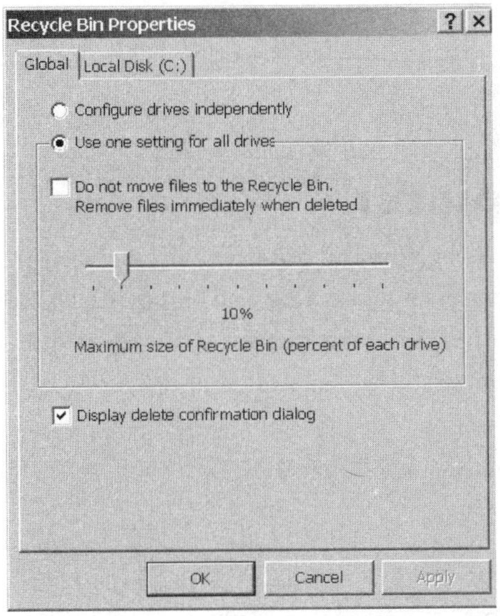

**FIGURE 2-6** Setting properties for the Recycle Bin

**Step 6** Microsoft gives you many ways to change the look of your Desktop to suit your personal preferences, from the color of the background to the size of the fonts. There are too many possible combinations to cover them all, so you'll look at only the most popular one, the background graphic. Follow these steps:

a) Alternate-click in an unused area of the Desktop, and select Properties.

b) Select the Desktop tab. (It's the Background tab in Windows 98/Me/NT/2000.)

c) Choose a background of your choice, and click Apply.

---

✔ **Hint**

When you become more familiar with Windows, you can use the Browse button to locate your own photo to use for the background.

---

**Step 7** One other thing to look at while you have the Display Properties dialog box open, which you should also remember for the A+ exams, is where to locate the Power Savings settings (except in Windows NT, which doesn't have this function):

a) Click the Screen Saver tab in the Display Properties dialog box.

b) At the bottom you should see the Energy Star icon. Click the Power button (the Settings button in Windows 98/Me) next to the Energy Star icon.

c) Look at all the different settings, and make notes to help you remember where to find them.

 30 MINUTES

# Lab Exercise 2.03: Windows Explorer

Windows Explorer is a program that enables you to see all the program and data files on a given storage device. Explorer works with both hard drives and removable media such as CDs and floppy disks. Both users and technicians alike use this program more than any other when they need to locate and manipulate files and folders.

## Learning Objectives

In this lab, you'll explore the Windows file structure.

At the end of this lab, you'll be able to

• Use Windows Explorer

• Understand and use the contents of the Windows and Program Files folders

## Lab Materials and Setup

The materials you need for this lab are

- A working computer running Windows 98/Me, Windows NT, Windows 2000, or Windows XP

---

✔ **Hint**

You can perform these steps on any Windows system, but some of them may involve functionality only available in Windows XP.

---

## Getting Down to Business

When you click (or double-click) a folder icon and a new window pops up, you're seeing Windows Explorer in action. It's really just a great graphical interface that enables you to see and manipulate files, folders, and their organizational structures quickly and easily, without memorizing a bunch of commands. Becoming familiar with its ins and outs is totally worth the effort.

**Step 1**   Begin by looking at the internal directory structure of Windows. Start Windows Explorer by selecting Start | Programs | Accessories | Windows Explorer (in Windows 98 the path is Start | Programs | Windows Explorer).

Look at the top of the list on the left pane of the Windows Explorer window; you'll notice an icon for the Desktop. Microsoft displays it there for your convenience, but actually, anything you put there is stored in a "Desktop" folder on your C: drive. Remember that C: is your root directory (on a standard Windows system), and no file stored on the hard drive is "outside" that. The first place to go exploring in the Windows directory structure is the root directory:

a)   Locate the My Computer icon in the left pane of Windows Explorer and click the plus sign (+). If it already has a minus sign (–) to the left, leave it there and continue.

b)   Locate the C: drive icon, and click it once to highlight it. There's no need to click the plus or minus sign at this time.

c)   In all Windows versions except NT, the right pane has will display the contents of the root directory of your C: drive (see Figure 2-7).

d)   Find the folders named WINDOWS (WINNT in Windows NT and sometimes Windows 2000) and Program Files. These two folders contain the majority of your operating system and program files.

e)   Click the plus sign next to the hard drive and then the WINDOWS (or WINNT) folder icon. Be sure to click the folder name in the left pane, not the plus sign. Look at Figure 2-8 for a sample of what you should see at this point if you're running Windows XP. If you're using Web view, Windows may require you to click a text link called Show Files (or something similar) before it will show you the folder contents.

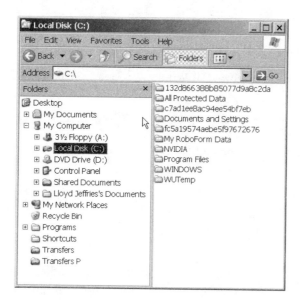

**FIGURE 2-7**  Viewing C:\ in Windows Explorer of XP

✔ **Hint**

My system is set up to view the files in the List view. Select View | List in Windows Explorer to display the files in the current folder in List View.

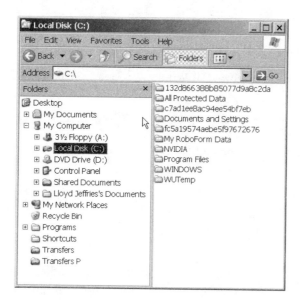

**FIGURE 2-8**  Exploring the WINDOWS folder

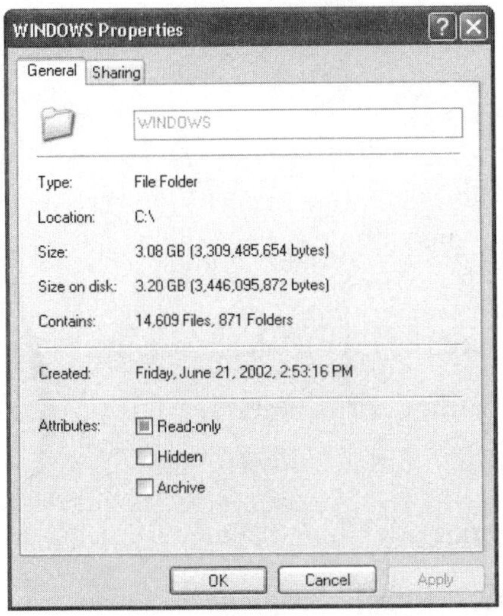

**FIGURE 2-9** Viewing the WINDOWS folder's properties

## ✖ Warning

Some system administrators may have changed the names of these folders, but in general this is not the best practice. When you call Microsoft for assistance, they always start by directing you to the default folder names, so changing them can increase your troubleshooting time.

Let's explore a little and have some fun. The WINDOWS folder in my system has more than 14,000 files in more than 800 folders (see Figure 2-9).

**Step 2** Alternate-click somewhere in the right pane, and select Properties. While looking at the different files and subfolders within the WINDOWS folder, try to locate some key files. (This exercise doesn't apply to Windows NT.)

a) Maximize your window by clicking the small box icon next to the × icon in the upper-right corner of the window. Then click the View icon in the toolbar at the top left of the screen, and select Details.

b) Notice the headings across the right pane, as shown in Figure 2-10. Click each of these headings to sort by that value. Click them again to sort in reverse order.

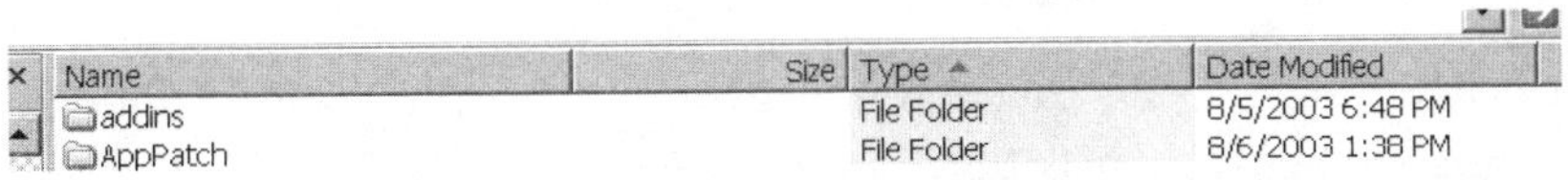

**FIGURE 2-10** Windows Explorer column headings in Details view

c)    Select Tools | Folder Options. (This step isn't necessary for Windows 98.)

d)    Select the View tab.

e)    In the Advanced settings area, remove the check mark next to *Hide extensions for known file types*, then click Apply and then OK. This directs Windows Explorer to display the filename extensions in Details view. This is useful generally for a tech, and these days also helps with things like identifying e-mail viruses hiding as (for instance) FILE.MP3.SCR.

f)    Sort the folders and files by Type, and see if you can locate the files with these extensions:

**.INI**    These are initialization files used to install and configure the system.

**.BMP**    These are Windows bitmap graphics.

**.EXE**    These are executable files (in other words, programs).

**.TXT**    These are text files containing only ASCII text and symbols, readable across a wide range of systems.

g)    Sort the list by Name, and locate these files:

**EXPLORER.EXE**    This is the Windows Explorer application you're using for these exercises.

**DESKTOP.INI**    This contains the configuration data for your Desktop.

**WIN.INI**    This contains configuration settings for the boot process.

---

### ✖ Warning

Do not alter these files in *any* way! You won't like the results.

---

**Step 3**    Although MS-DOS is no longer used as an operating system, some MS-DOS applications (commands) are still very much alive. There's likely to come a time when as a PC technician you'll need one of these DOS tools, so you'll now learn where to find them:

a)    While still in Windows select Explorer, select My Computer | C: | WINDOWS | System32 and open the folder. In Windows 98, select My Computer | C: | WINDOWS | Command. This folder stores all the MS-DOS applications. Again, Windows NT doesn't display the files, so this exercise won't work on that system.

b)    Sort the details list by Type, scroll down to the MS-DOS applications, and locate these files (see Figure 2-11):

**FORMAT.COM**    This is used to prepare hard drives and floppy disks for storing data

**EDIT.COM**    This text editor program can create and modify configuration files in the command line mode. The Windows equivalent is Notepad.

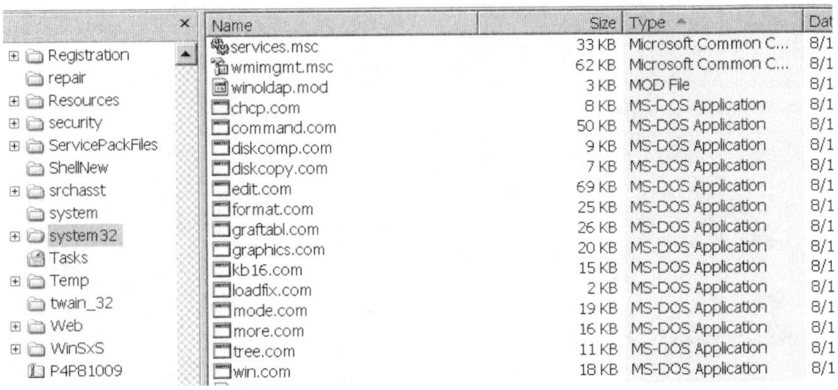

**FIGURE 2-11** Locating MS-DOS applications in XP

**Step 4**   Some of the other important folders and their contents are listed here. Look at each one to gain more experience using Windows Explorer. Remember, the location may be slightly different across the Windows family of operating systems. For instance, Windows 2000 uses WINNT as the default Windows folder. These are the folders you'll find:

**WINDOWS\CURSORS**   The folder where Windows stores the many different cursors you may use.

**WINDOWS\FONTS**   Windows stores all its fonts in this folder. Note that fonts usually have one of two extensions, .FON or .TTF. The .FON files are the old-style screen fonts and the .TTF files are modern TrueType fonts. Double-click a font icon to see what it looks like. The True-Type font icons will be the ones with two "T"s or the ones with a big "O." The .FON icons will have a red "A." Some users even print the font and keep them in a three-ring binder for later reference.

**WINDOWS\HELP**   This folder is the default location for all .HLP and .CHM (help) files. Open one to see what program uses it.

**WINDOWS\MEDIA**   This folder is the default location for sounds and audio clips. Double-click a file with a .WAV or .MID extension to hear sounds.

**WINDOWS\SYSTEM32**   This folder is the heart of Windows. Here you can see the core operating system files: GDI.EXE, KRNL386.EXE, and USER.EXE (Windows 98 has these three files in WINDOWS\SYSTEM). This folder also stores almost all of the .DLL files used by Windows 2000/XP.

**Step 5**   Collapse the WINDOWS folder, and expand the Program Files folder (see Figure 2-12). Windows 2000 and XP don't like people messing around in these folders, so you may have to look to the left and click Show Files to see the folders. This is the default location for applications installed on your system. (Remember to scroll down if you can't see the end of the list.)

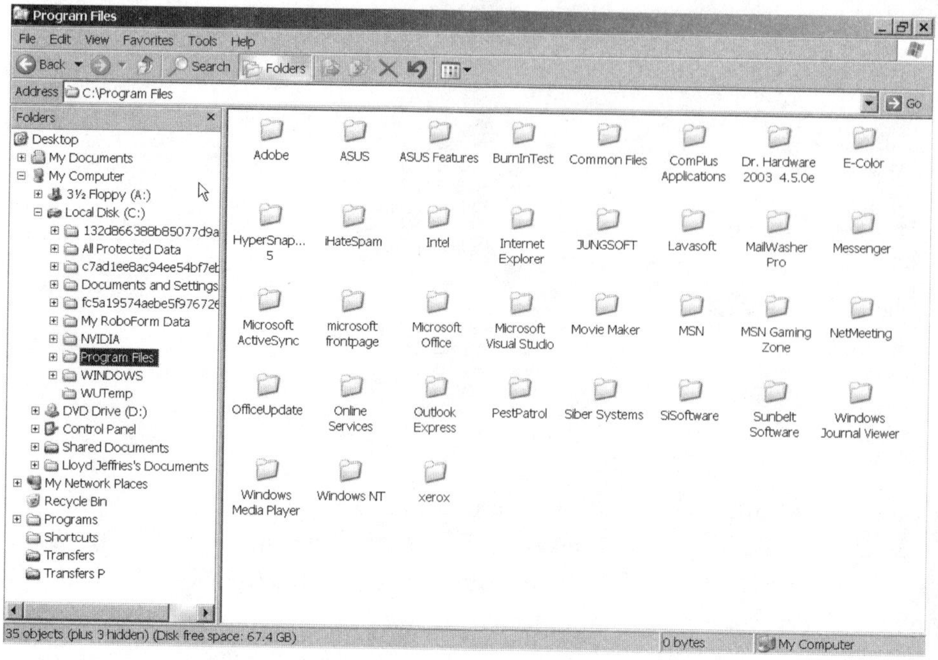

**FIGURE 2-12**  Exploring C:\Program Files in Windows Explorer

Follow these steps:

a)   Open the Windows Media Player subfolder, and find the application. Remember to look for the .EXE extension.

b)   Click the .EXE file icon to start the program.

c)   Close the program you just opened.

d)   Exit Windows Explorer.

30 MINUTES

# Lab Exercise 2.04: Windows Control Panel

The Windows Control Panel is the technician's toolbox. It contains the tools you need to do everything from changing the mouse settings to installing new device drivers. It isn't the purpose of this lab exercise to examine every icon in the Control Panel but just to go over a few so you'll be familiar with them. Some of the *applets* (as they're called) are specific to particular hardware, and others are for software configuration. Windows initially sets up defaults that work for most installations, but you, the technician, may need to tweak some of the settings. Also, not all the features are enabled in a normal installation, so you'll enable/disable features according to the needs of the user.

✔ **Cross-Reference**

For a refresher on the Windows Control Panel, refer to the "Control Panel" section of Chapter 2 of *Mike Meyers' A+ Guide to Operating Systems*.

## Learning Objectives

In this lab, you'll practice accessing the Control Panel and making configuration adjustments.

At the end of this lab, you'll be able to

- Navigate to the Control Panel
- Explain the use of some common Control Panel applets

## Lab Materials and Setup

The materials you need for this lab are

- A working computer running Windows 98/Me, Windows NT, Windows 2000, or Windows XP

## Getting Down to Business

The Control Panel is the toolbox, and one of the key tools in the Control Panel is the Device Manager. The Device Manager lists all your system hardware. From here you can load drivers, set resources, and configure other aspects of your hardware devices. You'll now get familiar with both.

**Step 1**   As a technician, you'll access the Control Panel and the Device Manager often. You really do need to know the path to these important tools in all versions of Windows. The A+ exam has numerous questions about paths to these tools.

✔ **Hint**

Throughout the rest of this manual, when a lab involves changing settings located in the Control Panel or the Device Manager, the directions will assume you know how to get that far, and the steps will begin with the Control Panel or Device Manager already open. Refer back to this exercise if you need a refresher on opening the Control Panel.

a)   To open the Control Panel, select Start | Settings | Control Panel. This path applies to all versions of Windows (XP in the Classic Start menu mode). The Control Panel dialog box opens, as shown in Figure 2-13.

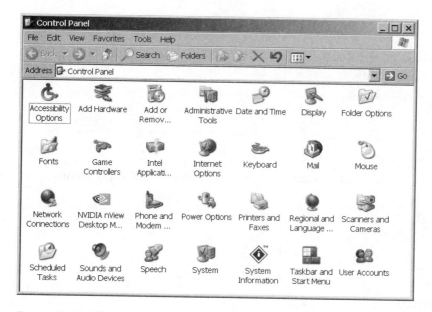

**FIGURE 2-13** The Control Panel in Windows XP

b) To open the Device Manager, follow these steps:

**Window 2000/XP in Classic mode**   Double-click the System icon to open the System applet, and select the Hardware tab. Click the Device Manager button.

**Windows 98/Me**   Double-click the System icon, and select the Device Manager tab. Note the list of hardware installed in your system. Expand various items to see the list of devices in each area. Highlighting any device, alternate-clicking, and selecting Properties will give you configuration information for that device. You'll return here later in the lab manual to configure these devices. Windows NT has no Device Manager but rather a Devices applet.

c) Close the Control Panel, as well as the Device Manager and the System window.

**Step 2**   You'll now examine some other applets in the Control Panel:

a) Double-click the Display icon. This is the same window you get if you alternate-click the Desktop and select Properties.

b) Notice the tab headings. Three are common to all flavors of Windows: Screen Saver, Appearance, and Settings. Windows 98 and 2000 also have Background, Web, and Effects tabs. Windows XP incorporates those three tabs into two new ones named Themes and Desktop. There's also a tab called Plus! in Windows NT.

---

**✖ Warning**

Clicking an Advanced button in the Display applet can give you access to many special features of your particular monitor/video card, including the refresh rate. Be sure you know what you're doing before you change these settings!

✔ **Hint**

If you click the Apply button instead of the OK button after making a change, the Display applet will remain open after the change takes effect—which is useful when you need to experiment a bit.

c)   Return to the Control Panel and double-click the Sounds icon (Windows 98), the Sounds and Multimedia icon (Windows 2000 and Me), or the Sounds and Audio devices icon (Windows XP) to open that dialog box.

d)   Again you'll see tabs at the top left of the dialog box. Most of your applets will be similar to this. Explore each tab, and become familiar with what each does. Make changes to see the results. Be sure you remember or record the original settings so that you can reset them.

e)   Reset all of your "experiments," and close the applet.

**Step 3**   Keyboard and mouse action settings are definitely a matter of personal preference. Be careful to tell the user if you make any changes to these. If you need to speed them up for your own use while troubleshooting a PC, remember to slow them down again so the user isn't frustrated by keys that repeat or a mouse cursor that races across the screen out of control. To adjust the Keyboard settings:

a)   Double-click the Keyboard icon in the Control Panel.

b)   Change the cursor's blink rate and test it.

c)   Change the key repeat rate and delay settings. A minor adjustment here can really help a heavy-fingered user.

d)   Close the Keyboard applet.

✔ **Hint**

The Mouse applet can have many different looks depending on whether the system uses a default Windows driver or special drivers for the particular mouse. You may have to explore your applet to find these settings.

e)   Double-click the Mouse icon to open the Mouse applet.

f)   Change from a right-hand to a left-hand mouse. Try it out. Brain hurt? Change it back. Ahhh.

g)   Change the double-click speed. Slow it down a bit. Easier? Slow it down more. Annoying? Speed it up. Can you click fast enough?

h)   Change the mini-icons that represent your mouse pointer, such as the arrow, hourglass, and so on. Try a couple of different sets. Can you think of situations where some of the alternate icon sets might be useful?

    i)    Change the pointer options. Change the speed at which it travels across your screen. Everyone has their own sweet spot for this, so experiment to find yours. Turn on pointer trails. Cool or annoying? If you have a Snap To option, turn that on. Now open a dialog box and watch the pointer jump to the active button. Convenient, or too much help? Turn off any features you don't want to retain.

    j)    Now that you've tweaked your mouse performance, close the applet.

**Step 4**    The A+ exam includes questions about user accessibility. Know where and what settings you can change to accommodate the hearing and visually impaired:

    a)    Double-click the Accessibility Options icon.

    b)    Notice there are Keyboard, Sound, Display, Mouse, and General tabs (see Figure 2-14).

    c)    Select the Display tab.

    d)    Turn on the Use High Contrast option, and click Settings (see Figure 2-15).

    e)    Choose a scheme you like, and click OK.

    f)    Click Apply in the Accessibility Options dialog box to see how it looks.

    g)    Turn off the Use High Contrast option, and click Apply and then OK.

    h)    Close the Accessibility Options dialog box.

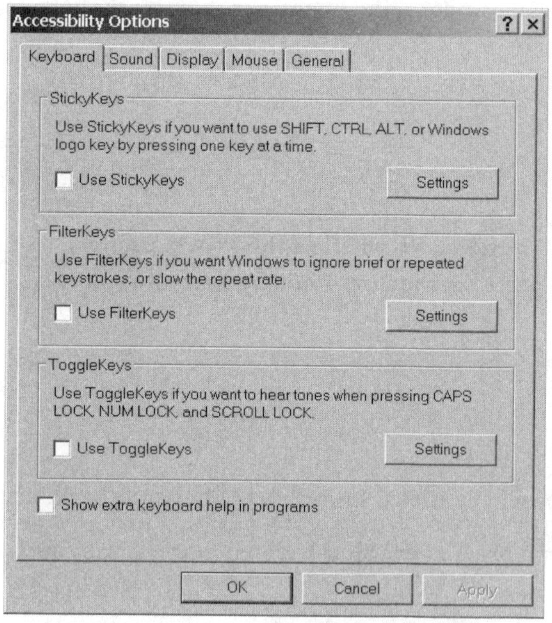

**FIGURE 2-14** Accessing the Accessibility Options dialog box

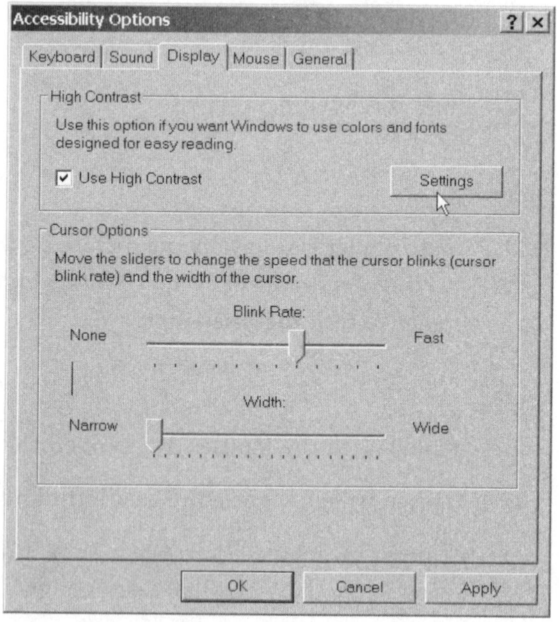

**FIGURE 2-15** Setting the High Contrast option for the visually impaired

**Step 5**    One more commonly used applet is the Date/Time applet.

Open the Date/Time applet in the Control Panel. This applet has been around since the dawn of time, more or less, when computers didn't automatically adjust themselves for Daylight Saving Time.

Adjust the date and time. Notice you can do this either by scrolling with the arrows or by highlighting the fields. This feature can come in handy if you travel and want to change the time zone on a portable computer.

 30 MINUTES

# Lab Exercise 2.05: Windows Registry

The Registry stores everything about your PC, including information on all the hardware in the PC, network information, user preferences, file types, and virtually anything else you might run into with Windows. The hardware, software, and program configuration settings in the Registry are particular to each PC. Two identical PCs with the same operating system and hardware can still be remarkably different because of user settings and preferences. Almost any form of configuration done to a Windows system involves editing the Registry.

> ✖ **Warning**
>
> When changing the Registry, proceed with great care—making changes in the Registry can cause unpredictable and possibly harmful results. To paraphrase the old carpenter's adage, think twice, change once!

## Learning Objectives

In this lab, you'll familiarize yourself with the Windows Registry and the REGEDIT command.

At the end of this lab, you'll be able to

- Access the Registry using REGEDIT

- Use the functions of the six Registry Keys

## Lab Materials and Setup

The materials you need for this lab are

- A working computer running Windows 98/Me, Windows NT, Windows 2000, or Windows XP

## Getting Down to Business

A technician needs to know how to access the Registry and modify the configuration based on solid support from Microsoft or other trusted sources. Your main interface to the Registry is the Control Panel. Changes made through the applets in the Control Panel result in modifications to the Registry settings. To see what's going on behind the scenes, though, you'll explore the Registry directly in this exercise using the REGEDIT command.

✔ **Cross-Reference**

For more detail on the Windows Registry and working with REGEDIT, refer to the "Registry" section of Chapter 2 of *Mike Meyers' A+ Guide to Operatiing Systems*.

**Step 1**   You almost never access the Registry directly. It's meant to work in the background, quietly storing all the necessary data for the system, updated only through a few menus and installation programs. When you want to access the Registry directly, you must use the Registry Editor (REGEDIT).

✔ **Hint**

Remember that the Registry is a binary file. You can't edit it using EDIT, Notepad, or any other text editor.

To edit the Registry directly, follow these steps:

a)   Select Start | Run, type **REGEDIT**, and then click OK (see Figure 2-16) to start the Registry editor.

b)   Note the five or six main subgroups or root keys in the Registry (see Figure 2-17). Some of these root key folders may be expanded. Click the minus sign by any expanded folders. Do a quick mental review—do you know the function of each Registry Key? You should!

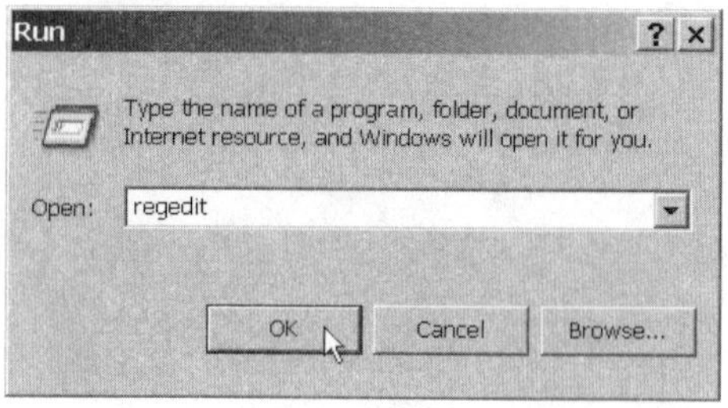

**FIGURE 2-16** Starting the Registry Editor

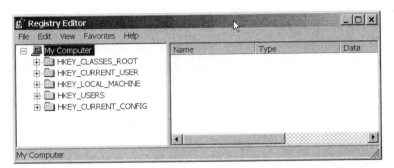

**FIGURE 2-17**  Viewing the five main subgroups of the Windows
XP Registry

c)   Now to test yourself for real. Referring to the textbook as necessary, match the listed keys
with their definitions by writing the definition number next to the corresponding key:

HKEY_CLASSES_ROOT          _5_

HKEY_CURRENT_USER          _6_

HKEY_LOCAL_MACHINE        _1_

HKEY_USERS                       _2_

HKEY_CURRENT_CONFIG      _4_

HKEY_DYN_DATA                _3_ (Windows 98)

1.   Contains the data for non-user-specific configurations and includes every device in your
PC plus those you've removed.

2.   Contains the personalization information for all users on a PC.

3.   Contains a snapshot of the hardware in use. This subgroup is built each time the system
boots and is stored in RAM.

4.   Contains additional hardware information when there are values in
HKEY_LOCAL_MACHINE such as two different monitors.

5.   Defines the standard class objects used by Windows. The information stored here is used
to open the correct application when a file is opened.

6.   Contains the current user settings, such as fonts, icons, and colors on systems that are set
up to support multiple users.

**Step 2**   Expand the HKEY_CLASSES_ROOT key by clicking the plus sign. Notice there are more subkeys
underneath it, some of which have subkeys of their own, and so on. Select any subkey folder, and note
that the values for the entries show up on the right.

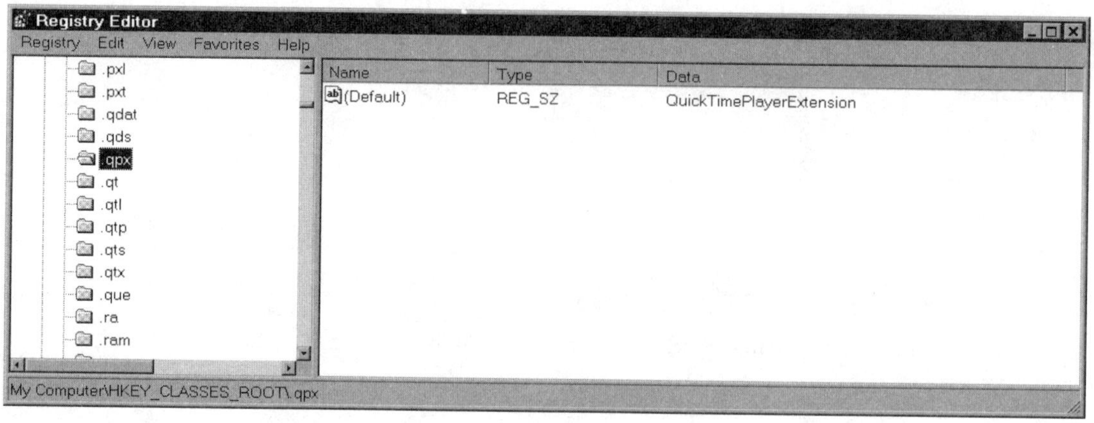

**FIGURE 2-18** QuickTimePlayerExtension key chosen

Before you start changing the Registry, it's a good idea to learn how to "back up" the keys by exporting and importing them:

a) Look for a subkey that won't affect your system's operation if it were to be erased for good. For instance, in the image shown in Figure 2-18, I've chosen the QuickTimePlayerExtension (.qpx).

b) Highlight the key, and open the Registry menu at the top left of the window. Scroll down to Export Registry File, and click. Save the key in a folder where you can find it again, and give it a useful name that you won't forget.

c) Highlight the key again, and press DELETE. You've eliminated that key from the Registry.

d) To retrieve it, open the Registry menu again, choose Import Registry File, and click. Navigate to where you saved the key, and double-click it. You should see a message that tells you the key was successfully imported.

✔ **Hint**

This next step has actually happened, and the user was really thankful when his misconfiguration was fixed.

**Step 3** Imagine you're in the Control Panel adjusting your mouse settings, and you adjust the mouse double-click speed to the maximum (fastest) and close the window without testing it. When you try to use the system, you can't double-click the mouse fast enough to even get back into the Control Panel to fix it. So what do you do? Follow these steps (the first three steps are just so that you can see where the slider is currently to compare it later):

a) Access the Control Panel, and open the Mouse applet.

b) Adjust the slider for the double-click speed to the middle position, and test to be sure it works.

c)   Click Apply and then OK. Close the Mouse applet and Control Panel.

d)   Open the Registry Editor, and make sure the entry My Computer is highlighted in the top of the left pane.

e)   Select Edit on the toolbar and then select Find to search for the mouse double-click speed. In the Find What field, type **doubleclickspeed** (be sure to spell it as one word, no spaces). Check the Match Whole String Only box. Click Find Next. You want only the *first* occurrence it finds. There are other things with that name that you don't want to change.

f)   When REGEDIT finds the file, alternate-click the word "doubleclickspeed" in the right pane and select Modify.

g)   Change the value to something between 100 and 900 (milliseconds); 100 is very fast.

h)   Click OK.

i)   Close the Registry Editor, and reopen the Mouse applet in the Control Panel.

Did the slider move from where it was? _____

j)   For more practice, set your double-click speed to the fastest setting in the Control Panel and go to the Registry to slow it down.

✔  **Hint**

The web site www.winguides.com/registry is full of working Registry fixes.

# Lab Analysis Test

1.   Your friend Brian calls you and asks if he can make his new Windows XP system look like the Windows 2000 system he uses at work. He says he doesn't like the bright, cartoonish style, and the Start menu is different. Explain to Brian what he can and can't do to change the look of Windows XP.

_____

_____

2.   Maria has deleted a set of pictures. She thought she had backups but now she can't locate them. Where should she check first if she wants to recover the deleted pictures?

_____

_____

3.  When you install Windows XP for the first time on Joe's PC, he notices that Desktop icons he's accustomed to seeing are missing. As a matter of fact, only the Recycle Bin icon is present. Where and how can you add the Desktop icons he's used to seeing in Windows 98?

    _____

    _____

4.  One of your clients using Windows XP called your Help Desk because he's experiencing difficulties using the mouse. He says his mouse moves too fast, and icons don't respond when he double-clicks them. What's wrong? Where would you direct him to go to fix his problems? Give the complete path.

    _____

    _____

5.  Which is a safer place for trained technicians to make changes or modifications: the Control Panel or the Registry? Explain your choice.

    _____

    _____

# Key Term Quiz

Use the following vocabulary terms to complete the following sentences. Not all the terms will be used.

Classic mode

Control Panel

Recycle Bin

REGEDIT

Start button

Taskbar

1.  The Registry contains all the configuration data and can be accessed directly using _REGEDIT_.

2.  When you delete files, Windows actually moves them into the _Recycle Bin_.

3.  The System, Display, and Mouse applets are found in the _Control Panel_.

4.  To give Windows XP the look of Windows 98, switch to the _Classic Mode_.

5.  The Start button and system tray are parts of the Windows _Taskbar_.

# Chapter 3

## Features and Characteristics of Windows

### Lab Exercises

**O**nce you've mastered the basics of the Windows interface, it's time to work with the quirks and features of the two families of Windows operating systems, Windows 9*x*/Me and Windows NT/2000/XP. The rest of the chapters in this book take you in depth into the utilities and configurations you'll use as a tech. This chapter gives you a first opportunity with three areas: customizing the boot menu in Windows 9*x*/Me, organizing users and groups in Windows NT/2000/XP, and working with NTFS permissions.

 30 MINUTES

# Lab Exercise 3.01: Customizing the Boot Menu in Windows 9*x*/Me

Windows 95, 98, and 98 SE offer a full boot menu that enable you to boot to various interfaces, including the command line, Safe mode, Safe mode with networking support, and more. Windows Me has some of the options, but offers a much more limited selection. The cool part about the boot menu is you can very easily customize it. Want to show a menu every time you boot your PC? Want to adjust how much time the user has to get to the boot menu before Windows tries to boot normally into the GUI? Editing the MSDOS.SYS file gives you almost complete control over the boot menu.

## Learning Objectives

This lab shows you how to configure a Windows 9*x*/Me system by editing a text file. The skill comes in handy for techs of all stripes.

At the end of this lab, you'll be able to

- Change file attributes in Windows

- Edit a system file successfully in Window 9*x*/Me

- Alter boot options in Windows 9*x*/Me

## Lab Materials and Setup

The materials you need for this lab are

- A fully functioning PC with Windows 98 or 98 SE installed (this lab will work with Windows 95 and Me, but the two versions of 98 offer more options and better stability)

## Getting Down to Business

Changing the boot menu in a Windows 9x/Me system requires you to edit the MSDOS.SYS file, a file with hidden, read only, and system attributes turned on by default.

**Step 1**    In My Computer or Windows Explorer, go to the root directory of your C: drive, alternate-click the MSDOS.SYS file, and select Properties. On the General tab, deselect the check boxes next to Hidden and Read-only. Click OK.

---

✔ **Hint**

If you don't see the MSDOS.SYS file in the root directory, chances are good that you have My Computer or Explorer set up to hide hidden and system files. (It's the default option, designed to protect unskilled users from deleting or corrupting necessary OS files!) As a tech, you need to see these files, though, so go to View | Folder Options, select the View tab, and scan through the list of check boxes for one that says something like "Do not show hidden files and folders" or "Show hidden files and folders." (Different versions of Windows 9x/Me differ slightly in the wording of these options.) Make sure to deselect the former and to select the latter. MSDOS.SYS should appear as soon as you click the OK button.

---

**Step 2**    Double-click the MSDOS.SYS file to bring up the Open with dialog box. Select a text editor such as Notepad to open the file. You should see something like Figure 3-1.

---

✔ **Cross-Reference**

Refer to the "Boot Menu" and "MSDOS.SYS" sections in Chapter 3 of *Mike Meyers' A+ Guide to Operating Systems* for details on startup options and edits you can make to MSDOS.SYS.

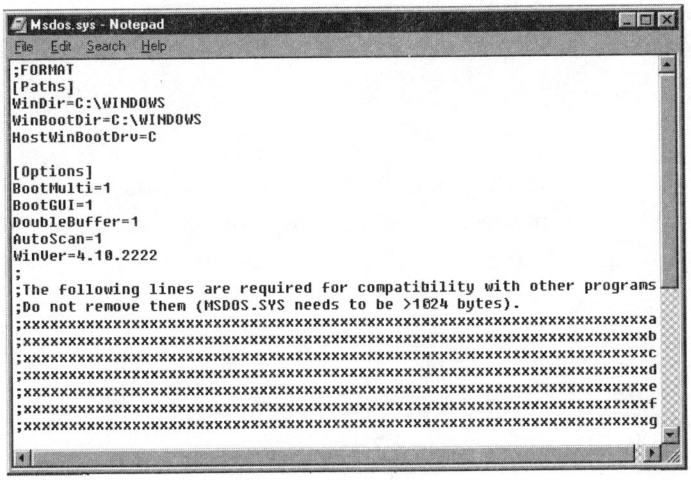

---

**FIGURE 3-1**  MSDOS.SYS open in Notepad

You can make changes to quite a few settings without too much worry, although backing up your MSDOS.SYS file at this point would probably be a good idea.

**Step 3**    Make a few changes to the settings under the [Options] section of MSDOS.SYS, although not all at the same time. Make one change, then save and exit; reboot to see the effects (if any) of the change you made. Then try something different, following the same procedure. Your instructor will tell you which changes to make, or you can follow these suggestions:

- Change BOOTMENU=0 to BOOTMENU=1 to force the menu to appear. That saves you from having to press F8 every time it says "Starting Windows 9x."

**✔ Hint**

If you don't see an option under the [Options] area of MSDOS.SYS, you can simply add it without worry.

- Change BOOTGUI=1 to BOOTGUI=0 to force Windows to boot straight to the command line interface. Note that you can type **win** at the prompt and press ENTER to load the GUI manually. Techs use this feature when they want quicker reboots and have a lot of work to do from the command line.

- Change BOOTSAFE=0 to BOOTSAFE=1 to force Windows to boot into Safe mode. This is a good option when you know you have a buggy system but have to get information off it. Saves you from having to press F8 or F5 when booting each time. Note that combining this option with changing BOOTWARN=1 to BOOTWARN=0 is a great practical joke to play on somebody. His or her system will boot "normally," but then show only 16 colors at 640 × 480 resolution and not tell the user the machine is in Safe mode!

**✘ Warning**

Do not actually *play* this practical joke on someone unless (a) you're sure you'll be around to explain and fix it, (b) you're sure it won't hurt anything, and (c) you aren't breaking the rules or otherwise getting yourself/others into trouble!

All of the options above offer little to no risk of messing up your system, but it's always a good idea to back up important data before you mess with system files. Also, don't forget to change MSDOS.SYS back to the defaults if this is your primary testing machine.

 60 MINUTES

# Lab Exercise 3.02: Organizing Users and Groups in Windows XP

Joan, the primary network administrator for your company, is on vacation in Tahiti when a sudden crisis erupts. Your company has hired three new workers (Maria, Fred, and Lisa), but nobody on staff knows how to give them access to the company data without compromising his or her own user account and password. It's up to you to create user accounts for the new workers and assign them to the proper groups. (In Lab Exercise 3.03, you'll check permissions on resources to make certain the new people have only the right level of access.)

## Learning Objectives

In this lab, you'll familiarize yourself with user accounts, passwords, and groups.

At the end of the lab, you'll be able to

- Create user accounts

- Set and change passwords for the accounts

- Assign accounts to various groups

## Lab Materials and Setup

The materials you need for this lab are

- A working computer, preferably running Windows XP Professional. The lab will also work with Windows NT or 2000, but uses the terminology and screenshots of the newer Microsoft operating system.

- The computer needs at least one partition formatted with NTFS.

✔ **Cross-Reference**

Refer to Chapters 3 and 5 of the *Mike Meyers' A+ Guide to Operating Systems* for information about NTFS.

## Getting Down to Business

Working with user accounts, groups, and passwords requires you to spend a good deal of time in the Control Panel, so open that up now and let's get to work!

**Step 1**   Create a user account in Windows XP Professional. Open the User Accounts applet and select the "Create a new user account" option. Pick a name for the new account. (This scenario assumes you'll create the user account Maria.) Your next window requires you to choose the level of access you want for that user. With a standalone machine, you have two choices: Computer administrator or Limited. Choose the former option for Maria.

✔ **Hint**

When you first set up a Windows XP machine, your first account must be a computer administrator. That does not include the built-in Administrator account.

**Step 2**   Assign a password to the newly created user account. Select the account and then the "Create a password" option. Use a proper password, such as one that combines letters and numbers to provide better security.

**Step 3**   Repeat steps 1 and 2, only this time create Limited accounts for Fred and Lisa. At this point you should have at least four accounts on the PC: Administrator, a Computer administrator account for Maria, and two Limited accounts, Fred and Lisa. (The rest of the steps in this lab assume these four accounts.)

**Step 4**   Open Administrative Tools in the Control Panel and open the Computer Management MMC. In Computer Management, select the Local Users and Groups from the System Tools area, then double-click Groups. Which groups do you have listed?

_____

_____

Go to Action | New Group and create a new group named Accountants (see Figure 3-2). Click Add to open the Select Users or Groups dialog box. In that dialog box, click the Advanced button to open the dialog box shown in Figure 3-3, and then click Find Now to produce a list of the user accounts on the PC, as shown in Figure 3-4.

**Figure 3-2**  New Group dialog box

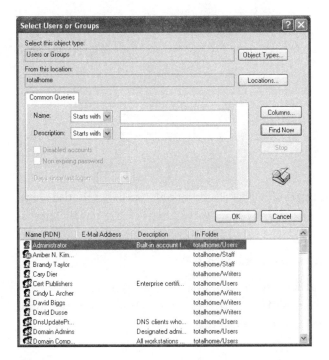

**FIGURE 3-3** Select Users or Groups dialog box

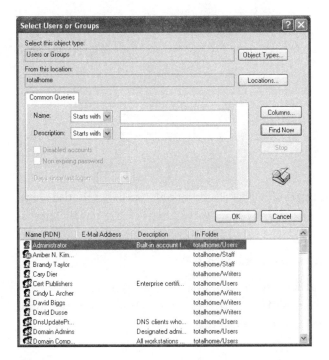

**FIGURE 3-4** User accounts listed

Select Lisa from the user accounts, then click OK to close the dialog box. Click OK again in the Select Users or Groups dialog box, then click Create in the New Group dialog box to complete the process.

**Step 5** Alternate-click the Accountants group and select the Add to Group option. This opens the Accounts Properties dialog box. You should see Lisa listed as the sole member. Click Add and type **Fred** in the text box. Then click OK to add Fred to the Accountants group.

**Step 6** Double-click three groups in the Groups folder—Administrators, Users, and Accountants—to see the members of those groups. Who is listed?

Administrators: _____

Users: _____

Accountants: _____

 30 MINUTES

# Lab Exercise 3.03: Working with Permissions in Windows XP

Now that you've set up the new users and put them into proper groups, you need to set the permissions on various files and folders to ensure the users have the correct level of access to resources.

## Learning Objectives

In this lab, you'll familiarize yourself with NTFS permissions.

At the end of the lab, you'll be able to

- Alter permissions on folders to block or allow access by members of various groups.

## Lab Materials and Setup

The materials you need for this lab are

- A working computer, preferably running Windows XP Professional. The lab will also work with Windows NT or 2000, but uses the terminology and screenshots of the newer Microsoft operating system.

- The computer needs at least one partition formatted with NTFS.

- The computer should be set up to have at least four accounts. This lab assumes the accounts created in Lab Exercise 3.02—Administrator, Maria, Fred, and Lisa—and the extra group, Accountants. Fred and Lisa are members of the Accountants group.

✔ **Cross-Reference**

Refer to Chapters 3 and 5 of the *Mike Meyers' A+ Guide to Operating Systems* for information about NTFS permissions.

# Getting Down to Business

The key to proper user management is to set the permissions for files and folders correctly. This enables you to control who gets access to a particular file and what he or she can do with that file. You'll need to log in and out quite a few times, so be prepared. Start by logging in as Administrator.

**Step 1** Open My Computer and create a folder on the root of the NTFS partition (call the folder Accounts, such as C:\Accounts) and create several subfolders in that folder. Create or drag and drop various files within those folders. Once you've finished with all the filing and "foldering," alternate-click the Accounts folder and select Properties. Which tabs do you see?

_____

**Step 2** In My Computer, go to Tools | Folder Options and select the View tab. Scroll all the way to the end until you reach the option that says Use Simple File Sharing (Recommended), and deselect the check box.

Alternate-click the Accounts folder and select Properties. Which tabs do you see now?

_____

Select the Security tab and examine the "Group or user names" area. Click through the various groups or users and note the different permissions for the various entries. Administrators, for example, should have check boxes selected to allow Full Control, Modify, Read & Execute, List Folder Contents, Read, and Write. What do Users have?

_____

**Step 3** Click the Add button and add the group Accountants in the text area of the Select Users, Computers, or Groups dialog box. Then click OK. In the Accounts Properties dialog box, select the Accountants group and then assign permissions. Select the check boxes to allow Read & Execute, List Folder Contents, Read, and Write.

**Step 4** Click the Add button again and this time add the user Fred. Click OK and then in the Accounts Properties dialog box, select Fred. In the permissions, select the check box to deny Fred the ability to Write.

**Step 5** At this point, you have your three new users set up and your Accounts permissions set. Now it's time to put your work to the test. Log off as Administrator and then log back in as Lisa. Access the Accounts folder and manipulate the folders and files. Can you open anything? Can you write to any of the files? Can you delete a file?

Now log off and log back in as Fred. Access the Accounts folder and manipulate the folders and files. Can you open anything? Can you write to any of the files? Can you delete a file?

Finish the lab off by logging in as Maria. Access the Accounts folder and manipulate the folders and files. Can you open anything? Can you write to any of the files? Can you delete a file?

# Lab Analysis Test

1. Joey wants to boot a Windows 98 SE PC to a command prompt by default, rather than boot into the GUI, because he has a legacy application that only runs from a clean command line interface. What would you suggest?

   _____

   _____

2. You get a tech call from an office that has a PC, recently "fixed" by a non-A+ Certified technician, that now boots into Safe mode automatically every time they power on the PC. What might cause such behavior?

   _____

   _____

3. William currently has a limited user account on a Windows XP Professional computer, but he needs to install a new application—a task beyond the scope of a limited user. What steps should he (or a supervisor) take to change his account type?

   _____

   _____

4. Marcy just recently got promoted from sales into management and needs her user account added to the Managers group. How would you do this?

   _____

   _____

5. Company X has a Windows XP computer used by data entry shift workers. Each day the workers compile new reports and save them into the Reports folder. Eileen has the only Administrator account on the machine. Outline the steps needed to make the contents of the Reports folder safe from being deleted by anybody but Eileen.

   _____

   _____

# Key Term Quiz

Use the following vocabulary terms to complete the following sentences. Not all the terms will be used.

Computer administrator

Limited

Local Users and Groups

MSDOS.SYS

permissions

user accounts

1.  Sylvia tried unsuccessfully to view the contents of a folder, but found that the _____ set on the folder did not allow it.

2.  Sylvia then tried to delete the folder, but found she only had a _____ account and couldn't do so.

3.  You use the _____ applet to create a new user account in a Windows XP PC.

4.  Alternatively, you could use the _____ option of the Computer Management MMC in Administrative Tools to create a user account.

5.  You can edit the _____ file to change boot options in a Windows Me PC.

# Chapter 4
## Using the Command Line

### Lab Exercises

**A**lthough A+ Certification has dropped the requirements of knowing MS-DOS inside and out, it does stipulate that PC technicians should know some of the basic commands and functions available at the command line interface in all versions of Windows. Why? Because they still work, and good techs use the command line often. The A+ Certification exams require you to have a solid understanding of several basic command line commands, such as CD and ATTRIB.

If you needed to install a new hard drive in a Windows 9x system, you'd need to access the command line in order to partition and format the thing, and you'd really need to know the proper commands for navigating around your folders and drives. Also when you start working with networks, the command line interface on all Windows systems is invaluable.

The command line often can offer a quicker way to accomplish a task than the graphical alternative. In cases where a virus, hard drive failure, or OS problem prevents you from booting to Windows, you should know how to get around with the command line. The following labs are designed to give you the chance to practice your basic command line skills, so that when the need arises, the command line will be your friend.

 30 MINUTES

# Lab Exercise 4.01: Using a Command Line Window

Before you can use the command line, you need to know the basics: ways to access it, manipulate it within the GUI, and close it down properly. This lab covers those basics.

## Learning Objectives

In this lab, you'll practice opening, resizing, and closing a command line window.

At the end of this lab, you'll be able to

- Open a command line window from within the Windows operating system

- Resize a command line window

- Exit a command line window

## Lab Materials and Setup

The materials you need for this lab are

- A PC with Windows installed

## Getting Down to Business

The first thing you'll need to do, obviously, is get to a command line. You'll spend the next several minutes becoming familiar with accessing the command line window.

---

✔ **Hint**

For details on how to access the command line at boot in Windows 9x, refer to the "Accessing the Command Line" section of Chapter 4 of *Mike Meyers' A+ Guide to Operating Systems*.

---

**Step 1** Turn on your system, and wait for the Desktop to appear. Then follow these steps:

a) Select Start | Run, and enter **cmd** (in Windows NT/2000/XP) or **command** (in Windows 9x/Me).

b) Click OK to display a command line window (see Figure 4-1).

**Step 2** There are three ways to change the size of the command line window for better viewing:

- Use the resize arrows along the edges of the windows (must not be maximized to work).

- Use the minimize/maximize button in the upper-right corner.

- Hold ALT and press ENTER to toggle between the full screen and a window.

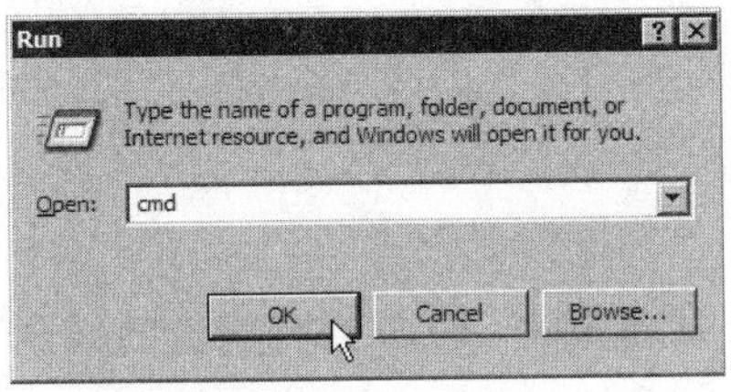

**FIGURE 4-1** Opening the Windows XP command line window

**Step 3**   In Windows NT and 2000, you should be looking at a black screen with your operating system information in the upper-left corner and a C prompt (C:\>) below. If you're using Windows 9x/Me, you'll see similar information in the upper left, but the prompt will look different (C:\WINDOWS\Desktop>). Windows XP will have yet a different prompt (C:\WINDOWS\Documents and Settings\*username*>). This just means that in Windows 2000 the command line opens as a default at the root of the C: drive, the Windows 9x/Me command line opens pointing at the Desktop subfolder in the WINDOWS folder on the C: drive, and Windows XP opens with pointing to the user's personal area in the Documents and Settings folder.

To the right of the prompt, you'll see a flashing cursor indicating it's waiting for your input. If you're using Windows NT/2000/XP, you'll notice also that there's a scroll bar along the right side of the window. Sometimes your command causes more information to be displayed than the window can hold, and it's really useful to be able to scroll back up and see what messages were displayed. Windows 9x, unfortunately, doesn't have this feature.

You'll now execute two versions of an important command, only for the purpose of exploring the scrolling issue. The Directory command lists the filename, extension, file size (in bytes), and creation date/time of the files in the current folder.

To execute it, type **DIR**, and then press ENTER. Depending on the contents of the current folder, the window may be able to display all of the information at once. If there's more than one screen's worth of information, it will keep scrolling out of sight until everything has been displayed. In Windows NT/2000/XP, you can use the scroll bar to go back a few screens' worth. If you have a scroll bar, try it.

In Windows 9x you can't scroll back, but there's a command you can use that forces the information to be displayed one screenful at a time. Type **DIR /P**, and then press ENTER. Adding the /p switch to the command tells it to *pause* after each screenful of text. Press the SPACEBAR to display the next screenful. You can't go back if you're too quick with the SPACEBAR, so take a good look at each screen!

**Step 4**   There are two normal ways to close a command line window:

- Click the × in the upper-right corner of the window. This method, however, isn't recommended if the window is actively running a program. You should wait until you see the prompt before clicking the ×.

- Type **exit** on the command line, and press ENTER. I prefer this way because I can be sure the window is inactive when I quit.

 30 MINUTES

# Lab Exercise 4.02: Understanding Basic Commands

Before you can really use the command line, you must know the basic commands needed to navigate around a drive to locate and modify files. In this lab exercise, you'll learn more basic command line commands that you would need to know when troubleshooting your or your client's PC.

✔ **Hint**

For the most part, mistakes such as spelling a command or file wrong won't be disastrous for you. It's possible to misspell just incorrectly enough to delete the wrong file, or something similar, especially if you're using wildcards (I'll get to those in a bit), but for the most part, the command line won't know what you're asking it to do and thus won't do anything.

## Learning Objectives

In this lab, you'll learn or review commands for directory and file management while using the command line.

At the end of this lab, you'll be able to

- Use commands to view, navigate, create, and delete directories using the command line
- Use commands to copy, move, rename, and delete files using the command line

## Lab Materials and Setup

The materials you need for this lab are

- At least one working computer running Windows XP

✔ **Hint**

Other Windows versions will work just fine as long as you understand that the results may appear differently on the screen.

## Getting Down to Business

Although there are scores of commands and extensions you could learn to use, several specific ones make up the cornerstone of command line navigation. These are the commands you'll use constantly when working with the command line.

**Step 1**   Follow these steps:

a) Select Start | Run, and enter **cmd** for Windows NT/2000/XP or **command** for Windows 9x/Me.

b) When you first open the command line window, your prompt might not be on the root directory. Because you want to focus on the root directory at this time, you must *change directories* to the root drive.

The Change Directory command (CD), changes the directory the system is focused on. When you use the CD command, you must type the command followed by a space and then the name of the directory you want to look at. This is true of all command line commands. First, type the command followed by a space and then the options. Because you want to focus on the root of C: and the name of the root is the backslash (\), you'd type in the following and press ENTER (assuming that you're in the C: drive to begin with):

```
C:\Documents and Settings\username>CD \
```

Notice the prompt has changed its focus to C:\> (see Figure 4-2).

**Step 2**    Probably the most frequently typed command is the request to display the contents of a directory (DIR). Because the command line interface doesn't continually display everything the way a GUI does, you have to *ask* (command) it for what you want to know or see displayed. The way you display the contents of a directory is to focus on the particular directory or subdirectory, and enter the command DIR.

Okay, let's see what's in your root (C:\>) directory. You should already be focused there from the previous step in this exercise. Type **DIR** at the command prompt, and press ENTER.

---

✔ **Hint**

From now on, when you see an instruction to type a command, you should assume that you should press ENTER last to complete the request (command). Otherwise, the command line will sit there, waiting patiently until the sun grows cold.

---

Now here's where it gets a little gray. Because I don't know what's in your root directory, there's no way to predict that your contents will look like mine. But in theory, your display should be similar to Figure 4-3. Windows NT/2000/XP will have the same basic look, and Windows 9x/Me is slightly different.

Notice that using the DIR command in any Windows operating system gives you the following information:

- Filename (Windows 9x shows the old 8.3 name, too)

- File extension

- Date and time of creation

```
D:\WINDOWS\System32\cmd.exe
Microsoft Windows XP [Version 5.1.2600]
(C) Copyright 1985-2001 Microsoft Corp.

C:\Documents and Settings\caryd>CD\

C:\>
```

**FIGURE 4-2** Changing the command line focus

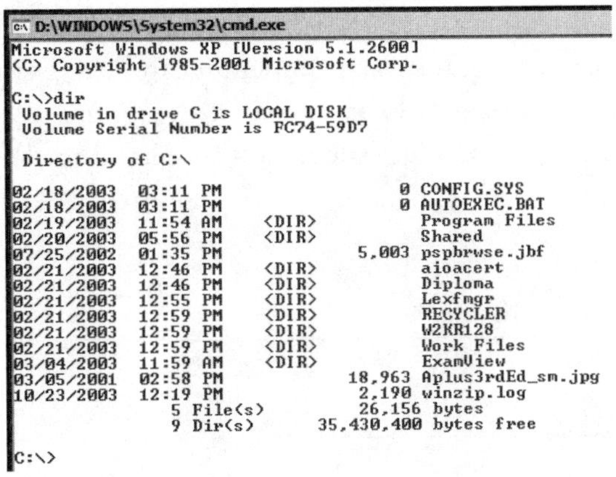

```
ː D:\WINDOWS\System32\cmd.exe
Microsoft Windows XP [Version 5.1.2600]
(C) Copyright 1985-2001 Microsoft Corp.

C:\>dir
 Volume in drive C is LOCAL DISK
 Volume Serial Number is FC74-59D7

 Directory of C:\

02/18/2003  03:11 PM                 0 CONFIG.SYS
02/18/2003  03:11 PM                 0 AUTOEXEC.BAT
02/19/2003  11:54 AM    <DIR>          Program Files
02/20/2003  05:56 PM    <DIR>          Shared
07/25/2002  01:35 PM             5,003 pspbruse.jbf
02/21/2003  12:46 PM    <DIR>          aioacert
02/21/2003  12:46 PM    <DIR>          Diploma
02/21/2003  12:55 PM    <DIR>          Lexfmgr
02/21/2003  12:59 PM    <DIR>          RECYCLER
02/21/2003  12:59 PM    <DIR>          W2KR128
02/21/2003  12:59 PM    <DIR>          Work Files
03/04/2003  11:59 AM    <DIR>          ExamView
03/05/2001  02:58 PM            18,963 Aplus3rdEd_sm.jpg
10/23/2003  12:19 PM             2,190 winzip.log
               5 File(s)         26,156 bytes
               9 Dir(s)     35,430,400 bytes free

C:\>
```

**FIGURE 4-3** Viewing a sample Windows XP
root directory

- Size in bytes

- If it's a directory (<DIR>) or a file

- The number of files in the directory

- The amount of free space on the drive

Look at your particular results and note the mixture of files, which display a size in bytes, and directories that have the annotation "<DIR>" after the directory name. In the preceding examples, Aplus3rdEd_sm.jpg is a file of 18,963 bytes, and Program Files, RECYCLER, and Work Files are directories.

Note whether you see the following files in your root (C:\) directory (you won't see them all):

| | | |
|---|---|---|
| AUTOEXEC.BAT | Yes ____ | No ____ |
| CONFIG.SYS | Yes ____ | No ____ |
| COMMAND.COM | Yes ____ | No ____ |
| WINDOWS | Yes ____ | No ____ |
| Documents and Settings | Yes ____ | No ____ |
| Program Files | Yes ____ | No ____ |

List the names of all the directories you see displayed in the root directory:

_____      _____

_____      _____

_____      _____

_____      _____

_____      _____

**Step 3** The biggest challenge when working with the command prompt is remembering what exactly to type to achieve your goal. Learning the commands is one thing, but each command can have switches and options to modify them. Also, you may have noticed the screen fills up and scrolls from top to bottom, making it difficult to view all the information you might need. Let's look at a command to clear the screen and another to provide assistance with how to use the commands.

Type in the command **CLS**. What happened?

_____

_____

 **Hint**

Clearing the screen is helpful sometimes, especially with Windows 9x because there's no scroll bar.

Type in **DIR /?**. What happened?

_____

_____

The question mark (/?) is a standard help switch for most commands. Even though I've used these commands for decades, I still use the /? switch occasionally to remember what options are available for a specific command.

 **Hint**

Be careful you don't confuse the backslash (\) and the forward slash (/). In a command line world, the path uses the backslash (\), and command switches use the forward slash (/).

Yes, I know there's a lot of help information displayed (see Figure 4-4) and you're now in command overload, but take comfort in the fact that DIR is the most complex command. Other commands are more straightforward with their help. You don't need to know what all the switches are; just know how to use the help switch (/?) to find them. The main thing to learn is the syntax of the commands.

```
D:\WINDOWS\System32\cmd.exe                                    _ □ ×
C:\>dir /?
Displays a list of files and subdirectories in a directory.

DIR [drive:][path][filename] [/A[[:]attributes]] [/B] [/C] [/D] [/L] [/N]
  [/O[[:]sortorder]] [/P] [/Q] [/S] [/T[[:]timefield]] [/W] [/X] [/4]

  [drive:][path][filename]
              Specifies drive, directory, and/or files to list.

  /A          Displays files with specified attributes.
  attributes   D  Directories                R  Read-only files
               H  Hidden files               A  Files ready for archiving
               S  System files               -  Prefix meaning not
  /B          Uses bare format (no heading information or summary).
  /C          Display the thousand separator in file sizes.  This is the
              default.  Use /-C to disable display of separator.
  /D          Same as wide but files are list sorted by column.
  /L          Uses lowercase.
  /N          New long list format where filenames are on the far right.
  /O          List by files in sorted order.
  sortorder    N  By name (alphabetic)       S  By size (smallest first)
               E  By extension (alphabetic)  D  By date/time (oldest first)
               G  Group directories first    -  Prefix to reverse order
  /P          Pauses after each screenful of information.
  /Q          Display the owner of the file.
  /S          Displays files in specified directory and all subdirectories.
  /T          Controls which time field displayed or used for sorting
  timefield    C  Creation
               A  Last Access
               W  Last Written
  /W          Uses wide list format.
Press any key to continue . . .
```

**FIGURE 4-4** Viewing the syntax of the DIR command

Everything in brackets ([]) is optional for the command. Notice that DIR is the only mandatory part in that command even though there are several switches and parameters. This is the same for all of the commands. The system will use defaults if you don't specify a switch or optional parameter. It's the *defaults* that can cause problems if you're not careful when using these commands. Now follow these steps:

a) Put a known good disk with files in the floppy drive.

b) Type in **DIR**, and listen for the floppy to read the disk.

   Did it read the disk? _____ Probably not because your prompt is still focused on the root directory of the hard drive.

c) Type in **DIR A:** and listen for the floppy to read the disk. Ah ha! The option of [drive:] was needed to see the floppy disk.

The [drive:] option will work for any of the drive letters. CDs, DVDs, and Zip drives are all fair game. And when you use that option, you can look at those other drives without switching from the directory you're in.

**Step 4** Type in **DIR /?** to look at two more optional switches, /P and /W. /P is used when all the information will not fit on one screen, and /W is used to see a condensed listing of the directory.

Let's focus on a different directory. Remember, the CD command will let you change the directory you want to focus on:

a) Type in **CD \WINDOWS**.

b) Type in **CLS**. Your prompt should look like the one in Figure 4-5.

```
C:\WINDOWS>_
```

**FIGURE 4-5** Focusing on the
WINDOWS subdirectory

c)    Type in **DIR** at the command prompt. This shows way too much data for the screen to display all at once.

d)    Type **DIR /P** at the command prompt. This very useful switch causes the display to stop scrolling (pause) after each screen and waits until you press the spacebar to show you more. In directories with lots of files, this is a lifesaver!

✔ **Hint**

If you want to stop a process that seems to be running forever, you can press CTRL-C. The process will end, and you'll get the prompt back.

e)    Now type **DIR /W** at the command prompt. This switch is convenient when you're simply looking to see if a particular file is actually in a particular directory because it shows a "wide" list with names but no details.

f)    Now practice moving around in the command window. Right now you're focused on the WINDOWS directory. Go back to the root directory by typing **CD \**. To change the focus to another directory, use the CD command as you've learned. Use the DIR command to see what directories you have available in your current folder.

g)    Try going to a subdirectory in another subdirectory and listing the contents. Look back at the list of directories you made previously and select one. Issue the CD command followed by a backslash (\) and the name of the target directory. For example, to switch to the Documents and Settings directory in the previous listing, type this:
C:\>**CD \DOCUMENTS AND SETTINGS**

Do this using several of the directory names you wrote down previously, and then type **DIR** to see what's there. Are there any subdirectories in this directory? Make a note of them.

_____    _____

_____    _____

_____    _____

✔ **Hint**

After you've changed the prompt focus many times, you may become confused as to where you are. You can always get to the root directory from anyplace you are by typing **CD \**.

**Step 5**    A normal Windows XP installation creates a Drivers directory in a System32 in the WINDOWS directory in the root of C: drive. To go to the Drivers directory, you don't have to do the CD command three times unless you really want. If you know the path, you can go directly to the subdirectory with one CD command.

Let's go to the Drivers subdirectory. Type this at the command prompt:

```
C:\>CD \WINDOWS\SYSTEM32\DRIVERS
```

Your prompt should now look like Figure 4-6.

Type **DIR** to see what's there.

One final navigation hint—you can change directories going back up toward the top level without returning directly to the root. If you want to go up a single directory level, you can type **CD** followed immediately by two periods. For example, typing this takes you up one level to the System32 directory:

```
C:\WINDOWS\SYSTEM32\DRIVERS>CD..
C:\WINDOWS\SYSTEM32>
```

Do it again to go to the Windows directory:

```
C:\WINDOWS\SYSTEM32>CD..
C:\WINDOWS>
```

And once more to arrive at the root directory:

```
C:\WINDOWS>CD..
C:\>
```

Take a minute and practice using the CD command. Go down a few levels on the directory tree, then jump up a few, jump back to the root directory, and then jump down another path. Practice is the only way to get comfortable moving around in a command-prompt environment, and a good PC technician needs to be comfortable doing this.

**Step 6**    Sometimes a technician needs to make a directory to store files on the system. This could be temporary for testing or maybe a place to store the diagnostic reports. In any case, it's important for you to know how to create and remove a directory. The A+ exam will test you on this. Follow these steps:

a)  Be sure you're in the root directory. If you aren't there, type **CD \** to return to the root directory, where you'll add a new top-level directory. Actually, you can make a directory anyplace in the file structure, but you don't want to lose track of where it is, so you'll make the new directory in the root. You do this using the Make Directory command (MD).

b)  Type **MD /?** to see how the command is structured and see what options are available (see Figure 4-7).

```
C:\WINDOWS\system32\drivers>_
```

```
C:\>md /?
Creates a directory.

MKDIR [drive:]path
MD [drive:]path
```

**FIGURE 4-6** Focusing on the Drivers subdirectory

**FIGURE 4-7** Using the MD command

c) At the command prompt, type the following:

`C:\>MD CORVETTE`

d) When the command line just presents a fresh prompt, it means that everything worked correctly. But to prove the directory was actually made, type **DIR** (that is, perform a DIR command) to see your new directory. It's as simple as that!

## ✖ Warning

Be careful—the new directory will always be created wherever the prompt is focused when you issue the command, whether that's where you meant to put it.

e) Be sure you're in the root directory (type **CD\**), and you'll remove your new CORVETTE directory.

Removing a directory requires the RD command and two conditions. The first condition is that the directory must be empty; the second is that you must not be focused on the directory about to be deleted.

f) Type this command:

`C:\>RD CORVETTE`

The directory has been deleted.

g) Type **DIR** to confirm CORVETTE has been removed.

## ✔ Hint

Be *very* careful when you remove directories or delete files in the command line. It isn't as forgiving as Windows—which allows you to change your mind and "undelete" things. When you delete a file or directory using the command line, it's gone. If you make a mistake, there's nothing left to do but pout. So use the computer version of the old carpenter's rule, "Measure twice, cut once." Do a DIR twice, and delete/remove once. Be sure you know *what* you're deleting before you do it, and you'll save yourself a great deal of agony. Also pay attention to the directory you're currently looking in. You need to be sure you're in the correct one.

**Step 7** Sometimes the technician knows the name of the file she wants to use but doesn't know the directory it's in. In this case, working with files and directories can become quite tedious. To easily help locate files, there are some switches and wildcards that can be used with the DIR command:

a) Look again at the results of the DIR /? command, and find the /S switch.

b) The /S switch will look for a file(s) in the specified (focus) directory and all subdirectories under that directory.

c)   Windows XP has a file named XCOPY.EXE somewhere on the drive. Locate the path to the XCOPY.EXE file using the /S switch.

d)   Start with your command prompt at the root directory (CD \).

e)   Type in this command:

```
C:\>DIR XCOPY.EXE
```

If the file isn't in the root directory, nothing will be displayed.

f)   Okay, now try the new switch you just learned about to search all subdirectories. Type in this command:

```
C:\>DIR /S XCOPY.EXE
```

g)   On my system, the file shows up in two places: in the C:\WINDOWS\system32 directory and in the C:\WINDOWS\system 32\dllcache directory (see Figure 4-8).

Another way to look for a file is to use a *wildcard*. The most common wildcard is the special asterisk character (*), which can be used in place of all or part of a filename to make a command act on more than one file at a time. Wildcards work with all commands that use filenames.

The * wildcard replaces any number of letters before or after the dot in the filename. A good way to think of the * wildcard is "I don't care." Replace the part of the filename that you don't care about with *.

For example, if you want to locate all the README files on a hard drive and you don't care what the extension is, type the following:

```
C:\>DIR /S/P readme.*
```

The result is a list of all the README files on the hard drive. Notice I used the /S switch to look in all the directories and the /P switch so I can view one screenful at a time (see Figure 4-9).

You can use the * wildcard for any number of characters. For example, not all companies use README.TXT as the help filename. Some use READ.ME, and others may use READ.TXT.

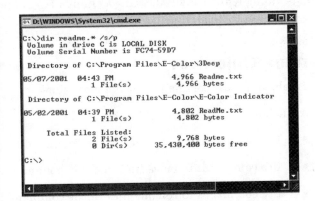

**FIGURE 4-8**  Locating the XCOPY.EXE file          **FIGURE 4-9**  Using a wildcard to locate files

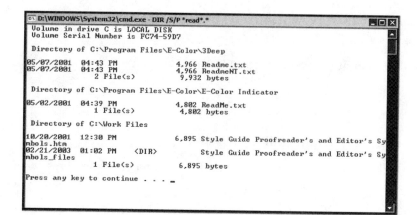

**FIGURE 4-10** Using a wildcard to locate *READ*.* files

Because "READ" is common to all those variations, let's find all the files with "READ" in the filename. But you should be willing to get a long list of every file with read in the name, not just the README files.

Type the following:

```
C:\>DIR /S/P *read*.*
```

Figure 4-10 shows the first screenful of results from my system. How many files and directories did you find with "READ" as part of the name?

 30 MINUTES

# Lab Exercise 4.03: Using Command Line Tools

Commands such as COPY, MOVE, RENAME, and DELETE are used for manipulating files, such as you would be doing while troubleshooting a client's PC. These are more of the commands that every working tech is soon very familiar with.

## Learning Objectives

In this lab, you'll use commands for file management.

At the end of this lab, you'll be able to

- Use commands to copy files in the command line

- Use commands to move files in the command line

- Use commands to rename files in the command line

- Use commands to delete files in the command line

## Lab Materials and Setup

The materials you need for this lab are

- At least one working computer running Windows XP

Other Windows versions will work just fine. However, the results may appear differently on the screen.

## Getting Down to Business

You might refer to these as the "second-tier" commands. Once you've used commands such as DIR and CD to navigate and create folders, the following commands are the ones you'll use to manipulate individual files.

**Step 1**    Okay, you'll now start playing with files! To play with a file safely, your first task is to create one. Close the command line window (type in **EXIT**), and open the Windows Notepad program:

a)    Select Start | Programs | Accessories | Notepad.

b)    Type some information into the new document. I suggest entering your name and the school/class you're attending.

c)    Select File | Save As.

d)    In the drop-down menu at the top, select Save In and choose your local drive C: (which is very important for this to work):

```
File name: = MYCLASS
Save as type: = Text Documents (*.txt)
```

e)    Click Save and close Notepad.

**Step 2**    Now follow these steps:

a)    Open a command prompt window by either selecting Command Prompt in the Start | Programs | Accessories menu or selecting Start | Run and typing **cmd** (**command** for Windows 9x/Me). This will give you a command line window to work in.

b)    At the command prompt, type **CD \** to be sure you're in the root directory.

c)    Now use the DIR command to make sure your new file is there.

Is it there? _____ If it isn't there, contact the instructor for help.

You'll now create a new directory in the root called STUDY so you can do some copying and moving. The only difference between copying and moving is that COPY leaves the original file in the same place (as a backup) with a duplicate made elsewhere, but using the MOVE command relocates the original file to a new location with no backup available. They're otherwise similar, so once you've learned the COPY command, you've pretty much learned the MOVE command! Follow these steps:

a)   Make a directory named STUDY by typing the following:

```
C:\>MD STUDY
```

b)   Verify the directory is there by using the DIR command.

Follow these steps for copying your file named MYCLASS.TXT to the new STUDY directory:

a)   Change the focus of the command prompt to the STUDY directory:

```
C:\>CD STUDY
```

b)   Copy the MYCLASS.TXT file to the STUDY directory:

```
C:\STUDY>COPY C:\MYCLASS.TXT C:\STUDY\MYCLASS.TXT
```

COPY is the command, C:\MYCLASS.TXT is the current location and name of the file, and C:\STUDY\MYCLASS.TXT is the target location and name of the file.

The entire command and response looks like this:

```
C:\STUDY>COPY C:\MYCLASS.TXT C:\STUDY\MYCLASS.TXT
1 file(s) copied
```

c)   Run the DIR command to see if you copied the file. If the file isn't there, repeat the previous steps or ask the instructor for help.

d)   Change your directory focus back to the root drive (**CD \**) and run the DIR command to see if the original MYCLASS.TXT file is still there.

---

### ✔ Hint

If you're already in the target directory, you don't need to include the target path in the command. My idea of copying or moving files is to first be in the directory to which you want to copy the files. Then you can bring the files to where you are. Each time you copy or move a file, you can run the DIR command to see if it's actually there. The other way of sending a file to a directory can be troublesome if you're moving files because you may accidentally send them a wrong directory and waste time looking for them.

---

### ✔ Hint

Another good use of the COPY command is to make a backup copy of a file and rename it at the same time so it can be in the same directory. An example command is C:\>copy MYCLASS.TXT MYCLASS.BAK.

**Step 3**   Suppose you don't want two copies of the same file using the same name, and you really want to keep the original as an archive backup file. In this situation, you can use the rename command (REN). To change MYCLASS.TXT to MYCLASS.SAV, type the following:

```
C:\>REN MYCLASS.TXT MYCLASS.SAV
```

Notice that the command window doesn't confirm what it has done—it simply presents you with a fresh prompt. You must do a DIR to check your results. (Are you getting the idea that DIR is going to be your favorite command?)

Change back to the STUDY directory and delete the copy of MYCLASS.TXT that you copied there. If you're not sure how to get back to the STUDY directory, review Lab Exercise 4.03. To remove the file, you'll use the DEL command:

```
C:\STUDY>DEL MYCLASS.TXT
```

Once again, note that the command window not only doesn't ask if you're sure you want to delete this file, but it also doesn't confirm that it has done the delete. However, if you do a DIR, you'll find the file is indeed gone. And remember that there's no Recycle Bin when using the command line.

# Lab Analysis Test

1.  Will this command work? Why or why not? What will it do?
    C:\>copy A:\diags.*

    _____

    _____

2.  Which command(s) would you use to make a full copy of a file in the same directory under a different name?

    _____

    _____

3.  The XCOPY.EXE file is in the System32 directory, which is in the WINDOWS directory that's in the root directory of the primary hard drive. What's the complete command line path to the file?

    _____

    _____

**4.** Explain the 8.3 rule. What does the 8 mean? How about the 3?

_____

_____

**5.** John Steven was messing around one day and deleted a file named CRITICAL.DLL from the System32 directory. His friend gave him a copy on a floppy disk. What's the exact command he'd use to copy it back to the correct place?

_____

_____

# Key Term Quiz

Use the following vocabulary terms to complete the following sentences. Not all of the terms will be used.

RD

CD

MD

DIR

/?

/P

COPY

/W

REN

DEL

**1.** The command to create a new directory is _____.

**2.** The command used to create a duplicate file is _____.

**3.** The _____ switch is used to get help about command syntax.

**4.** When there are too many files to show on the screen while using the DIR command, add the _____ switch.

**5.** For a brief listing of just the names of a directory's contents, use the _____ command with the _____ switch.

# Chapter 5
## Implementing Hard Drives

### Lab Exercises

Once you've installed a new drive on a PC and it has been recognized by the system, you've got two more steps to complete before you can start storing data—partitioning and formatting.

> ✔ **Hint**
>
> Make sure you're clear on the distinction between partitioning and formatting because you must do them in the proper order. Partitioning the disk simply means defining physical sections that are used to store data. Formatting means *configuring the partition* with a file system.

In the Windows 9x world, your hard disk drive has to be partitioned and formatted before you run the installation setup routine. Windows NT, 2000, and XP incorporate these disk preparation steps into the installation routine itself. However, it's still important for you to know how to perform these tasks from scratch, both for the CompTIA A+ Core exam and as part of your basic PC tech repertoire.

You have a number of tools at your disposal for performing partitioning and formatting tasks. The command line utilities FDISK and FORMAT are included on the useful Windows 9x bootable floppy diskette. Windows 2000 and XP include the Disk Management utility, which enables you to create and modify partitions. Windows NT has a similar tool called Disk Administrator. Note that Windows 9x doesn't have an equivalent tool—to create or modify partitions from within Windows 9x you need a third-party tool such as Partition Magic. However, all versions of Windows enable you to format drives from within My Computer.

After looking at how we create and format partitions using the command line tools, you'll start up Windows to look at how to accomplish these tasks using the built-in tools. After an introduction to creating and using dynamic disks, you'll look at the procedures for performing regular hard disk maintenance and troubleshooting tasks.

30 MINUTES

# Lab Exercise 5.01: Creating Partitions with FDISK

The first step in making a newly installed hard drive usable is to configure partitions. All versions of Windows come with utilities for partitioning a hard drive. Windows 9x/Me PCs use the FDISK utility included on the bootable system diskette that came with the OS. Windows NT uses a tool called Disk Administrator, and Windows 2000/XP systems use the built-in Computer Management console's Disk Management utility, an updated version of Disk Administrator.

✔ **Cross-Reference**

For details about partitioning drives with FDISK, refer to the "FDISK" section of Chapter 5 of *Mike Meyers' A+ Guide to Operating Systems.*

## Learning Objectives

In this exercise, you'll use the FDISK program to partition a hard drive for use.

At the end of this lab, you'll be able to

- Set up a primary, active partition on a hard drive

## Lab Materials and Setup

The materials you need for this lab are

- A working PC with two hard disk drives, one that holds your Windows OS, and a second blank hard disk drive (or a hard disk that you can safely erase)

- A bootable Windows 9x floppy disk with the FDISK command line utility

✖ **Warning**

Partitioning a hard disk drive destroys any data on it! Only practice this lab on disks that don't store any data that you need.

## Getting Down to Business

In this exercise you'll start the system using a bootable floppy diskette, use the FDISK utility to examine your second hard drive's partitions (if any exist), and then create a new active, primary partition on the second hard drive.

**Step 1**  If it isn't already, set your floppy disk drive to be the first boot device in CMOS. Boot the PC using the Windows 9x boot diskette.

**Step 2**  Type **fdisk** at the command prompt.

**Step 3**  You're presented with an option menu with four choices:

1. Create DOS partition or logical DOS drive

2. Set active partition

3. Delete partition or logical DOS drive

4. Display partition information

Since your system has more than one physical hard drive, you'll actually have a fifth choice:

5. Change current fixed disk drive

Figure 5-1 shows the main FDISK screen.

**Step 4**  Choose option 5 to switch to the second hard drive, and then at the next screen enter the disk number for your second hard drive.

**Step 5**  With FDISK focused on your second hard drive, choose option 4 to view current partition information. If it's a blank disk, there won't be much to see. If the disk has previously been partitioned, then you'll see listings for each partition that include the partition's status (active or not), type, volume label, size in megabytes, and percentage of space used.

Once you've viewed the current configuration, press ESC to return to the main menu.

**Step 6**  If your second hard drive is blank, choose option 1 to create a new partition and proceed to the next step. If a partition currently resides on the hard drive, choose option 3 from the menu to delete the partition, and follow the prompts so that you're left with an unpartitioned disk. Return to the main FDISK menu and choose option 1, and proceed to the next step.

```
                    Microsoft Windows 98
                   Fixed Disk Setup Program
            (C)Copyright Microsoft Corp.  1983 - 1998

                        FDISK Options

Current fixed disk drive: 1

Choose one of the following:

1. Create DOS partition or Logical DOS Drive
2. Set active partition
3. Delete partition or Logical DOS Drive
4. Display partition information
5. Change current fixed disk drive

Enter choice: [1]


Press Esc to exit FDISK
```

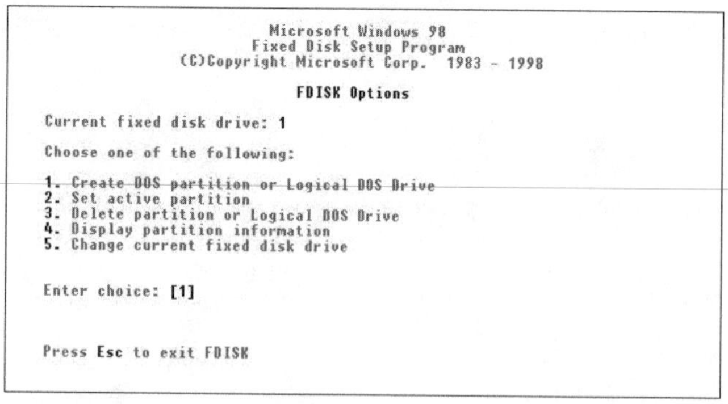

**FIGURE 5-1**  Main FDISK screen

Viewing partition information is completely safe, but performing any other actions with FDISK will destroy all data on your disk! Proceed to the next steps only if you can erase data on your subject hard disk without regrets.

**Step 7**    You're presented with a submenu listing the following choices:

1. Create primary DOS partition

2. Create extended DOS partition

3. Create logical DOS drive(s) in the extended DOS partition

Figure 5-2 shows the partition options submenu.

**Step 8**    Choose the option to create a primary partition. You're then asked if you want to use the maximum available space for your new partition. Choose No, and enter a partition size of 2048 megabytes (2 GB). Leave the rest of the space on your hard drive unpartitioned so that you can create additional partitions at a later time.

**Step 9**    If this is the first partition created on your new hard drive, you'll be prompted to set the partition as the active partition. Do this, and follow the remaining prompts to complete the partitioning process.

Deleting a partition is just as easy. Selecting option 3 from the main FDISK menu brings you to a submenu of deletion options. Simply follow the prompts to confirm to FDISK that you really, really want to delete the partition and that you understand the dire consequences.

```
                 Create DOS Partition or Logical DOS Drive
     Current fixed disk drive: 1

     Choose one of the following:

     1. Create Primary DOS Partition
     2. Create Extended DOS Partition
     3. Create Logical DOS Drive(s) in the Extended DOS Partition



     Enter choice: [1]




     Press Esc to return to FDISK Options
```

**FIGURE 5-2** Partition options submenu

 30 MINUTES

# Lab Exercise 5.02: Formatting Partitions with FORMAT

The other command line disk preparation tool is the FORMAT utility. Running FORMAT does two important things: creates the file system on your hard disk partition, and creates the root directory that your OS uses to build its file and folder structure. The file system is the index that tells the OS where files and folders are stored on the hard disk partition.

---

### ✔ Cross-Reference

For details about the FORMAT utility, refer to the "Formatting a Partition" section of Chapter 5 of *Mike Meyers' A+ Guide to Operating Systems*.

---

The version of FORMAT that's included on the Windows 9x bootable floppy diskette can create either the FAT16 (usually just called FAT) or FAT32 file systems. Windows NT's version of FORMAT creates either the FAT or NTFS4 file systems, while the version of FORMAT that ships with Windows 2000 and XP can create the FAT, FAT32, and NTFS5 file systems.

Windows 2000 and XP's version of FORMAT also offer the /fs: *file system* parameter switch, which enables you to specify whether to format the partition with FAT or NTFS. Note that Windows 2000 automatically formats partitions of 2 GB or less with FAT, and greater than 2 GB with FAT32.

In this lab exercise, you'll format the partition that you just created with the FAT file system.

## Learning Objectives

In this lab exercise, you'll practice formatting a hard drive.

At the end of this lab, you'll be able to

- Use the FORMAT command line utility to create a file system on a blank partition

## Lab Materials and Setup

The materials you need for this exercise are

- The same hard disk drive that you partitioned in Lab Exercise 5.01

- A bootable Windows 9x floppy disk with the FORMAT command line utility

---

### ✖ Warning

The FORMAT process will destroy any files residing on the partition. Make sure the partition you're formatting contains nothing you need!

---

# Getting Down to Business

Running FORMAT is fairly straightforward. The steps below work on all versions of FORMAT.

**Step 1** Boot the PC using the Windows 9x boot diskette (remember to set your floppy disk drive as the first bootable device in CMOS).

**Step 2** Type **format d: /s** at the command prompt.

Here's a quick review of the FORMAT syntax:

- Typing **format** starts the FORMAT.EXE program on the Windows 9x boot diskette.

- Typing **d:** tells FORMAT to create file system on the partition with the drive letter d:. If this isn't the correct drive letter for partition you created on your second hard drive, change it.

- Typing **/s** tells FORMAT to copy system files (IO.SYS, MSDOS.SYS, SYSTEM.INI) onto the partition, making it bootable.

**Step 3** You're warned that all data will be lost; press Y to proceed, or N to cancel. In this case, press Y.

**Step 4** A counter shows you what percentage of the formatting process has been completed. Once the counter reaches 100 percent, you're prompted to enter a volume label for the newly formatted partition. Volume labels are optional, but handy if you want to give the partition a descriptive name to go along with its drive letter. For now, press ENTER to skip this step.

**Step 5** Once the file system structure is complete, you'll see a summary telling you how much disk space is free on the partition, as shown in Figure 5-3. Eject the floppy diskette and restart the system.

FORMAT doesn't have to be run from a bootable floppy diskette. It works just fine when run from a command line window within the Windows OS. You can't, of course, use it on the partition that holds your current OS (think about it), but you can certainly use it to format a second hard disk drive or partition.

Now that you've looked at the command line utilities used to partition and format hard disk drives, let's look at the built-in GUI tools supplied with Windows.

```
A:\>format C:/s

WARNING:  ALL DATA ON NON-REMOVABLE DISK
DRIVE C: WILL BE LOST!
Proceed with Format  (Y/N)?y


Formatting  30709.65M
Format complete.
System transferred

Volume label (11 characters, ENTER for none)?

32,197,017,600 bytes total disk space
         262,144 bytes used by system
32,196,755,456 bytes available on disk

     491,520 bytes in each allocation unit.
     982,455 allocation units available on disk.


Volume Serial Number is 3166-11D9
```

**FIGURE 5-3** FORMAT complete

 30 MINUTES

# Lab Exercise 5.03: Creating Partitions with Disk Administrator and Disk Management

Windows NT, 2000, and XP include tools that let you create and modify partitions "on the fly" from within Windows. Windows NT's tool is called Disk Administrator. Windows 2000 and XP use an updated version called Disk Management.

### ✔ Cross-Reference

For details about the creating partitions using Disk Administrator and Disk Management, refer to the "Disk Administrator" and "Disk Management" sections of Chapter 5 of *Mike Meyers' A+ Guide to Operating Sysgtems*.

This lab exercise assumes that you want to create a partition on a new, second hard drive installed on a Windows NT, 2000, or XP system. Follow the steps below to create a new partition.

## Learning Objectives

In this exercise, you'll use Disk Administrator or Disk Management program (depending on whether you have Windows NT or Windows 2000/XP) to partition a hard drive for use.

At the end of this lab, you'll be able to

- Set up a primary, active partition on a hard drive

- Set up an extended partition and logical drives in that partition

## Lab Materials and Setup

The materials you need for this lab are

- A Windows NT, 2000, or XP PC with a second hard disk drive (either blank or safe to erase)

### ✖ Warning

Partitioning a hard disk drive destroys any data on it! Only practice this lab on disks that don't contain any data that you need.

# Getting Down to Business

The steps for partitioning disks in Windows NT, 2000, and XP are very similar. The following steps list the procedures using both Disk Administrator and Disk Management.

**Step 1**    The first step is to open the appropriate tool using the following steps:

- In Windows NT, select Start | Programs | Administrative Tools (Common) | Disk Administrator.

- In Windows 2000, select Start | Setting | Control Panel | Administrative Tools | Computer Management. Under the Storage node, click the Disk Management icon.

- In Windows XP, select Start | All Programs | Control Panel | Performance and Maintenance | Administrative Tools | Computer Management. Under the Storage node, click the Disk Management icon.

**Step 2**    Start the process of creating a partition by alternate-clicking an unpartitioned section of disk space and telling the utility what type of partition you wish to create—primary or extended.

- In Disk Administrator, highlight your second hard disk drive and select a section of unpartitioned space labeled as Free Space, and then select Create from the pop-up menu to create a primary partition.

- In Disk Management, highlight your second hard disk drive and select a section of unpartitioned space labeled Unallocated, and then select New Partition from the pop-up menu to start the New Partition Wizard (see Figure 5-4).

**Step 3**    Click Next, and then select Primary partition from the partition type pull-down menu. At the next screen, enter the size of your new partition in megabytes.

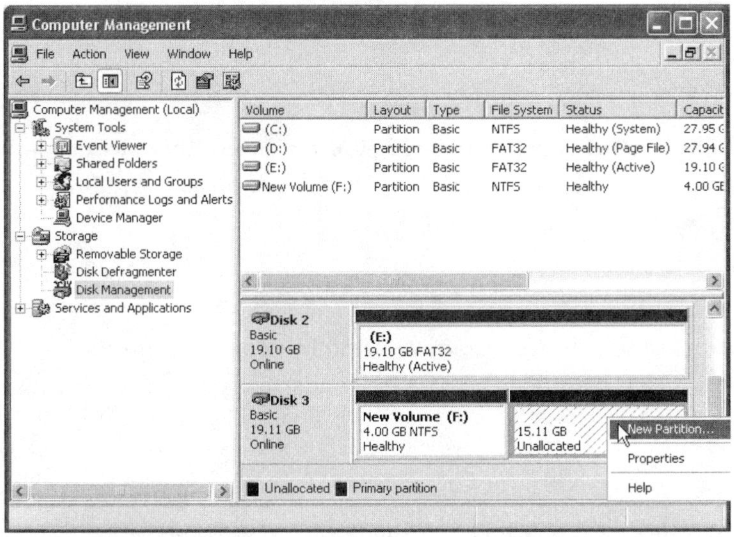

**FIGURE 5-4** Creating a new partition in Disk Management

**Step 4** Your next step depends on which tool you're using:

- In Disk Administrator, once the partition is created, you must alternate-click the partition and select Commit Changes Now. Click the Yes button on the confirmation dialog box the opens. Disk Administrator then alerts you that the disks were updated successfully and reminds you to update your Emergency Repair Disk. Click OK to close this dialog box.

- In Disk Management, the next screen is where you assign a drive letter or mount the partition to an empty folder. For now, go with the default drive letter assignment and click Next again.

The next step is formatting the partition. If using Disk Administrator, this is a separate process, so you can skip ahead to the next lab exercise. If you're using Disk Management, you'll note that the next screen in the New Partition Wizard offers you the option of formatting the new partition. One-stop shopping!

For now, however, select the Do Not Format This Partition radio button and click Next, and then click Finish to exit the wizard.

 30 MINUTES

# Lab Exercise 5.04: Formatting Partitions with Disk Administrator, Disk Management, and My Computer

Just as with the command line tools, the next step after creating a partition with Disk Administrator or Disk Management is to format it with a file system. Either of these tools also has the capability of formatting the partition that you just created, but you can also use another Windows utility that you should be intimately familiar with by now: My Computer.

✔ **Hint**

Remember that different versions of Windows support different file systems: Windows 9x supports only FAT, either FAT16 or FAT32; Windows NT supports only FAT16 and NTFS4; Windows 2000 and XP support FAT16, FAT32, and NTFS5.

Note that you're not given a choice as to which file system you can format partitions with—Windows NT automatically formats with NTFS4, Windows 2000/XP automatically formats with NTFS5.

✔ **Hint**

NTFS5 is completely backward compatible with NTFS4, but Windows NT systems must have Service Pack 4 installed to read NTFS5-formatted partitions.

## Learning Objectives

In this exercise, you'll use Disk Administrator or Disk Management program (depending on whether you have Windows NT or Windows 2000/XP) to format a hard disk drive partition with a file system.

At the end of this lab, you'll be able to

- Format a partition with a file system

## Lab Materials and Setup

The materials you need for this lab are

- A Windows NT, 2000, or XP PC with a blank hard disk drive (or a hard disk that you can safely erase)

### ✖ Warning

Partitioning a hard disk drive destroys any data on it! Practice this lab only on disks that don't store any data that you need.

## Getting Down to Business

In the following steps, you'll complete what you started in the previous exercise and format your new partition with a file system.

**Step 1**   Open the appropriate tool and locate the newly created partition.

**Step 2**   To format the new partition with a file system, alternate-click it and select Format from the pop-up menu.

**Step 3**   Select the file system (FAT or NTFS in Disk Administrator; FAT, FAT32, or NTFS in Disk Management) and enter a volume label if you wish. Then click Start or OK, in Disk Administrator or Disk Management, respectively. Figure 5-5 shows this selection screen in the Disk Management utility.

**Step 4**   The utility will warn you that formatting will erase all data on the disk. Click OK to begin formatting.

**Step 5**   My Computer also enables you to format partitions, but generally speaking you'll only use this method to format removable disks such as floppy diskettes, Zip disks, USB thumb drives, and so on.

Simply alternate-click a drive icon in My Computer and select Format from the pop-up menu to start the formatting dialog box shown in Figure 5-6. Then proceed as listed previously.

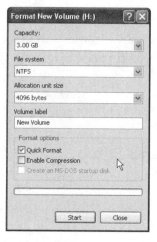

**FIGURE 5-5** Formatting a partition in Disk Management

**FIGURE 5-6** Formatting a partition in My Computer

 30 MINUTES

# Lab Exercise 5.05: Creating and Managing Dynamic Disks with Disk Management

By now, you've created and formatted your new hard drive partitions—think you're finished? With Windows 2000 Professional and Windows XP Professional, you can turn those basic disks you just partitioned and formatted into dynamic disks using the Disk Management utility.

---

✔ **Hint**

Remember that different versions of Windows have different names for the same basic utility. Disk Administrator is only found in Windows NT 4.0 while Disk Management is part of Windows 2000 and Windows XP. Some techs incorrectly use the term Disk Administrator when they really mean Disk Management.

---

Dynamic disks are great because they're flexible. With dynamic disks, a user can make two separate volumes on physically separate hard drives appear as one large volume when viewed in My Computer. Likewise, a user can *stripe* data across two separate partitions to increase the hard drive write speed of a particular system. Before you can start to explore all the features of dynamic disks, however, you have to take the partitions you just formatted and get them ready.

## Learning Objectives

In this exercise, you'll use the Disk Management utility to convert basic disks into dynamic disks.

At the end of this lab, you'll be able to

- Convert a basic disk into a dynamic disk

- Span a simple volume

- Stripe two simple volumes

## Lab Materials and Setup

The materials you need for this lab are

- A Windows 2000 Professional or Windows XP Professional PC with a freshly formatted and partitioned hard drive installed (the machine you used for Lab Exercise 5.04 will work just fine)

✔ **Hint**

In order to take full advantage of the dynamic disk features of Disk Management, you need to have a second hard drive installed in your PC (or an extended partition with a logical drive created on your primary hard drive), otherwise, some of the dynamic disk features will not apply. Also, be sure that you have properly backed up any data on that hard drive, just in case.

## Getting Down to Business

In the following steps, you'll build on what you accomplished in the previous exercise and convert your basic disks into dynamic disks.

**Step 1** Open Disk Management. Use the method that you prefer.

**Step 2** To convert a basic disk into a dynamic disk, alternate-click the name of the disk. Select Convert to Dynamic Disk, as shown in Figure 5-7.

**Step 3** Select any additional disks you want to convert to dynamic disks and click OK.

**Step 4** Double-check your choices in the dialog box that pops up. When you have verified your choices, click Convert to begin the conversion process (see Figure 5-8).

✖ **Warning**

Do not convert any basic disks that contain operating systems into dynamic disks; if you do, you won't be able to boot to these disks!

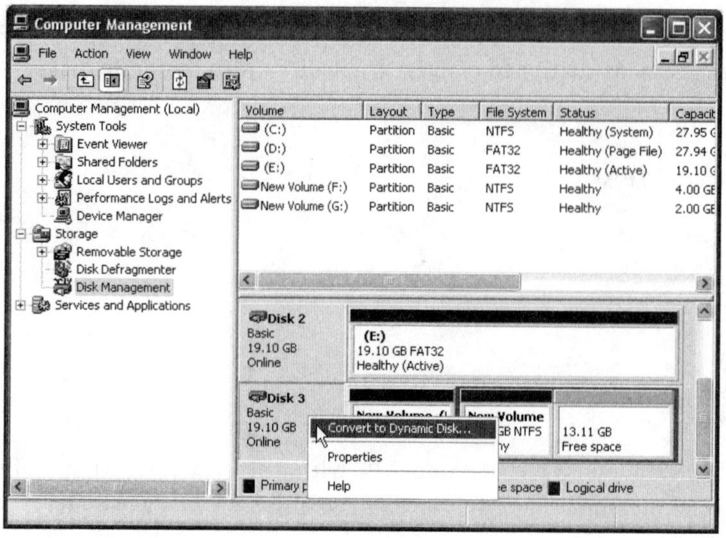

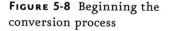

**FIGURE 5-7** Converting to dynamic disk

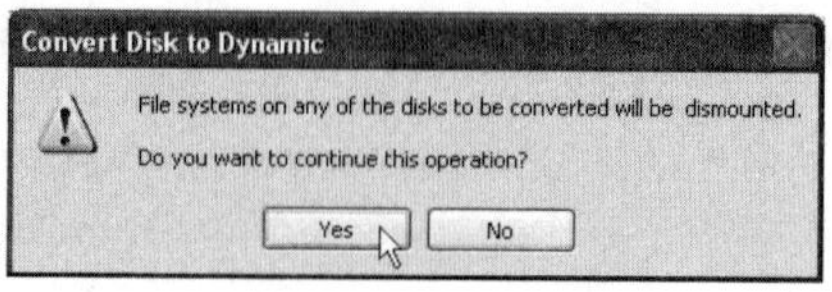

**FIGURE 5-8** Beginning the conversion process

**Step 5** Take a look at Disk Management now. You should see something like Figure 5-9, showing your new dynamic disks.

Now that you've got your dynamic disks set up, let's explore some of the things that can be done with them. The first thing to do now that you've set up your dynamic disks is to make a simple volume.

**Step 6** Alternate-click an unallocated area of the dynamic disk in Disk Management and select New Volume from the menu. You'll be asked to specify certain values, like file system and size. Repeat this step to make a second simple volume on your dynamic disk, but be sure to leave some free space open on the dynamic disk.

---

### ✔ Cross-Reference

For details about working with dynamic disks, refer to the "Partitioning Dynamic Disks" section of Chapter 5 of *Mike Meyers' A+ Guide to Operating Systems*.

---

**Step 7** One of the most common tasks performed with dynamic disks is spanning. Spanning simply means taking a simple volume and extending it to grab up free space on either the same or another dynamic disk, making the two separate areas of a disk or disks act like and appear to be a single volume.

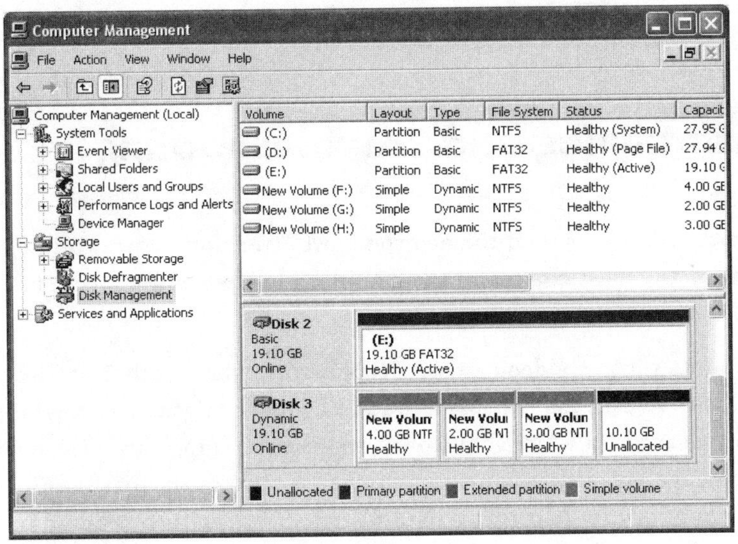

**FIGURE 5-9** Dynamic disks revealed

Alternate-click one of the simple volumes you've created in Disk Management and select Extend Volume. Follow the instructions presented by the wizard. Span the volume you chose with the free space available at the end of the dynamic disk. Voila! It's that simple. You've created a volume that is *spanned* across two separate areas of the disk.

Now that you've mastered the art of spanning dynamic disks, let's try *striping* dynamic disks.

**Step 8** Select two unallocated spaces on dynamic disks in Disk Management. Do this by holding the CTRL key while selecting two unallocated simple volumes by clicking them with your mouse. You might need to remove the spanned volume you created earlier or create some new simple volumes on the dynamic disk. You can remove a spanned volume by alternate-clicking the volume and selecting Delete Volume from the menu.

**Step 9** Alternate-click these selected volumes and select New Volume. Choose the option for creating a striped volume and enter the appropriate values. Once that's finished, take a look at the Disk Management screen. Your striped volume should have a single drive letter, but should be just as large as the total of the two unallocated volumes you initially selected.

✖ **Warning**

Be careful to back up data when you try striping. If one portion of the striped volume fails, the whole volume fails since data that is written on one portion depends on the other portion, and vice versa.

1 HOUR

# Lab Exercise 5.06: Maintaining and Troubleshooting Hard Disk Drives

Of all the devices installed on a PC, hard disk drives tend to need the most attention. Maintaining and troubleshooting hard disk drives is one of the most common tasks you'll undertake as a PC tech, but also one of the most important.

After all, the loss of other components such as video cards or NICs is inconvenient, but hardly disastrous. The loss of a hard disk drive, however, means the loss of data. This data might be as trivial as your favorite bookmarked Web pages or a saved Half-Life game, or it might be as important as your business records, family photos, or the 1200-page novel that you've spent the last two years writing! Unless you want to spend valuable time and money trying to retrieve data from a damaged or corrupted hard disk drive, you should familiarize yourself with the built-in Windows disk maintenance tools. These tools include

**Error-checking**   This GUI tool enables you to examine the physical structure of the disk and retrieve data from bad clusters. Command line utilities that perform the same duties are called CHKDSK and SCANDISK.

**Disk Defragmenter**   This tool reorganizes disorganized file structures into contiguous clusters.

**Disk Cleanup**   This tool reclaims wasted space on the hard disk drive by deleting unneeded files and compressing files that are rarely accessed.

## Learning Objectives

At the end of this lab, you'll be able to

- Use Error-checking to scan for and fix physical errors on the hard disk drive
- Use the Disk Defragmenter utility to reorganize the hard disk drive's file structure
- Use the Disk Cleanup utility to reclaim wasted disk space

## Lab Materials and Setup

The materials you need for this lab are

- A fully functioning Windows PC

## Getting Down to Business

There are a number of reasons why you should perform regular maintenance on your hard disk drives. The first is if you're getting obvious disk-related errors, such as error messages indicating that your disk has bad clusters or cannot be read from, or that files are missing or corrupt. Another sign that your disk needs a tune-up is excessive disk activity, or disk "thrashing." It's also a good idea after a serious system crash or virus infection to scan your disk for damage or fragmentation.

**Step 1**   To scan a hard disk drive for physical problems, open My Computer and alternate-click the drive's icon. Select Properties from the pop-up menu, and then select the Tools tab, shown in Figure 5-10. Click Check Now to start the Error-checking utility.

On Windows 9x systems, you're prompted to select either Standard or Thorough error-checking, and given the option of automatically fixing errors. Windows 2000/XP systems give you essentially the same options. Select the appropriate check boxes to have the utility do a thorough scan and automatically fix errors, and click Start.

✔ **Hint**

The Error-checking utility must have *exclusive* access to the drive to finish scanning it. If you have services or applications running in the background, the utility will halt. In some cases, the utility will schedule itself to run the next time you restart your PC.

The Error-checking utility has two command line equivalents, CHKDSK (used on Window NT, 2000, and XP) and SCANDISK (used on Windows 9x). There's no inherent advantage to running these utilities as opposed to the GUI version, except that you can launch the utilities as part of a scripted batch file.

**Step 2**   To launch the Disk Defragmenter, click Defragment Now. Windows 2000/XP's version of the Disk Defragmenter, shown in Figure 5-11, is somewhat more sophisticated looking than Windows 9x's version, but they both do the same thing.

**FIGURE 5-10**  Disk Properties Tools tab

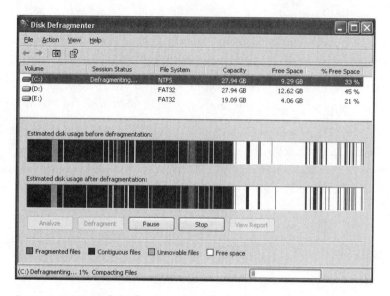

**FIGURE 5-11** Disk Defragmenter

Windows 9x's Disk Defragmenter starts running immediately after launching, but Windows 2000/XP's version does not; it offers you a choice: you can click Analyze to examine the disk to see if a defragmenting operation is needed, or simply click Defragment to start the process without first analyzing the drive.

**Step 3** Select properties for a drive and click Disk Cleanup on the General tab. Disk Cleanup calculates the space you'll be able to free up, and then displays the Disk Cleanup dialog box, shown in Figure 5-12.

Near the top it tells you how much disk space (maximum) it could free up. But look carefully! Depending on which categories in the list of Files To Delete are checked, the actual amount of disk space you'll gain could be much smaller than the estimate at the top. As you select and deselect choices, watch this value change.

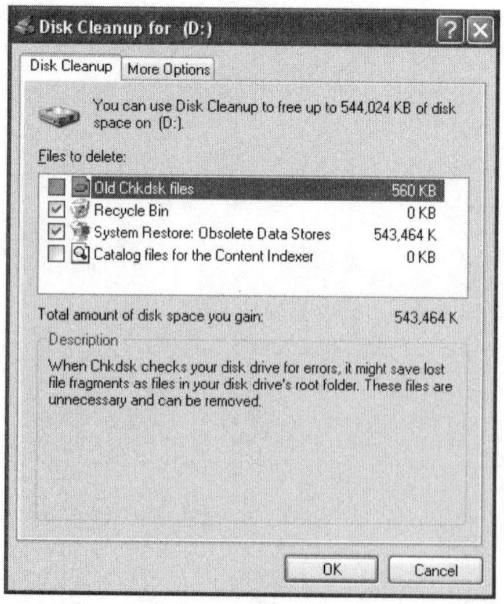

**FIGURE 5-12** Disk Cleanup

Pretty cool, but wait, there's more—Disk Cleanup does more than just delete files! If you scroll down through the list you'll see a choice to compress old files. In fact, this file compression trick is where Disk Cleanup really, uh, cleans up. File compression is where you'll gain the most space. The other big heavyweight category is temporary Internet files, which you usually want to be sure you have Disk Cleanup delete for you.

# Lab Analysis Test

**1.** Name at least two indicators that you should perform maintenance on your hard disk drive.

_____

_____

**2.** What are the two command line versions of the Windows Error-checking utility?

_____

_____

**3.** Jackie argues that a hard drive must be formatted before you can set up the partitions. Pam says the drive must be partitioned first. Who is correct and why?

_____

_____

**4.** The FORMAT C: /S command puts three files on the partition to make it bootable. What are their names?

_____

_____

**5.** What is the maximum number of logical drives you can configure using FDISK?

_____

_____

# Key Term Quiz

Use the following vocabulary terms to complete the following sentences. Not all of the terms will be used.

CHKDSK

defragmentation

Disk Cleanup

Disk Management

dynamic disk

Error-checking

FDISK

format

partition

SCANDISK

1. To _____ a hard drive in Windows 9x you can use the _____ program from a command line.

2. Use a _____ tool to fix noncontiguous file clusters on a hard drive.

3. The _____ tool enables you to partition and format drives in Windows XP.

4. To create a FAT or NTFS file structure, you must _____ the hard drive.

5. If your hard disk drive is running out of free space, you should use the _____ utility.

# Chapter 6

## Installing and Upgrading Windows

### Lab Exercises

**A**s a PC technician, you'll spend a lot of time installing and upgrading operating systems. For this reason, it's important that you become familiar with the tasks involved—otherwise, you might find yourself in a tight spot when Windows XP Professional Edition won't install on the laptop that your boss needs to have working for a presentation in an hour.

A number of different operating systems are in use today, including Apple MacOS X, several different flavors of Linux, and of course the Microsoft Windows family. Because CompTIA's A+ Certification focuses on Microsoft products and because Microsoft products represent the majority of the market, these lab exercises are limited to Windows.

Just about anyone can install software if everything goes right and no problems come up during the process; plenty of people with minimal software knowledge have upgraded Windows without the slightest incident. Even an experienced technician may have problems, though, if the system has incompatible expansion cards, broken devices, or bad drivers. As an A+ technician, you have to be prepared to handle both the simple installations—the ones with only new, compatible components—and the more complex installations on older and more problematic systems.

Installing and upgrading Windows is more than popping in the installation CD and running the install program. You need to plan the installation thoughtfully, check for component compatibility, and thoroughly understand the installation options and how to configure them. You should know ahead of time whether the new installation or upgrade has a chance of succeeding.

Be sure to have everything you need before you start, from the installation CD to the disks containing your device drivers. If you should start to feel a bit over-prepared, remember the old adage: "Measure twice, cut once." Believe me, it's no fun to start over on an installation or upgrade if you mess it up! Do it right the first time—you'll be glad you did.

 30 MINUTES

# Lab Exercise 6.01: Pre-Installation Planning

Your client has asked you to upgrade his system to Windows XP Home Edition. He's currently running Windows 98 Second Edition (SE), and everything works fine. He has the documentation that came with his system, which states that it has an ASUS TX97 motherboard. He isn't sure how fast the processor is, but he does know that he's already using the maximum amount of memory that the system can take. Where do you start the planning process?

---

**✔ Cross-Reference**

To review the details of pre-installation planning, refer to the "Preparing for Installation or Upgrade" section of Chapter 6 of *Mike Meyers' A+ Guide to Operating Systems*.

---

## Learning Objectives

In this lab exercise, you'll become more familiar with using the Internet to help answer pre-installation questions.

At the end of this lab, you'll be able to

- Access the Microsoft support web site

- Determine the minimal requirements for a system installation

## Lab Materials and Setup

The materials you need for this lab are

- A working PC

- Internet access

## Getting Down to Business

The first step in a successful Windows installation or upgrade is to determine whether the hardware meets the requirements of the new operating system. Your first stop in this process is the Microsoft support web site.

Microsoft has invested massive amounts of energy and time in building its support web site. Sometimes digging through all of the articles on the huge number of web pages can be overwhelming, but I'm a firm believer in this site's usefulness. When I have a question that directly concerns a Windows operating system (or any Microsoft product, for that matter), I check this site first, and I'm rarely disappointed. In fact, while searching for the answer to a problem or question, I usually learn two or three new, sometimes unrelated, things just by reading through the search results. Also, my search techniques improve with each visit. I consider the Microsoft support web site an invaluable tool and resource.

**Step 1**    Start by looking up the requirements for Windows XP Home Edition. Go to www.microsoft.com/windowsxp/home/howtobuy/upgrading, and view the four choices that will help you determine whether your client's machine is actually capable of running Windows XP (see Figure 6-1).

---

**✔  Hint**

Web sites are infamous for losing information that was once relevant to a particular subject—or sometimes disappearing altogether. If any of the links in this lab manual are no longer active or don't seem to contain information relevant to the exercise in question, please direct your browser to www.mikemeyersaplus.com to find an updated list of links or modified lab exercises.

---

Select the first option, Check Your System Requirements, and then answer these questions:

What's the recommended/minimum CPU speed? _____

What's the recommended/minimum amount of RAM? _____

How much hard drive space is required? _____

What video resolution is required? _____

At a minimum, what other devices are required? _____

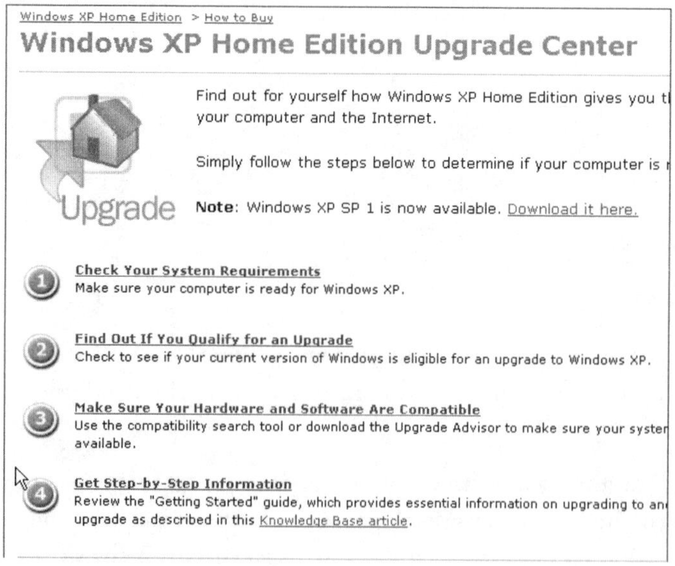

**Figure 6-1**  Using the Windows XP Home Edition Upgrade Center

Click your browser's Back button, select Find Out If You Qualify for an Upgrade, and then answer these questions:

Can Windows XP Home Edition be used to upgrade Windows 98 SE? _____

Can Windows XP Home Edition be used to upgrade Windows 2000 Professional? _____

Can Windows XP Professional Edition be used to upgrade Windows 98 SE? _____

Can Windows XP Professional Edition be used to upgrade Windows 2000 Professional? _____

Click your browser's Back button, and this time select Make Sure Your Hardware and Software Are Compatible.

Select Search the Windows catalog. On the resulting screen, enter the following components to see if they're compatible (see Figure 6-2):

Is the ASUS P4G8X Deluxe motherboard compatible with the recommended settings for Windows XP? _____

Is the ASUS TX97 motherboard compatible with the recommended settings for Windows XP? _____

Close all open windows.

**Step 2**   Because the ASUS TX97 motherboard isn't listed, you'll now try to find out why.

Open an Internet browser window, and perform a search on "ASUS TX97." You might find references to other versions, such as ASUS TX97-xe—be sure to look for the specifications of the basic TX97 model.

Why is this motherboard not on the Windows XP compatibility list?

_____

_____

**FIGURE 6-2** Searching the Windows catalog

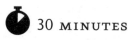 30 MINUTES

# Lab Exercise 6.02: Installing/Upgrading Considerations

You get a call from a client who wants to standardize the Windows operating systems that her employees use. She explains that as her company grew over the past few years, she bought new PCs and kept whatever version of Windows came pre-loaded on them. Now, some employees are using Windows 2000 Professional, while others with newer systems have Windows XP Professional Edition; team members on the same project are using different operating systems, and your client feels that this is a drain on productivity. She wants you to come in and upgrade all the Windows 2000 machines to XP.

### ✔ Cross-Reference

For a refresher on the considerations that come into play when you install or upgrade to Windows 2000/XP, refer to the "Upgrade Advisor" section of Chapter 6 of *Mike Meyers' A+ Guide to Operating Systems*; for details on the Files and Settings Transfer Wizard, read the section of the same name in Chapter 2.

## Learning Objectives

You'll review the steps for upgrading from Windows 2000 to Windows XP Professional Edition. The basic concepts are the same whether you upgrade to Windows XP from Windows 98 SE or from Windows Me.

At the end of this lab, you'll be able to

- Use the Microsoft Upgrade Center to check hardware compatibility for upgrading Windows

- Use the Upgrade Advisor

- Use the Files and Settings Transfer Wizard

## Lab Materials and Setup

The materials you need for this lab are

- A PC running Windows 2000 Professional Edition (Windows 98 SE and Windows Me are viable options, but may not work in all of the steps)

- Access to the Internet

- Blank formatted floppy disks—you may need as many as three—to save the settings during step 3 of this exercise

## Getting Down to Business

You need to upgrade a Windows 2000 system to Windows XP; this exercise assumes that you've done the preliminary research and collected all of the Windows XP drivers for your components. After looking at all of the issues, you've decided to do an upgrade rather than a clean install. You've visited the Microsoft Upgrade Center, and it appears that all of your hardware is compatible. Everything seems ready, but there's one final step you should take. Microsoft offers a tool to help check your software compatibility and provide a final check of the hardware compatibility. This tool is called the Upgrade Advisor, and it's a good idea to use it.

**Step 1** To begin verifying that your system is ready for an upgrade, make sure that the system's existing devices are getting along with one another under the current OS:

a)  Go to Device Manager (see Figure 6-3), and check for the symbols that indicate problems.

b)  If you find any conflicts, you should resolve these before you do the upgrade. Consult with your teacher to be sure this happens correctly.

**Step 2** Insert the Windows XP CD-ROM into the CD drive, close the tray, and wait for the Welcome to Microsoft Windows XP screen to appear.

---

✔ **Hint**

If the CD doesn't auto-start, try this alternate method to get started: Open My Computer and alternate-click the CD-ROM icon. Select Explore, and then double-click the SETUP.EXE icon.

---

**FIGURE 6-3** Checking Device Manager in Windows 2000 Professional for possible device conflicts

Microsoft has built the Upgrade Advisor into the installation routine, so you can look once more at the compatibility of your system from the operating system's point of view. It's always best to run the Upgrade Advisor prior to upgrading to XP to make sure that you've addressed any issues before the upgrade begins.

a)    Click Check System Compatibility to start the Upgrade Advisor (see Figure 6-4).

b)    On the screen that asks "What do you want to do?" click Check My System Automatically.

---

✔  **Hint**

Clicking Visit the Compatibility Web Site links you to a page that resembles an online retail store. You have to search around a little to make any progress on this web site, but you'll eventually find where the compatibility lists are stored.

---

If you're connected to the Internet and your teacher says it's okay, select "Yes, download the updated Setup files (Recommended)," as shown in Figure 6-5. If you have no Internet connection, select "No, skip this step and continue installing Windows."

When the Upgrade Advisor completes the check, it will display a report, as shown in Figure 6-6. If there are no errors, the system is ready to upgrade from Windows 2000 Professional to Windows XP Professional Edition.

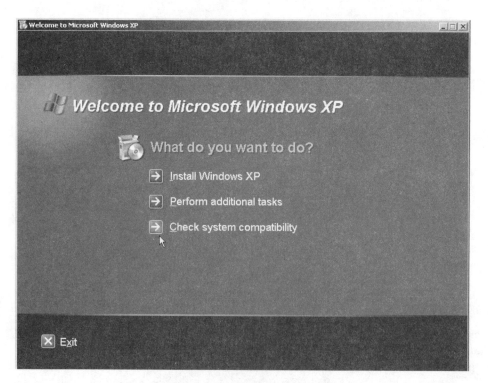

**FIGURE 6-4**  Launching the Windows XP Upgrade Advisor

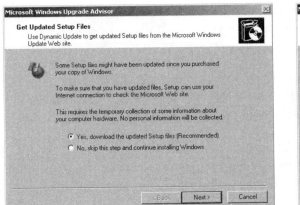

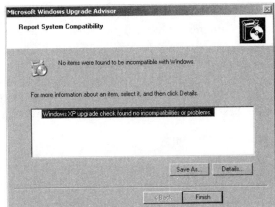

**FIGURE 6-5** Getting updated setup files    **FIGURE 6-6** Finding no incompatible items

---

✔ **Hint**

If the Upgrade Advisor informs you that an application or piece of hardware you have loaded is incompatible with Windows XP, you should do a little more searching—possibly on the manufacturer's web site—before you decide to remove the offending item. The Upgrade Advisor isn't always correct! If you do determine, however, that something should be removed, then by all means remove it; if you don't, you may be in for some serious upgrade headaches.

---

c)   Click Finish, then Back—but *do not* exit the Windows XP Welcome screen.

---

✔ **Hint**

Microsoft also provides the Update Advisor as a free download. I recommend using a high-speed connection to download it because it's a very large file—about 32 MB. I have a copy of this file stored on a separate CD so that I can test systems before giving my clients the bottom line on upgrading. If you do this, be sure to update the file periodically because new hardware and software are continually added to the list. The download site is www.microsoft.com/windowsxp/pro/howtobuy/upgrading/advisor.asp.

---

**Step 3**   There's another tool on the Windows XP CD that's worth mentioning. If you've upgraded operating systems before, you know how aggravating it is to lose some of your settings, such as your Internet Explorer settings, folder options, screensaver selection, and so on. The Files and Settings Transfer Wizard allows you to transfer all your personalized settings during an upgrade. Follow these steps:

a)   Click Perform Additional Tasks.

b)   Click Transfer Files and Settings, and then click Next (see Figure 6-7).

What you actually save will depend on your specific situation and the storage media you have available. Remember that a floppy disk will hold only about 1.44 MB, so if you need to back up 25 MB of files and settings, you'll have a real problem. For the purpose of this exercise, you'll practice saving just enough settings to fill a floppy disk or two.

In Figure 6-8, you'll note that there are several transfer methods you can use. For large amounts of data, it's best if you can save to a network server, or another PC on a network.

Follow these steps:

a) Just for grins, select Other, and click the Browse button to look around. If you're on a network, you may find a shared hard drive some place to transfer your data. Or you might have a Zip drive or other media available.

b) Click Cancel after you've looked around, and return to the Select a Transfer Method screen.

c) Click Floppy Drive, and then click Next.

   This next step is to determine what files/settings you want to transfer (see Figure 6-9). As you can see, there is a multitude of choices, but don't let that discourage you. The system will recommend certain folders and file types (defaults) that it thinks you need to transfer, but you can customize that to narrow the list down to what you really need. You only want enough to fill one or two disks for this exercise.

d) Click Settings Only.

e) Click the check box at the bottom left to select a custom list.

f) Click Next. The Select Custom Files and Settings screen appears (see Figure 6-10).

g) From this screen, it's possible to customize the settings you transfer by adding or removing items. For this exercise, accept the defaults by clicking Next. The system will calculate the amount of bytes to transfer and inform you of the number of disks you'll need (see Figure 6-11).

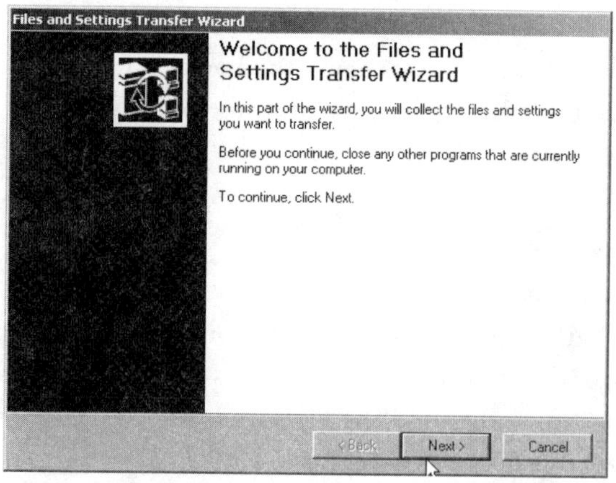

**Figure 6-7** Using the Files and Settings Transfer Wizard

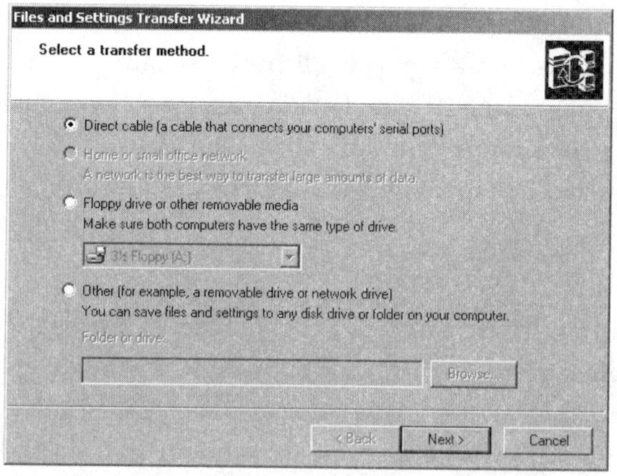

**Figure 6-8** Selecting a transfer method

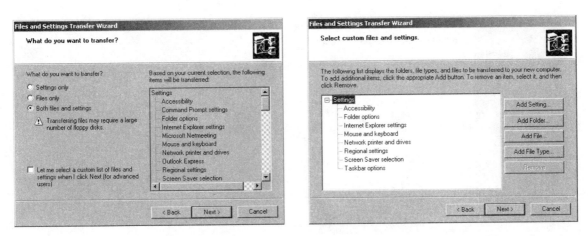

**FIGURE 6-9** What do you want to transfer?   **FIGURE 6-10** Selecting custom files and settings

h) Insert the first disk, and click OK.

i) Insert any other disks as needed.

j) The last screen displayed tells you how to transfer your saved data to the system after the upgrade is complete (see Figure 6-12).

k) Click Finish to close the wizard.

l) Click Back to return to the installation screen.

m) Exit the installation/upgrade wizard.

---

✔ **Hint**

The Files and Settings Transfer tool is located by selecting Start | Programs | Accessories | System Tools | Files and Settings Transfer Wizard on Windows XP systems. Once you save your files and settings and install/upgrade to Windows XP, you'll need to launch this wizard to transfer the settings to the new system. When you launch the wizard, select New Computer to let the system know you're importing the settings.

---

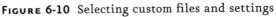

**FIGURE 6-11** Number of diskettes needed for transfer

Files and Settings Transfer Wizard

**Completing the Collection Phase**

You have successfully collected the files and settings from your old computer. Now go to your new computer and continue running the wizard to transfer the files and settings you collected.

If the wizard is not already running on your new computer, click Start, click All Programs, click Accessories, click System Tools, and then click Files and Settings Transfer Wizard.

To close this wizard, click Finish.

[< Back] [Finish] [Cancel]

**FIGURE 6-12** Completing the collection phase

**3 HOURS**

# Lab Exercise 6.03: Upgrading a Windows Operating System

A client of yours, who has a high-end system but still uses Windows 98 SE, decides to modernize by moving to a more recent OS. He asks you to upgrade his system to Windows 2000 Professional. You agree, and make the upgrade for him, only to find the next day that he's been thinking and reading up on the Web about Windows XP, and would *really* prefer to use that OS instead. Without missing a beat, you determine that his system meets the requirements for XP, and upgrade his system a second time.

## Learning Objectives

You need to finish at least one complete upgrade, both for practice and to prepare for questions asked on the A+ exam.

At the end of this lab, you'll be able to

- Upgrade an operating system

### ✔ Cross-Reference

To refresh your memory about the ins and outs of performing a Windows upgrade, read the "Windows 2000 Installation/Upgrade Process" section of Chapter 6 of *Mike Meyers' A+ Guide to Operating Systems*.

## Lab Materials and Setup

The materials you need for this lab are

- A working PC with a hard drive that you can write to without negative consequences

### ✔ Hint

To complete the exercise as described, you should begin with a system that has a copy of Windows 98 SE installed. For the full effect of this lab, you should have copies of both Windows 2000 Professional Edition and Windows XP Professional Edition. If you're unable to start with Windows 98 SE and upgrade in two steps—first to Windows 2000 and then Windows XP—you can modify the lab to complete at least one upgrade from an earlier version of Windows to a newer version.

## Getting Down to Business

You'll need quite a bit of time to complete this lab; most of that time will be spent waiting for Windows to install files. The exercise will walk you through upgrading a Windows 98 SE system to Windows 2000; you'll then upgrade the system to Windows XP. Depending on the systems and software licenses you have available, you may not be able to do this lab exactly as it's laid out here. The important thing is that you actually perform a Windows upgrade, to see the questions that are asked during the installation, and to become familiar with the process so that you're prepared for the A+ OS exam. If time constraints make it necessary, you can complete this lab in two separate sessions: the upgrade from Windows 98 SE to Windows 2000, and the upgrade from Windows 2000 to Windows XP.

When you start the installation process, you'll be asked what type of file system you want to install—FAT16, FAT32, or NTFS—and where you want the files installed. The program will set the default location as the C: drive. You should think about this before you begin, referring to the textbook for guidance on this issue. The next step is the big file copy process. Finally, you'll be asked a series of questions about naming your system and what networking configuration is applicable to your situation.

### ✘ Warning

While I would normally encourage you to answer the installation questions on network configuration yourself after consulting the information on networking settings covered in Chapter 9 of *Mike Meyers' A+ Guide to Operating Systems*, if you're in a classroom environment, you should ask your instructor about these settings before you begin the upgrade process.

**Step 1**    You've completed the compatibility exercise in the earlier labs, and you know that your system can handle Windows XP. With few exceptions, any system that can successfully load Windows XP can also load Windows 2000. For this lab, you'll do an upgrade rather than a clean installation; note that you'll also be migrating to NTFS during the upgrade to Windows 2000.

If you're starting with Windows 98 SE, the first step is to upgrade to Windows 2000. Ask the instructor (or decide for yourself, if you aren't in a classroom environment) what naming conventions you'll use and gather the information for any network you'll be connecting to, if applicable. Be sure that you have the Windows 2000 Professional CD handy, then follow these steps:

a) Insert the Windows 2000 CD. The Setup Wizard will start automatically. If it doesn't, go to My Computer, locate your CD drive, and browse to and double-click SETUP.EXE.

b) From the Setup Wizard screen, select Upgrade to Windows 2000 (see Figure 6-13).

c) Follow the instructions on the screen, which you'll find are pretty straightforward. When asked what file system you want to use, choose NTFS and continue.

d) When prompted, enter your user information and the information about your network, if applicable.

e) When the installation is complete, start Windows and navigate to Device Manger to confirm that there are no conflicts.

f) Ask the instructor whether you should continue with the next step at this time.

**Step 2** Be sure that you have the Windows XP Professional Edition CD handy, along with the appropriate network and user data—again, in a classroom environment, check with your instructor for this information. Then follow these steps:

a) Insert the Windows XP CD. The Setup Wizard will start automatically. If it doesn't, you can go to My Computer, locate your CD-ROM drive, and then browse to and double-click SETUP.EXE.

b) From the Setup Wizard screen, select Install Windows XP.

c) Follow the instructions on the screen; again, they're pretty straightforward.

d) When prompted, enter your user information and the information about your network, if applicable.

e) When the installation is complete, start Windows XP and navigate to Device Manger to confirm that there are no conflicts.

This would be an excellent time to practice installing the files and settings data that you saved onto floppy disks in Lab Exercise 6.02.

**FIGURE 6-13** Selecting Upgrade to Windows 2000

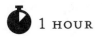 1 HOUR

# Lab Exercise 6.04: Performing a Clean Installation

Your boss usually orders new workstations already assembled and loaded with the desired Windows OS. She recently decided, though, that with her great in-house techs, she should be buying PC parts from a wholesaler instead, and having you and your team build the systems. You've enjoyed choosing the various hardware components and building these custom machines, but now it's time to bring your creations to life! You need to load Windows XP Professional Edition onto these new machines that have never seen the light of day.

## Learning Objectives

You should complete at least one clean Windows installation, both for the experience and to prepare for questions asked on the A+ exam.

At the end of this lab, you'll be able to

- Install a Windows operating system on a blank drive

## Lab Materials and Setup

The materials you need for this lab are

- A working PC with a blank hard drive, or with a hard drive that you can write to without negative consequences

- A Windows XP Professional Edition CD-ROM with a valid product key

## Getting Down to Business

In this exercise, you'll be putting an operating system onto a drive that doesn't currently have one. If the hard drive that you plan to use currently has data on it (even data that no one needs), then you must wipe that drive clean before you begin the exercise. Once you have a clean hard drive, you can proceed as directed.

### ✔ Cross-Reference

If you need to refresh your memory on how to format a hard drive, review the "Formatting Hard Drives" section of Chapter 5 of *Mike Meyers' A+ Guide to Operating Systems*.

**Step 1**   Insert the Windows XP CD-ROM into the CD drive, close the tray, and wait for the Welcome to Setup text screen to appear.

**Step 2**   Follow the directions to install the OS. Read the End User License Agreement thoroughly and agree to it to proceed. When the setup program prompts you to partition your drive, set up a single NTFS partition that uses all the available drive space. Then you'll simply need to wait and watch while the setup program does its magic and reboots the computer.

**Step 3**   When the computer has rebooted, work through the graphical portion of the installation process by carefully reading each screen and filling in the appropriate information. Be sure to enter the product key correctly, as you won't get past that screen with an invalid key.

**Step 4**   When you come to the Networking Settings screen, ask your instructor (if you're in a classroom setting) whether to use Typical or Custom settings, and what specific information to use.

**Step 5**   On the Let's Activate Windows screen, DO NOT activate at this time. Instead, select "No, log me off" and click Next. You should see a blank Windows Desktop, signifying that you've completed a successful installation of Windows XP.

# Lab Analysis Test

1.   Betsy just bought a new computer with Windows XP Professional Edition installed. She had been using Windows XP Professional Edition on her older and slower PC. Is there any way she can transfer her old settings to the new PC? If so, explain how.

2.   What's the recommended CPU speed and amount of RAM needed to install Windows XP Professional Edition?

3.   Dwight wants to upgrade his Windows 98 system to Windows XP Professional Edition, but he isn't sure about his hardware. What Microsoft tools would you recommend that he use to check his system?

4. Joe is just starting to study PC repair and has been reading about file systems. He asks you, the veteran tech, to explain why it's best to use NTFS for a new installation. What do you tell him?

_____

_____

5. What happens if you don't complete the Microsoft Product Activation (MPA) for Windows XP Home Edition within 30 days of installation?

_____

_____

# Key Term Quiz

Use the following vocabulary terms to complete the following sentences. Not all of the terms will be used.

CD-ROM drive

floppy disks

installation

network drive

upgrade

Upgrade Advisor

Windows 2000 Professional

Windows XP Home Edition

Windows XP Professional Edition

1. If you plan to install Windows XP onto a system, it must have a _____.

2. You can start with a blank hard drive to perform a full _____ of Windows 2000.

3. During a files and settings transfer, you can use a _____ to transfer large files.

4. Installing Windows XP on top of Windows 98 is known as a(n) _____.

5. You cannot upgrade directly from _____ to Windows XP Home Edition.

# Chapter 7

# Maintaining, Optimizing, and Troubleshooting Windows 9x/Me

## Lab Exercises

**E**very tech loves the idea of tweaking their Windows system to make it run faster, better, or prettier. Sadly, Windows 98 and Me are pretty well optimized right out of the box. There's not too much in the way of tweaks to make a Windows system run faster or better. You may have seen some of the many third-party products supposedly designed to make Windows function better, but generally they only take the same tweaks that are available to you and automate them with pretty front ends and help screens. There's nothing wrong with these tools, but reading a couple of good magazines and books on Windows hints and tips just as easily helps you optimize the OS for less money.

When I talk about optimizing Windows 9x/Me, I mean checking the status of and possibly adjusting certain OS settings, which in all probability are usually already set properly with their defaults. It's the product enhancements, proper device drivers, service packs, and so on that make the difference between a well-oiled machine and one that's generally troublesome if not downright difficult. To keep things running smoothly, you should take advantage of Microsoft's updates and keep your drivers current as you add new components. Microsoft has made it easy by adding the Windows Update tool.

Installing a new hardware device can bring with it a multitude of issues. What if the device you installed has a driver written specifically for Windows 98 and you later upgrade to Windows 98 SE or Me? The device itself may be on the Hardware Compatibility List, but in order for it to run correctly, you must make sure you have loaded the latest software driver for the version of Windows installed. And then if it still doesn't work properly, you must determine if the new driver requires that a corresponding update be made to the operating system.

These labs give you essential skills for maintaining, optimizing, and troubleshooting a Windows 9x/Me PC.

**30 MINUTES**

# Lab Exercise 7.01: Updating and Patching Windows 9*x*/Me

Your company has a new client that has a dozen Windows 98 PCs. Your boss assigns you the joyful task of updating and patching the systems so they run more stably.

It might come as a shock to some of you but every version of Windows has certain flaws or bugs. Shocking, but true! One of the essential tasks for techs is to update or apply specific patches to clients' machines. Not every Windows 9*x*/Me system requires every patch and update that Microsoft puts out, but instead a technician must analyze and install the patches for the version that's in the system at the time. Microsoft has released literally hundreds of fixes, patches, and updates for the Windows 9*x*/Me family, but the majority of them are important only for those that have a particular problem that the patch was designed to fix. Installing every patch for your version may cause you additional problems if the programs or features they fix (such as world languages or a tape drive you don't have) aren't enabled or installed on your system. Your job as a technician is to check for updates and patches and decide what applies to a specific system.

> ✖ **Warning**
>
> One thing to keep in mind is that some patches need to be installed before another patch can be used. This creates a unique situation where the patch order is quite important. You should install the oldest patch first unless the new one says it incorporates all patches before it.

## Learning Objectives

The student must know how to determine what version of the operating system is currently running on a system and how to download and install the appropriate fixes and patches.

At the end of this lab, you'll be able to

- Find the operating system version level
- Check the system for patches
- Access the Microsoft web site to download and install patches and updates

## Lab Materials and Setup

The materials you need for this lab are

- A PC running Windows 9*x*/Me
- Access to the Internet

```
C:\WINDOWS\Desktop>ver

Windows 98 [Version 4.10.2222]

C:\WINDOWS\Desktop>_
```

FIGURE 7-1  Checking the Windows 98 SE version number

## Getting Down to Business

This lab steps you through identifying which version of Windows is running on a system and what patches are needed. There are several ways to determine what version of Windows you're running. The A+ exam asks about this information, so be sure you know it.

**Step 1**    To verify the software version of your operating system, begin by opening a command line window:

a)    Select Start | Run and type **command** in the Run dialog box. Then click the OK button.

b)    From the command prompt, type **VER**, and press ENTER. See Figure 7-1 for a sample of the results from a Windows 98 SE system.

What's your operating system? _____

What's your version number? _____

**Step 2**    Select Start | Programs | Accessories | System Tools | System Information.

What version is listed for your system? _____

Does this agree with the VER command results from step 1? _____

My lab system is using Microsoft Me version 4.90.3000 (see Figure 7-2).

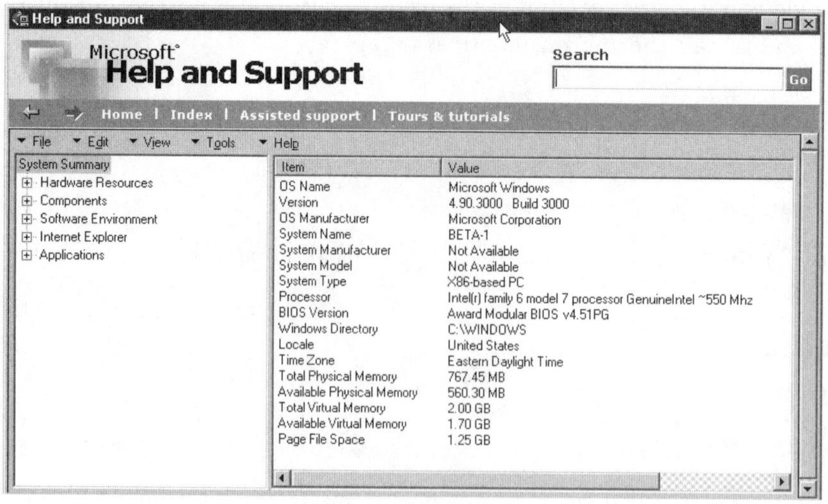

FIGURE 7-2  Windows Me version displayed in Help and Support

**Figure 7-3** My Computer's Properties

**Step 3**   There's one more place to look for the version level. Alternate-click My Computer and select Properties from the options. Read the version under System on the General tab (see Figure 7-3).

**Step 4**   Compare your operating system with the released updates/upgrades. Look at your release version and compare it to the following list.

### Versions of Windows 9x/Me

- Windows 95 (original) = Windows 95 4.00.950

- Windows 95 SP1 = Windows 95 4.00.950a

- Windows 95 SR2 = Windows 95 4.00.950b

- Windows 95 SR2.5 = Windows 95 4.00.950c

- Windows 98 (original) = Windows 98 (Windows 98 version 4.10.1998)

- Windows 98 Second Edition = Windows 98 Second Edition (Windows 98 version 4.10.2222)

- Windows Millennium Edition = Windows Me 4.90.3000

Most of the Microsoft system files and drivers have been modified or completely rewritten since their original release. Keep in mind that every time motherboard features or devices are improved, the operating system has to know how to communicate with the device. At first Microsoft used hot fixes and patches to modify the system files. When someone complained, Microsoft would send them a new, improved file to replace the broken one. This quickly became too much to keep up with so Microsoft created a web site where technicians could go and get the fixes or patches they needed. This idea eventually evolved into a feature called Windows Update.

**Step 5**   Click the Start button, and look at the top section of the menu for the Windows Update icon (see Figure 7-4).

When you click Windows Update (don't do it now), it uses the Internet to access the Microsoft web site. A local program on your system reports to Microsoft a table of information, calculated from the Registry, about what's installed in your system. Based on what's already installed, Microsoft reports what upgrades or patches are available for your system to be downloaded and installed.

With Windows 98, clicking the Windows Update menu item starts the process of checking for update. More recent versions of Windows, however, have an Automatic Update feature. This is available in Windows Me, 2000, and XP. When you turn this feature on, your PC will check for, download, and install critical updates for you. This eliminates the need for you to check for updates manually.

If your system has Windows Me installed, try this:

a)   Go to the Control Panel, and find the icon for Automatic Updates (see Figure 7-5).

b)   Double-click it to open the Automatic Updates Wizard, and review the choices for updating (see Figure 7-6):

- Automatic

- Notify Me First

- Manual

c)   Set your system according to your needs, and click OK.

---

### ✖ Warning

In the next step, I'm using a system running a rather old copy of Windows Me that hasn't been updated. This allows me to show you some good figures of what you may see. Remember that your system will definitely be different. The important thing is to learn the concepts presented here so you can apply them to your clients' PCs.

---

**FIGURE 7-4** Viewing the Windows 98 Start button menu

**FIGURE 7-5** Viewing the Automatic Updates icon in the Windows Me Control Panel

**FIGURE 7-6** Checking out Windows Me
Automatic Updates options (Windows 2000
looks slightly different)

**Step 6**   So let's do some updating already! If your Internet connection is ready, you're halfway there:

a)   Select Start | Windows Update. This connects you to Microsoft and displays the screen shown
in Figure 7-7.

b)   Click Scan for Updates (near the center of the screen).

The update program will report what needs to be installed. Notice in Figure 7-8 it reports that
Windows Me needs 2 critical and 37 other patches downloaded and installed.

c)   Click Review and Install Updates.

Because two updates are critical, it'll show you the details separately for these updates first (see
Figure 7-9).

**FIGURE 7-7** Using Windows Update

**FIGURE 7-8**  Picking the updates to install

d)    Click Install Now.

e)    Accept the license agreement.

Sometimes the patch can be added without a reboot, but other times you must restart your system to complete the installation.

Once the patch is added (and any necessary rebooting has occurred), go back to Windows Update and finish installing any other updates you require.

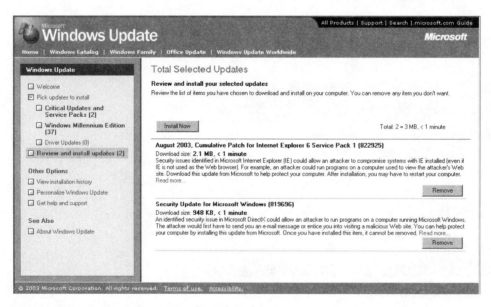

**FIGURE 7-9**  Viewing the total selected updates

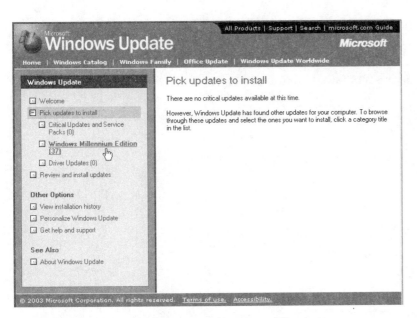

**FIGURE 7-10** Selecting other upgrades to install

In the left panel, select the updates you want to review (see the mouse pointer in Figure 7-10), then, when they appear, choose which ones you want to install by clicking the Add button in the right frame. Looking at my selections, I see that 33 of the 37 updates are for foreign language support, which I don't need.

Once you've selected all the updates you want to add, click Review and Install Updates, and then click Install Now.

 30 MINUTES

# Lab Exercise 7.02: Optimizing Windows 9*x*/Me

In addition to installing patches and updates, you can customize several tools and settings to optimize the performance of your Windows operating system. There are two categories of tweaks you can use for optimization. The first category includes settings that tell Windows how to use the available system resources. The second category consists of a group of tools that lets you monitor the resources being used by your system and control all the programs that run in the background. As you add programs to a PC, you build up an annoying list of programs that run in the background and drain system resources. Shutting down the background programs that you don't really need can free up resources and greatly improve the performance of your system.

## Learning Objectives

To optimize your system, you need to learn what tools are available to customize the operation of Windows and how to use them.

At the end of this lab, you'll be able to

- Locate and optimize your virtual memory swap file settings

- Turn on, locate, and use the Windows Resource Meter

- Turn on, locate, and use the System Monitor

- Locate and use the Task Manager

## Lab Materials and Setup

The materials you need for this lab are

- A PC running Windows 9x/Me

## Getting Down to Business

This lab walks you through the tools you can use to customize your Windows system and to monitor and optimize the usage of your system resources.

**Step 1**    In this step, you'll adjust the virtual memory settings for a PC. All versions of Windows use virtual memory. Virtual memory manifests itself in Windows via a swap file on the hard drive that acts like RAM. This allows your system to have more programs open on the screen than it could actually hold in real RAM. The swap file in Windows 9x/Me is called WIN386.SWP.

Windows sets the initial size of the swap file automatically during installation. Although automatic settings work fairly well, there are occasions when you might want to tweak the settings.

For Windows 9x/Me, you configure the swap file as follows:

a)    Alternate-click My Computer and select Properties.

b)    Select the Performance tab and click the Virtual Memory button (see Figure 7-11).

The most common reason for changing the default swap file is to move it to some drive other than C:. Systems tend to fill up the C: drive and when there's little or no room left for an adequate size swap file, Windows tends to act erratically. You always want to avoid filling up the drive that holds the swap file!

If you have two or more hard drive (or partition) letters, try moving your swap file:

a)    Click the "Let me specify my own virtual memory settings" radio button, and select another drive (see Figure 7-12).

b)    Once you're seen how this works, return the settings to the C: drive unless you're short of space on the primary hard drive, in which case leaving it on a secondary drive may improve your performance.

Notice the minimum and maximum swap file sizes. Windows 9x/Me sets the minimum to zero and the maximum to the size of the free space on the drive. Leaving these settings at their defaults creates enormous swap files, far larger than you really need. The current consensus is to reduce the swap file size down to around two or three times the amount of RAM.

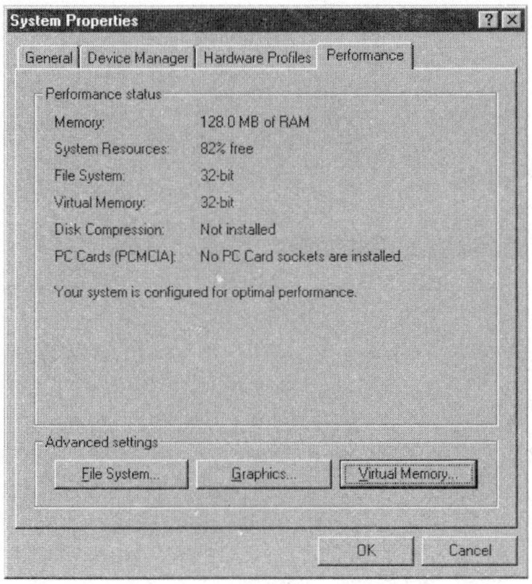

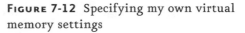

**FIGURE 7-11** Virtual Memory button on the Performance tab

**FIGURE 7-12** Specifying my own virtual memory settings

It can also be useful to put the swap file on either the fastest drive or the least-used drive. That way the computer is likely to access the swap file and exchange the data therein more quickly.

Record the current settings for your system. It's always good to note current settings before you make changes.

Minimum: _____

Maximum: _____

Setting the minimum and maximum to the same size can help reduce fragmentation, which is another thing that can contribute to a slow system. Change both the minimum and maximum settings to an amount equal to three times the amount of RAM in your system.

What did you set it to? _____

Click OK to save the new settings.

**Step 2**   You can spend the time optimizing your Windows operating system and yet still find that your system operates poorly. This can be caused by an inefficient use of available resources by the other programs you're running. Windows has several built-in tools that allow you to track and optimize resource use by other programs, but they may not be enabled unless you did so during the install process. In this step, you look at two of these valuable tools: System Resources and System Monitor.

Follow these steps:

a)   System Resources is one tool that many technicians use to observe resource allocation information on a Windows 9x/Me system. The System Resources percentage on the Performance tab of System Properties is the first place to look (see Figure 7-13).

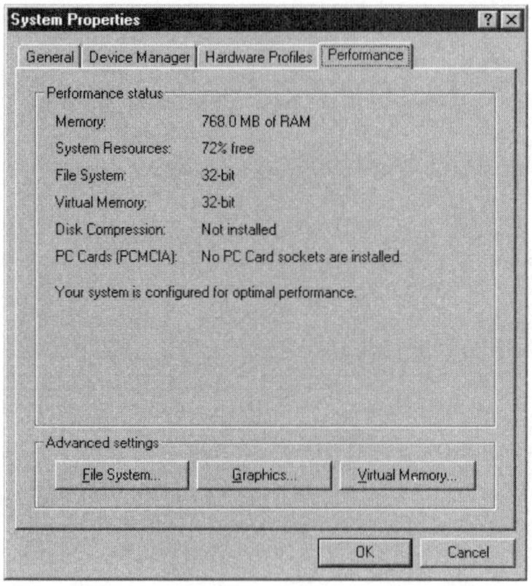

**FIGURE 7-13** Checking the System Resources percentages

**FIGURE 7-14** Adding System Tools from the Windows Setup tab of the Add/Remove Programs applet

b)   If you look for the Resource Meter and System Monitor and they're not there, you can turn them on by going to the Add/Remove Programs applet in the Control Panel. Open the applet, and look under the Windows Setup tab to find System Tools. Select System Tools, and click Details (see Figure 7-14).

c)   Scroll down the list, and select the check box by both tools (see Figure 7-15). Then click OK, click Apply, and then click OK. Windows may ask you for the Windows 9x/Me CD to complete the install.

d)   Alternate-click My Computer, and select Properties. Now look under the Performance tab for the amount of free system resources.

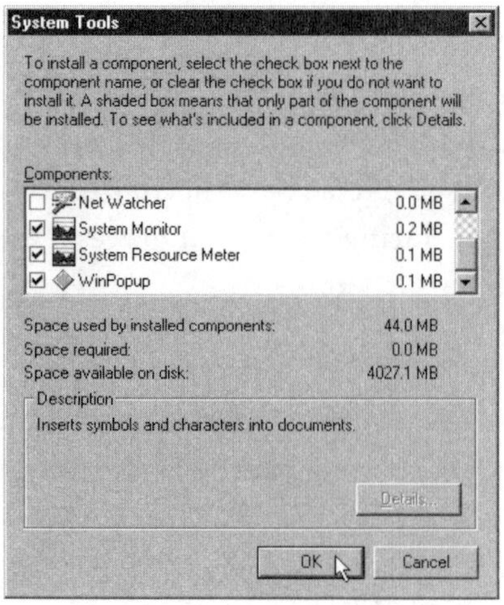

**FIGURE 7-15** Enabling System Monitor and System Resource Meter

e) The Resource Meter is a tool that gives a quick overview of resource usage. Select Start | Programs | Accessories | System Tools, and click Resource Meter. Also notice that you can choose System Monitor as well. Don't panic if these tools aren't there. If they weren't installed during the Windows installation, you'll have to install them from the Windows installation CD.

f) Clicking Resource Monitor will activate it and place an icon in your system tray that will allow you to monitor the resource usage.

g) You'll get a warning that reminds you that the Resource Meter itself uses resources and may slow down your system. Click OK.

h) By hovering your pointer over the icon in the system tray, you can check the system resources (see Figure 7-16). Alternate-click the icon in the system tray, and select Details (see Figure 7-17).

i) If your system is already a resource hog, don't leave the Resource Meter enabled for very long. It takes resources away from important programs. To close the Resource Meter, alternate-click the icon in the system tray and select Exit.

A+ Certification exams put great emphasis on the Resource Meter tool, but I find that I use the System Monitor much more.

**Step 3** The System Monitor is my favorite tool for checking system problems. It provides a graphic snapshot of a broad number of system processes. You can track free physical memory, CPU usage, and network throughput. In fact, almost any process where you need to see what's happening on your PC is shown by the System Monitor.

To open the System Monitor, select Start | Programs | Accessories | System Tools | System Monitor.

To produce the results shown in Figure 7-18, I transferred 24 files from the system I'm using to another system on the network to generate a spike in resource usage.

Become familiar with this tool; it can provide a lot of useful information. Take a look at some other things it can tell you:

- Select Edit | Add Item to open a dialog box with a selection of system activities you can choose to monitor.

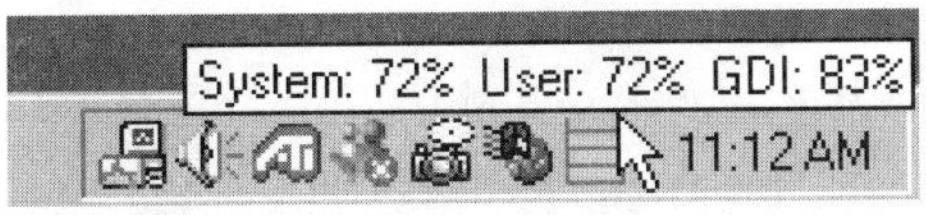

**FIGURE 7-16** Quickly checking resource usage

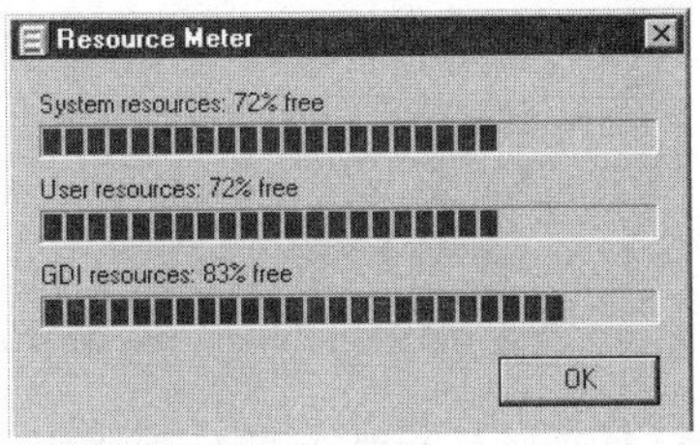

**FIGURE 7-17** Getting the Resource Meter details

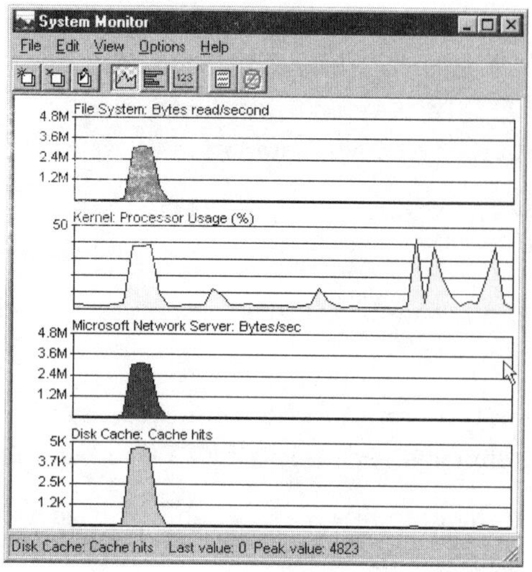

**FIGURE 7-18** Using the System Monitor

- Monitor a variety of system activities. In particular, select Cache Hits under Disk Cache, Processor Usage (%) under Kernel, and Allocated Memory under Memory Management.

  Can you explain how these would be useful?

  _____

  _____

- On the main System monitor screen, select Options | Chart to open the Options dialog box. Use the slide bar to increase and decrease the update interval.

- Explore other settings.

  Which do you think are the most useful settings for you to use as a technician?

  _____

  _____

**Step 4** The Task Manager is another tool that you can use to track and control resources. Sometimes a program will lock up for some unknown reason. The Task Manager is a good way to end the program or task.

Press CTRL-ALT-DELETE and the Task Manager comes up, showing all of the running programs, including some hidden ones. I often use the Task Manager in concert with the System Resource Meter and System Monitor to close background programs that seem to defy all other attempts to shut them down. It's also a good tool for closing an unresponsive program without having to crash the entire system.

Try closing some of the programs running in the background on your system and watch the effect it has on the System Monitor. Remember not to close Explorer or Systray because these two programs must run in order to keep Windows running.

 30 MINUTES

# Lab Exercise 7.03: Installing Devices with Windows 9*x*/Me

The non-profit company where you work has just received a stack of donated scanners and other equipment that plug into proprietary expansion cards. The cards range from legacy ISA to Plug and Play (PnP) PCI cards. Your job is to get the expansion cards installed so folks can use the scanners.

When installing a legacy device, or a newer one that you're not sure of, follow these basic rules:

**Physical Compatibility**   Where will this device plug into the system? Be sure you have a way to connect it. Does your system have an open slot of the right type?

**System Compatibility**   You must consider the possibility of system incompatibility. What if you have an open PCI slot and want to install a second video card into your Windows Me system to use two monitors? Will this PCI card, motherboard, and BIOS support a two-monitor system?

**Driver Check**   Always check the version of drivers that come with a device. Most hardware today comes with drivers for more recent operating systems such as Windows XP but may not have drivers for older operating systems such as Windows 9*x*/Me. Also find out whether you have the latest drivers. A large percentage of devices don't ship with the latest drivers. Driver updates frequently occur while the device is sitting on the shelf at the store. A quick check at the manufacturer's web site can usually settle this issue quickly. If the driver disk that comes with your new device doesn't have the latest driver, be sure to download and the new driver before you begin an installation.

**Resource availability**   Does the new device have jumpers or is it a jumperless PnP card? Do you have available IRQs, I/O addresses, and DMA channels to assign to the new device?

## Learning Objectives

You should be prepared to add any given device to a working PC system or explain why it can't be done. You should also be able to reboot a system that has locked up because of problems caused by installation errors that create software/hardware conflicts.

At the end of this lab, you'll be able to

- Create a emergency startup disk
- Determine Device Manager errors
- Determine the correct drivers to install

## Lab Materials and Setup

The materials you need for this lab are

- A working PC with Windows 9x/Me installed

- A blank floppy disk

## Getting Down to Business

The first step before you begin any troubleshooting should be to create a startup disk. If you make a mistake and your system locks up, you might not be able to recover unless you have a startup disk handy.

**Step 1**  What if you add a device and somehow the software gets messed up and your system won't boot? Windows 9x/Me both have the capability to create an emergency startup disk with CD-ROM support. A startup disk is a bootable floppy disk that, in case of an emergency, enables you to access an A: prompt. Follow these steps:

a) Open the Control Panel.

b) Locate the Add/Remove Programs icon, and click it to start the applet.

c) Click the Startup Disk tab.

d) Insert a blank floppy disk into the floppy drive.

e) Click Create Disk.

f) After Windows has created the startup disk, take it out of the floppy drive, label it, and set it aside for later. I hope you won't need it.

✔ **Hint**

On some systems, Windows prompts for the Windows installation CD; on others, it won't. The startup disk that Windows creates contains just enough files to perform basic troubleshooting.

✔ **Cross-Reference**

Windows 95 startup disks lack the capability to provide access to the CD drive. You need to copy two files and edit two others so that a Windows 95 startup disk can access CDs. Read Chapter 7 in the *Mike Meyers' A+ Guide to Operating Systems* to see how to make a Windows 95 boot disk with CD support. Many technicians, including me, use a Windows 98 startup disk when working on Windows 95 systems—it works just fine!

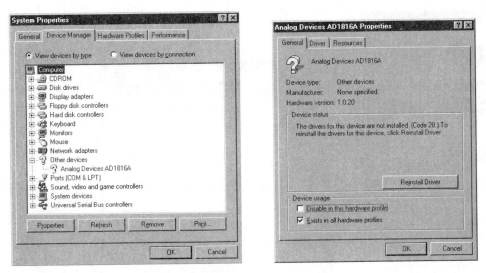

**FIGURE 7-19**  Using the Device Manager          **FIGURE 7-20**  Driver problem

**Step 2**   The Device Manager is the primary tool for dealing with devices and device drivers in Windows, a fact you'll recall from Chapter 2 of the main textbook. Device Manager displays every device that Windows recognizes. Figure 7-19 shows a typical Device Manager screen with all installed devices in good order with the exception of a device named Analog Devices AD1816A (a sound card). If Windows detects a problem, it shows the device with a yellow question mark (?) or exclamation point (!), as you see in Figure 7-19.

a)   Open your Device Manager, and look for any problems. Expand every device type including System Devices, and look for yellow question marks and exclamation points or a red ×.

b)   List any devices that aren't fully functional on your system.

_____

_____

c)   By double-clicking a questionable device (or by selecting the device and clicking the Properties button), you can see the device status. According to Figure 7-20, the analog device needs the driver reinstalled. Most likely it needs an updated driver.

Some legacy systems have trouble allocating resources, so the Device Manager gives you a way to "adjust" some of the resources. Of course, I'm assuming you have already made all the configuration adjustments to the physical device (jumpers and so on) and BIOS settings (enable/disabling COM ports and stuff) when I covered that earlier in the manual.

d)   Double-click any device (or select the device and click the Properties button) and then click the Resources tab, and you can see the resources used by that device.

e)   Figure 7-21 confirms a driver problem because the Resource tab shows no conflicts.

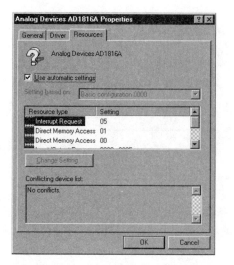

**FIGURE 7-21** Seeing no resource conflicts

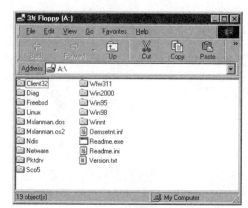

**FIGURE 7-22** Linksys NIC drivers

**Step 3** When installing drivers, make sure you locate the driver for the correct operating system. Take care and select the right operating system folder on the driver disk. If you tell the system, especially Windows 9x/Me, to install the driver for the wrong operating system, it may do so and cause problems. This can create a huge mess! Not only does the device not work, but the operating system requires you to delete the device from Device Manager and try again. In some cases, installing the wrong driver wreaks even more havoc: Windows copies a device INF file to the \INF folder, so even if you delete the device from the Device Manager, Windows keeps reinstalling the wrong driver! To stop this action, you must find and delete the INF file and the references to it in the Registry.

Look at Figure 7-22. This is the driver disk for a Linksys LNE100TX PCI network card. You see that you have an open PCI slot so you install the card and your Windows Me PnP operating system finds it.

When you're asked for the location of the driver, where will you look?

_____

_____

 30 MINUTES

# Lab Exercise 7.04: Working with Windows Me System Restore

The first three labs dealt with upgrading and resolving conflicts in the software and hardware. Many times these problems are self-inflicted due to something you installed or changed. In these cases, the best thing you can do is to put the system back to the state it was in before you started. This lab focuses on restoring the system to a previously working state.

## Learning Objectives

The successful technician knows how to restore a working Windows Me system that has encountered problems beyond those associated with installation and configuration problems.

At the end of this lab, you'll be able to

- Manually create a restore point in Windows Me

- Restore a Windows Me system to a restore point

## Lab Materials and Setup

The materials you need for this lab are

- A working PC with Windows Me installed

## Getting Down to Business

Windows Me has a great utility to help you restore your system after a botched program or driver installation. It watches for any system changes and records them in a diary. To restore a system to a previous state, just open the diary and point to a day and time you want to restore.

**Step 1**  In this step, you'll manually create a restore point in Windows Me. Windows Me automatically creates restore points each day, as well as any time you install an application, update a driver, or add a piece of hardware. You also have the option to create your own restore points whenever you want and give them unique names that are meaningful to you. You might decide to create a restore point before tweaking a bunch of settings in the Control Panel, for example, and name the restore point "B4Tweaking" system settings.

a)   To create a restore point, select Start | Programs | Accessories | System Restore to open the System Restore utility (see Figure 7-23).

b)   At the welcome screen, choose Create a Restore Point from the radio buttons on the right side of the screen, and then click Next.

c)   Type **My Test Restore Point**, and click Next.

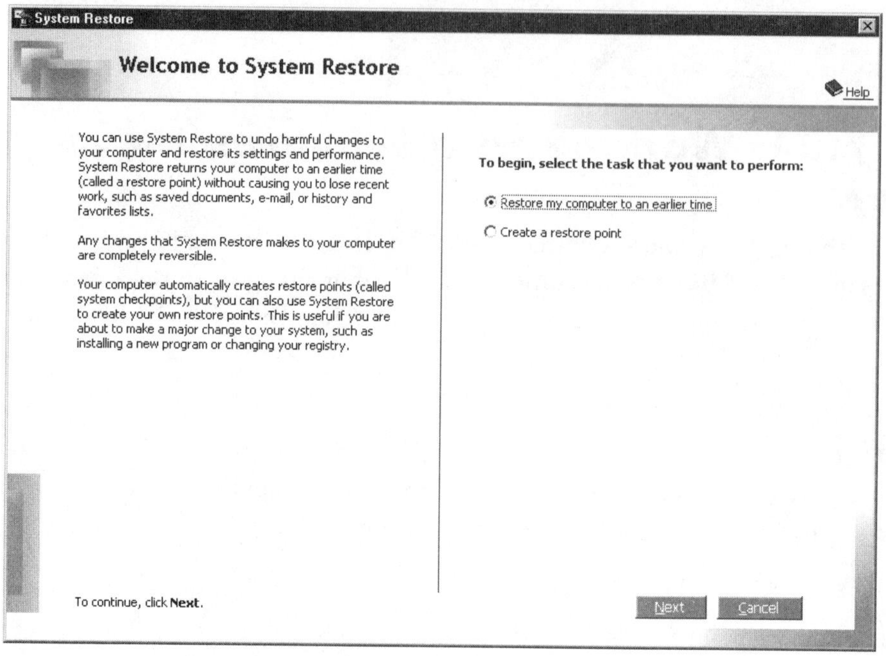

**FIGURE 7-23** Using System Restore

d) The system will take some time building the restore file information and then display a confirmation screen (see Figure 7-24). Click OK to continue.

You're done! That was easy!

**Step 2** To restore the system to an earlier time, return to the System Restore utility, but this time, select Restore My Computer to an Earlier Time.

When you click the Next button, the Select a Restore Point screen displays, with a calendar and a listing of the most recent restore points (see Figure 7-25). Based on your knowledge of when your system started having problems, select a restore point and follow the prompts to complete the restore operation.

System Restore is pretty powerful. Even if you crash hard and can only boot to Safe mode, you can still run the System Restore utility to recover your system. It sure beats the alternative!

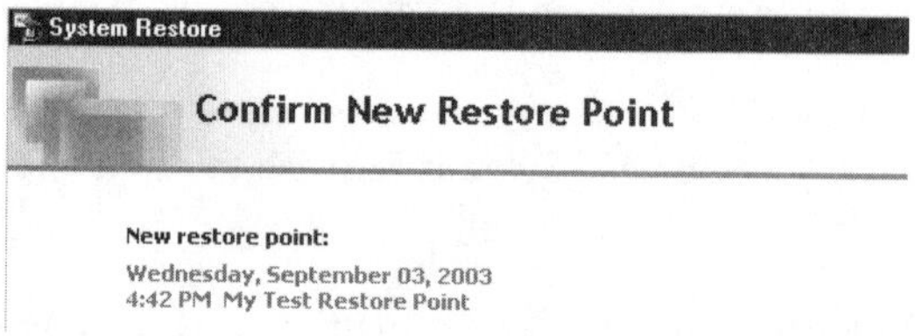

**FIGURE 7-24** Confirming the new restore point

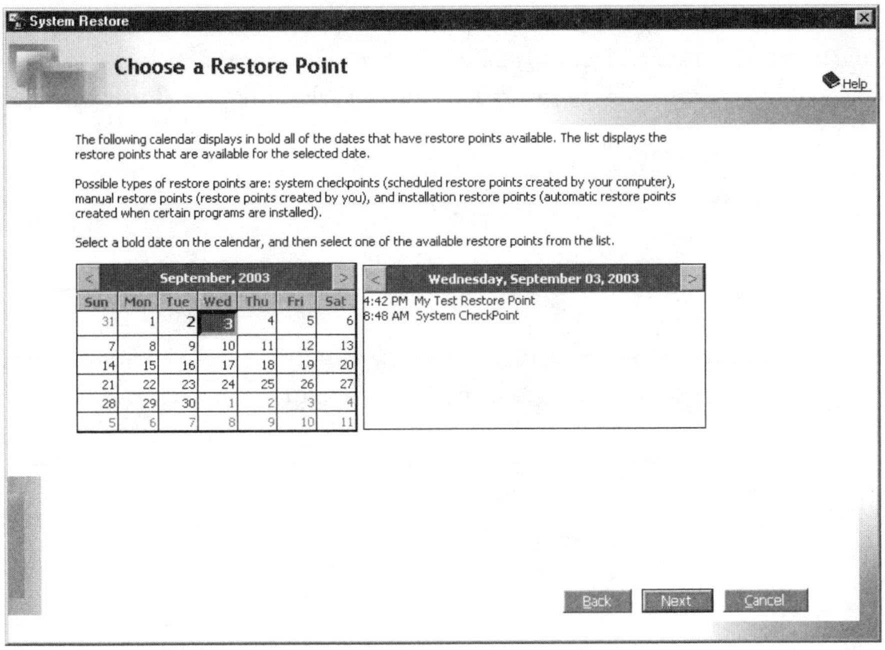

**FIGURE 7-25** Choosing a restore point

# Lab Analysis Test

1. Joe was wondering what release of software he's using so you told him to type in **VER** at a command prompt and tell you the numbers he saw. He said it was 4.10.2222. What operating system is he using?

_____

_____

2. Kal is quite the computer guru and is always fiddling with his system. Recently he made some tweaks and now he gets a lot of Not Enough Memory errors. What might be cause of this? Where would he check it?

_____

_____

3. Where would Teresa go to create a startup disk using Windows 98 SE?

_____

_____

**4.** John complains his Windows Me system gives him a lot of grief. He tries to tweak the settings and then forgets what he changed, and it takes him days before he can straighten it back out. What tool would you recommend he use to create a way to revert his system back to the way it was before he starts all the tweaking?

_____

_____

**5.** John's C: drive is almost full, but he has a new drive D: that's completely empty and ready for his MP3 collection. What optimization would you suggest to get his machine running better?

_____

_____

# Key Term Quiz

Use the following vocabulary terms to complete the following sentences. Not all of the terms will be used.

Automatic Updates Wizard

Resource Meter

restore point

swap file

System Monitor

System Restore

Task Manager

virtual memory

Windows Update

**1.** To set up a Windows Me system so you don't have to worry about patching it, you'd run the

_____.

**2.** If you suspect a system is a resource hog, you can use the _____ to verify it.

**3.** The _____ enables you to close programs running in the background.

**4.** You can use the _____ to return a Windows Me machine back to an earlier state.

**5.** When the system will not boot, use the _____ to get a command prompt.

# Chapter 8

## Maintaining, Optimizing, and Troubleshooting Windows NT, 2000, and XP

### Lab Exercises

Imagine, if you will, that a department in your company's remote office has put in a request for all new PCs. You know that their computers are just over a year old and equipped with hardware that should be more than adequate for their needs, yet they insist that their machines are running so slowly it's affecting productivity. Since you're looking at a replacement expense of thousands of dollars, you decide it would be worthwhile to spend a day trying to figure out if anything can be done to make the machines run faster.

After checking out a few of the systems, you determine that no hardware-related issues are slowing them down. What could it be? Well, if it's not the hardware causing problems, it's got to be the software, right? The first place to start looking for software-related issues is the main program running on the PC—the Windows operating system itself. Even though most versions of Windows are pretty well optimized when they're installed, time and use can alter that fact significantly. It's important, therefore, to be able to take what you know about navigating and manipulating the Windows environment and put it to work figuring out what needs to be fixed or improved. Sometimes a simple tweak is all it takes to make a sluggish system act like it's fresh out of the box.

One of the easiest software-related fixes you can make on a PC is updating the device drivers. With that in mind, the first lab will have you stepping through driver installations specifically in Windows 2000/XP. In the following labs, the focus will shift to various troubleshooting tools for Windows 2000/XP.

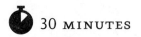 30 MINUTES

# Lab Exercise 8.01: Installing Device Drivers in Windows 2000/XP

Installing new devices under Windows 2000 and XP is easier than it has ever been. Assuming, of course, that you're starting with compatible hardware, Windows 2000 and XP will detect the new device and install the correct driver with little prompting. Often, Windows already has a useable driver and will install it without any action on your part. It's better, though, to use the driver that came with the device, and it's better still to download the newest driver from the manufacturer's web site.

It's a good idea to check for newer drivers periodically, even for devices that have been working fine. Manufacturers occasionally release new drivers aimed at optimizing the device or enabling it to work with some new technology. Keep in mind, however, that a new driver may cause unexpected problems with your operating system. Because of this, Windows XP has included a new feature that enables you to roll back to the previous (working) driver if something should go wrong with a driver update.

One of two wizards will assist you when you need to load a driver: the Found New Hardware Wizard or the Add New Hardware Wizard. Windows starts the Found New Hardware Wizard when it discovers some new hardware device while booting. If Windows has a driver in its database, it proceeds on its own. If not, the Found New Hardware Wizard will prompt you for one. The Add New Hardware Wizard allows you to add or update hardware manually at any time. There's a lot of overlap in how the two wizards work, so you'll look at just the Add New Hardware Wizard because you can activate it at any time.

## Learning Objectives

Loading and removing device drivers is one of the basic skills of a good PC tech. The following lab exercise walks you through the process.

At the end of this lab, you'll be able to

- Load a device driver in Windows 2000 and XP

- Roll back to a previously working driver in Windows XP

## Lab Materials and Setup

The materials you need for this lab are

- A working PC with Windows 2000/XP installed

- An Internet connection

## Getting Down to Business

The following labs cover the steps for installing and updating device drivers. You'll also look at the steps for rolling back (uninstalling) device drivers that turn out to be incompatible.

**Step 1** The first step before you begin installing any new device should be to check the Hardware Compatibility List (HCL) for the device you're trying to load, as discussed in Chapter 6. The most current HCL is available on the Microsoft web site at http://www.microsoft.com/whdc/hcl/default.mspx. Devices on the list are guaranteed to work with the Windows OS. Always check there before purchasing a device for your Windows 2000 or XP PC.

**Step 2** Now let's walk through the process of adding a device using the Add Hardware Wizard:

    a)   Go to the Control Panel and double-click Add Hardware (in Windows 2000 or Classic mode XP).

    b)   This launches the wizard, so click Next.

---

✔ **Hint**

If the wizard doesn't find any new hardware it asks, "Have you already connected this hardware to your computer?" Select Yes or No, and follow the directions.

---

    c)   Select the device you want to install or update by either selecting from the given list or choosing the Add a New Hardware Device item in the list box. For this lab, select the last item in the list: Add a New Hardware Device.

    d)   Click Next.

    e)   Click the Install Hardware That I Manually Select from a List option button.

    f)   Click Next.

    g)   Select the type of hardware you're trying to install or update from the list. If your device doesn't fit the descriptions, select the Show All Devices item.

    h)   Click Next. If you chose the Show All Devices item, the wizard displays the Select the Device Driver You Want to Install for This Hardware screen. If you chose a specific type of hardware, you'll be led through a bevy of options for that type of hardware.

    i)   Either choose the Windows driver for your device or click Have Disk and point to the location of the new driver you'd like to install. This will generally either be on the installation CD that came with the device or be a file you downloaded from the manufacturer.

    j)   Click Next. Windows is ready to install the driver.

    k)   Click Next again.

    l)   Click Finish.

You should now have a driver that runs your newly loaded device. If the device isn't working properly and you're sure the driver loaded correctly, you'll want to check online and see if there's a newer driver that you can download from the manufacturer's web site. If the device just won't work after you've updated the driver, you'll want to perform step 3, but we're getting ahead of ourselves.

**Step 3** What if you have a device already installed and you want to update the driver to address a problem, improve performance, or just add a new feature? This step will take you through updating new drivers:

a) Begin by locating the updated driver. In most cases, the best way to obtain the updated driver is to search the Internet for the manufacturer's web site. Search its site for your specific model, and download the most recent driver.

b) Go to Device Manager, and expand the appropriate device category. Locate the device you want to update.

c) Alternate-click the device and select Properties.

d) Select the Driver tab and click the Update Driver button (see Figure 8-1). This will launch a wizard similar to the Add New Hardware Wizard.

---

**✔ Hint**

In Windows XP, you can alternate-click the device in question (in Device Manager), and update the driver without accessing its properties.

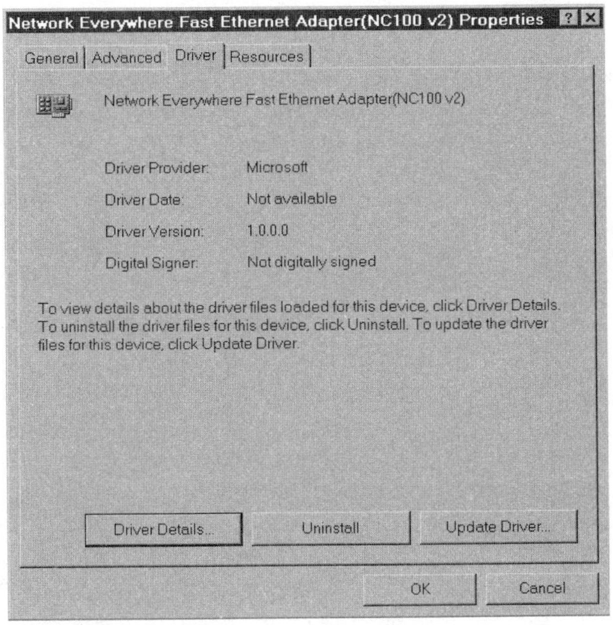

---

**FIGURE 8-1** Viewing the Windows 2000 Update Driver button

For Windows 2000, click Next at the Welcome screen. Select Display a List of Known Drivers for This Device, and click Next. On the next screen, select Have Disk and browse to the location of the updated driver.

For Windows XP, select Install from a list or specific location and click Next. Select Include This Location in the Search, and browse to where you have saved the new driver.

But now you ask, "What if I load a new driver, and my system doesn't work correctly anymore?" Well, if you're using Windows XP, you're in luck! Read the next step, and your question will be answered.

**Step 4**   If a driver is corrupt or if the wrong driver is installed, Windows has a bad habit of stopping dead in its tracks, rendering your PC useless. Windows XP has a feature that keeps track of the drivers you install on a system and allows you to roll back to a previous one when a new one isn't working as it should:

a)   Go to the Device Manager and locate the device you want to roll back.

b)   Alternate-click the device, and select Properties.

c)   Select the Driver tab. You can revert to the previous driver by clicking Roll Back Driver (see Figure 8-2).

At this point, you should be pretty familiar with drivers and how to load and update them. More and more devices are being sold as hot-pluggable, but I doubt that user-installed drivers will be going away in the near future. Loading and maintaining drivers will probably be a part of the PC technician's job for a while yet to come.

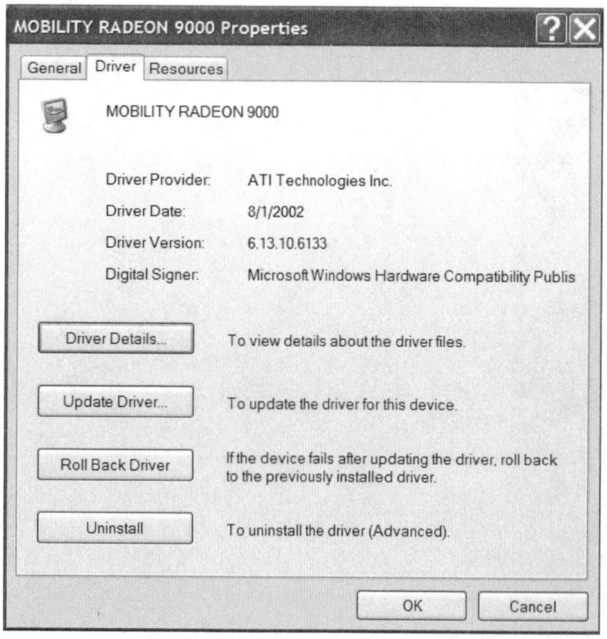

**FIGURE 8-2**  Windows XP Roll Back Driver button

 30 MINUTES

# Lab Exercise 8.02: Configuring a Custom Microsoft Management Console (MMC) Toolbox

You're about to learn how to customize your "toolkit." I think every do-it-yourselfer has a toolkit where they keep their hammer, saw, screwdrivers, pliers, wrenches, sockets, and so on. They buy new tools ("Because they were on sale" is a common excuse) and add them to an already overflowing toolbox. How do you organize all of this, and how do you find your favorite tools when you need them?

To help organize your PC technician's toolbox, Microsoft created the MMC. The MMC not only organizes all of those useful tools but it also provides a consistent look and feel between different systems and even different operating systems, which makes it easier to use them.

✔ **Cross-Reference**

For details on working with the MMC, refer to the "Microsoft Management Console (MMC)" section of Chapter 8 of *Mike Meyers' A+ Guide to Operating Systems*.

## Learning Objectives

In this exercise, you'll learn how to create an MMC. You'll also create a Desktop icon that you can use to access this customized software toolkit whenever you need it.

At the end of this lab, you'll be able to

- Create an MMC
- Add tools (Snap-ins) to the MMC

## Lab Materials and Setup

The materials you need for this lab are

- A PC system with Windows 2000 or XP installed

## Getting Down to Business

The MMC is a shell program that holds individual utilities called *Snap-ins*. The first time you create an MMC, you get a default blank console. A blank MMC isn't much to look at; like a new toolbox, it starts out empty.

**Step 1** To create your MMC, select Start | Run, type **mmc**, and then click OK. A console has been created (see Figure 8-3)!

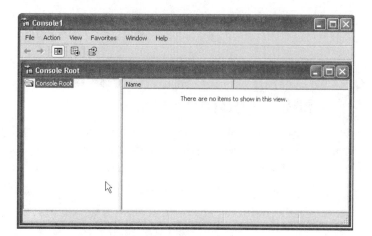

**FIGURE 8-3** Looking at a blank MMC

Notice in the upper-left corner that the name is "Console 1."

Before you actually configure an MMC, you need to understand a few points. First, you can have more than one MMC; successive consoles will be given default names such as "Console 2," "Console 3," and so on. Second, you can rename the MMCs that you create and choose where to save them so that you can easily find them again. Finally, once you've created an MMC, you can modify it by adding or taking away tools—just like your toolbox at home.

Now follow these steps:

a) Click File (Windows XP) or Console (Windows 2000) | Save As and fill in the boxes as follows:

**Save in**   Desktop

**File name**   My First MMC

**Save as type**   Microsoft Management Console Files (*.msc)

b) Click Save to continue. (*Don't* exit the MMC!)

c) Notice the upper-left corner of the open window (MMC). The name has changed.

d) Move the window (if necessary) so that you can see the new icon that's been created on the Desktop (see Figure 8-4). This icon bears the same name as your new MMC, and will enable you to access the MMC in the future with just a double-click.

**FIGURE 8-4** Viewing the MMC desktop icon

**Step 2**   When you add Snap-ins, they'll show up in the Add/Remove Snap-in dialog box (see Figure 8-5).

You'll now add some tools (Snap-ins):

a)   Click File | Add/Remove Snap-in (Windows XP) or Console | Add/Remove Snap-in (Windows 2000).

b)   Click Add, and let the fun begin (see Figure 8-6). I bet you haven't had this many selections since your last visit to Sears' hardware department!

c)   You'll add the Device Manager for the first tool. Select Device Manager, and click Add.

When you add a Snap-in, you have a choice of adding it for either your local computer or another computer. With the proper access permissions, in other words, you can look at the Device Manager on a networked system. More than likely, you don't have the necessary permissions to do this, so you'll just move on.

d)   Select Local Computer, and click Finish.

---

### ✖  Warning

I can't emphasize strongly enough that the best way to get a systems administrator mad is to go snooping around on the network. As a technician, your main concern is to do no harm. If you accidentally find your way to an unauthorized area, it's your duty to report it to an administrator.

---

While you're here, you'll add one more Snap-in: the Event Viewer. You'll use this tool in the next lab. Adding it here will provide an alternate way to access this tool:

a)   Select Event Viewer from the list.

b)   Select Local Computer and Finish to close out the wizard.

**Figure 8-5**  Adding or removing Snap-ins          **Figure 8-6**  Adding a stand-alone Snap-in

c)    Click Add to close the list window and OK to close the Add/Remove window.

d)    Your MMC should now show two Snap-ins.

e)    Be sure to save your MMC.

You now have a toolbox with quick access to Device Manager and Event Viewer. You can use these tools in the same way as if you navigated to them through the conventional method.

Click Device Manager to expand the list of devices. Notice that it looks the same and works the same as if you opened it through the Control Panel.

**Step 3**    If everything has worked correctly up to now, continue with this step (if you had problems creating your MMC, ask the instructor for assistance):

a)    Double-click the Desktop icon for My First MMC.

b)    Your Device Manager and Event Log are now available directly from your Desktop (see Figure 8-7).

---

✔  **Hint**

I only scratched the surface here showing you how to create an MMC. Your customizing options are only limited by the number of Snap-ins available and your imagination. I suggest you go back and do this lab again if time permits, and let yourself be creative this time.

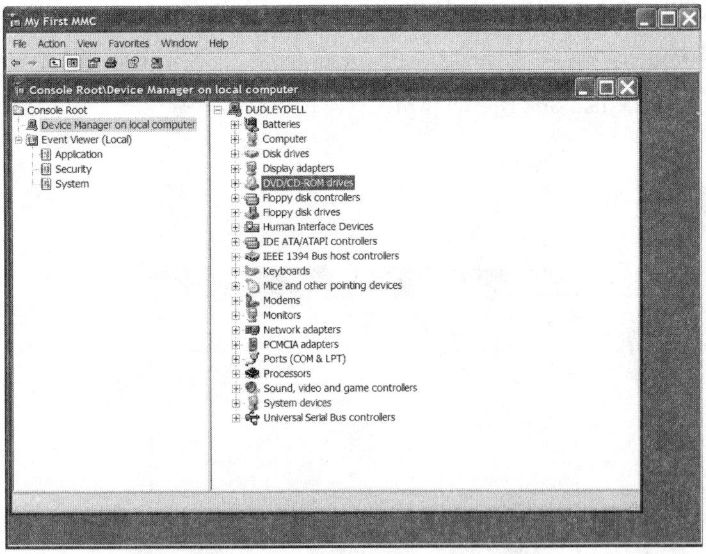

---

**FIGURE 8-7**  Accessing Device Manager from a custom MMC

30 MINUTES

# Lab Exercise 8.03: Examining and Configuring Log Files in Event Viewer

The Windows Event Viewer, available in Windows NT, Windows 2000, and Windows XP is a valuable tool to anyone who maintains or troubleshoots these systems. It's mostly run as a stand-alone program, but it can also be added as a Snap-in to your MMC, as shown in the previous lab.

Event Viewer monitors various log files and provides data about the health of the operating system. Real-time statistics are reported but normally only used with servers. Desktop computer users are less proactive and usually depend on the after-the-fact log files to help determine the cause of a problem.

## Learning Objectives

You'll become familiar with using Event Viewer to analyze the different logs kept by the system.

At the end of this lab, you'll be able to

- Run the Event Viewer program

- Examine an event log entry

- Save the event log

## Lab Materials and Setup

The materials you need for this lab are

- A working PC with Windows NT/2000/XP installed

## Getting Down to Business

You can start Event Viewer from the Control Panel using the Administrative Tools applet. If you've added Event Viewer to your MMC, you can also access it there. For practice, you'll do this lab by accessing it the conventional way, but you should confirm that everything works the same through the MMC.

**Step 1**  Go to the Control Panel and double-click the Administrative Tools icon. Then double-click the Event Viewer icon to start the applet. Event Viewer will display events from three log files: Application, Security, and System. (More log files are available in the server versions of Windows 2000.) Figure 8-8 shows the contents of the system event log in Event Viewer.

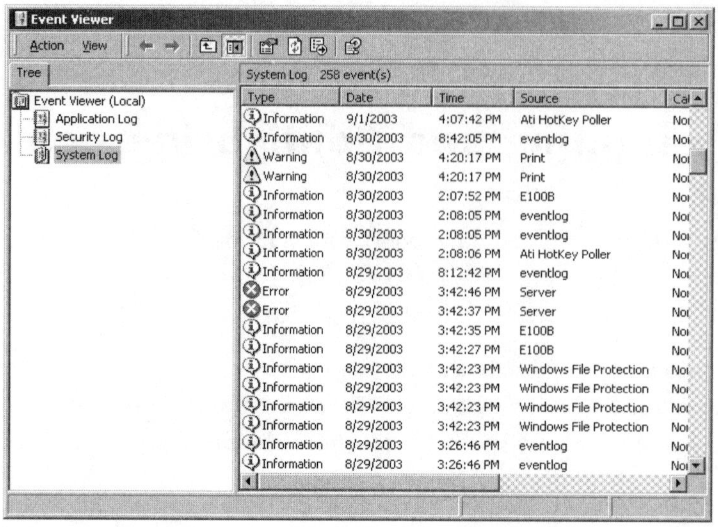

**FIGURE 8-8** Viewing the system log in Event Viewer

Notice in Figure 8-8 that there are three kinds of log entries for the system and applications logs: Information, Warning, and Error. The security event log shows two types of entries: Success Audit and Failure Audit. The success audit and failure audit events are only logged when auditing is turned on, which is usually done only on servers.

Double-clicking any entry will give you details of the event.

**Step 2**    Follow these steps to change the size of a log file:

a)   In Event Viewer's left panel, alternate-click System and select Properties.

b)   Change the number in the Log Size box to **1024** (512 is the default).

c)   Select Overwrite Events As Needed (see Figure 8-9).

d)   Do this for all three event logs: application, security, and system.

Sometimes the log can be completely full before you get a chance to look at the entries. Scrolling through all of the events can be tedious, but you can fix that with filter settings.

e)   Click the Filter tab, and look at the filter settings (see Figure 8-10). You can filter events based on type, source, category, ID, user, computer, and date. This only controls what Event Viewer displays; all the event information will still be logged to the file, so you can change your mind about filter settings.

f)   Click OK to close the Properties dialog box.

**Step 3**    To clear, archive, and open a log file, follow these steps:

a)   Clear the system log by alternate-clicking System and selecting Clear All Events (see Figure 8-11).

b)   When you're prompted to save the system log, click Yes.

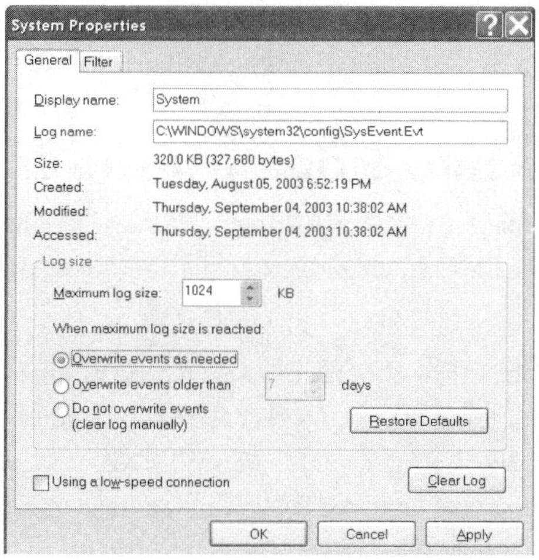

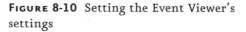

**FIGURE 8-9** Selecting Overwrite Events As Needed

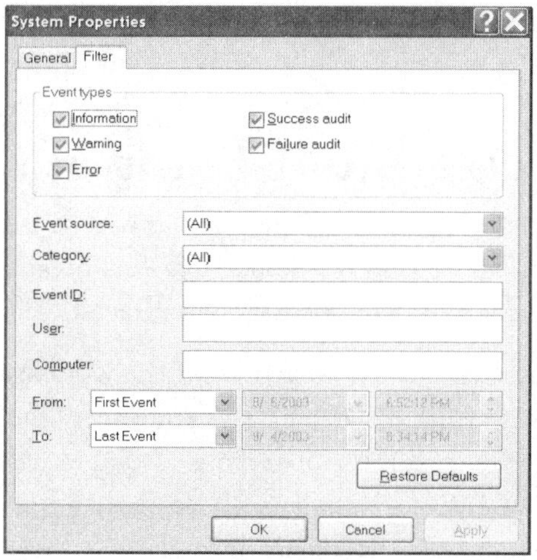

**FIGURE 8-10** Setting the Event Viewer's settings

c) You can archive log files using different filenames each time (recommended) and select a location other than the default.

d) Give your file a name you can remember and save it.

e) To open a saved file, click the Action menu and select Open Log File.

f) Select the file.

g) Select the log type (the System, Application, or Security option).

h) Click Open. The saved log file will open.

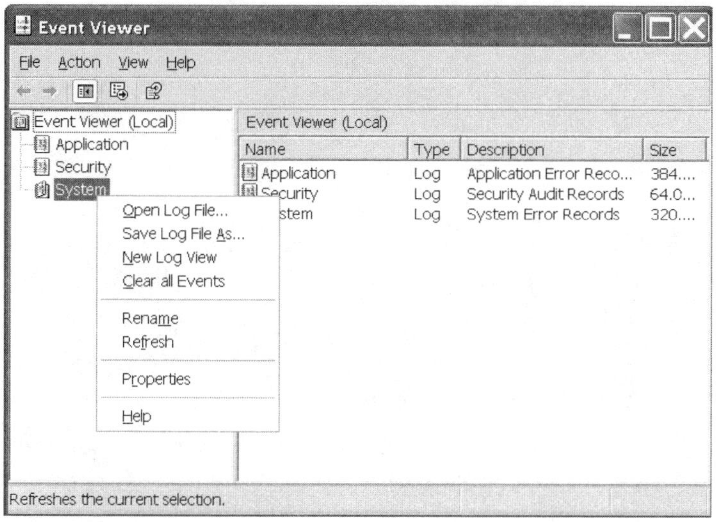

**FIGURE 8-11** Alternate-click System to select Clear all Events

 30 MINUTES

# Lab Exercise 8.04: Using Alternative Boot Methods

An errant upgrade or a poorly written driver can cause the system to lock up. Some software problems will even prevent the system from booting. This means that you must be ready to use alternative methods to boot the system to make repairs or replace files.

Windows has several ways to boot, and the ways are as different as the operating systems themselves. A Safe Mode boot is available with all the Microsoft operating systems. Windows NT/2000 uses a four-disk set of boot floppies to install the operating system or access troubleshooting tools. Windows XP has a single, limited-use, MS-DOS startup disk. There's also a nice recovery tool that comes with Windows 2000 and Windows XP known as the Recovery Console.

## Learning Objectives

You'll become familiar with alternate methods of booting a faulty system.

At the end of this lab, you'll be able to

- Create a four-disk set of boot floppies for Windows 2000

- Create a MS-DOS startup disk for Windows XP

- Install the Recovery Console for Windows XP

## Lab Materials and Setup

The materials you need for this lab are

- Working PCs with Windows 2000 and Windows XP installed

- Windows 2000 and XP CDs

- Five blank floppy disks

## Getting Down to Business

If your system won't boot normally because of some system problem, you need a way to gain access to the hard drive and your files to troubleshoot the problem. There are, happily enough, troubleshooting tools that enable you to access these files if the normal boot process won't work. Remember—each operating system has its own version of these tools, and they're not necessarily compatible. For instance, you can't use a Windows 98 boot disk to access files stored on an NTFS partition in a Windows XP system.

**Step 1** Put the Windows 2000 CD in the CD drive of a working Windows 2000 system and, when the setup screen appears, select Browse This CD. Then open the BOOTDISK folder and double-click MAKEBOOT.EXE.

A command line window will open, asking where you want to create the image (see Figure 8-12). Type **a** to answer the question, and it'll ask you to insert a floppy disk. Follow the instructions for all four floppies until the operation is complete.

```
××××××××××××××××××××××××××××××××××××××××××××
This program creates the Setup boot disks
for Microsoft Windows 2000.
To create these disks, you need to provide 4 blank,
formatted, high-density disks.

Please specify the floppy drive to copy the images to: ▪
```

**FIGURE 8-12** Creating Windows 2000 boot disks

**Step 2** Now that you have a Windows 2000 boot disk set, insert disk 1 and press CTRL-ALT-DELETE to reboot your system. Insert each disk when prompted until you see a screen that reads as follows:

```
Windows 2000 Professional Setup
  Welcome to Setup
  This portion of the Setup program prepares Microsoft
Windows 2000™ to run on your computer
            To set up Windows 2000 now. Press ENTER.
            To repair a Windows 2000 installation, press R.
            To quit Setup without installing Windows 2000, press F3.
```

Because the operating system is already installed, press R to do the repair function. The next screen to appear gives two choices. It shows the following:

```
To repair a Windows 2000 installation by using
            the recovery console, press C.
```

or the following:

```
To repair a Windows 2000 installation by using
            the emergency repair process, press R.
```

Press C to open the Recovery Console.

**Step 3** Follow the instruction by putting setup disk 4 back into the drive, and press ENTER.

What you'll see is a command line interface asking which installation to log onto. If you have a dual-boot system, you'll have to choose which operating system to log into. Type the number and press ENTER. Then type the administrator's password. This is the password for the first account created when you initially installed the operating system. You now have a command line prompt from which to work.

---

## ✖ Warning

Be sure you know what you're doing here. You have access to files that you can add, change, rename, or delete. The old DOS set of commands is only partly available.

Now, follow these steps:

a)    To see a list of commands, type **help**.

b)    Type a command followed by **/?** to get an explanation of the command.

I'll explain some of the new commands later when you install the Windows XP Recovery Console.

c)    Type **exit** to quit the Recovery Console; the system will reboot.

**Step 4**    Use a Windows XP system for the following steps.

Windows XP has only a limited-use MS-DOS startup disk, but you never know when it'll come in handy:

a)    Put a blank floppy disk in the A: drive.

b)    Open My Computer.

c)    Alternate-click the 3.5-inch floppy and select Format.

d)    Select Create an MS-DOS Startup Disk, and click Start (see Figure 8-13).

e)    Close the floppy window.

What you have now is a disk that will boot the system, but not much else can be done with it. It performs one function and one function only. It gets you to the A:\ prompt from a cold boot.

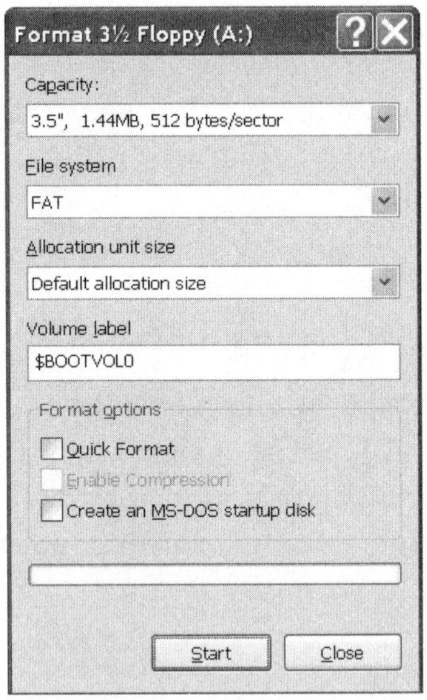

**FIGURE 8-13**  Creating a Windows
XP MS-DOS startup disk

✔ **Hint**

Windows XP has the equivalent of the Windows 2000 four-disk boot set. However, it doesn't ship with XP, and you can't make one from the Windows XP CD. Where can I get Windows XP boot disks, you ask? Microsoft provides downloads to create XP boot disks. Microsoft continues to release service packs and therefore needs updated boot disks. You must download the correct set of boot disks for your version of XP (you can't use XP Home Edition boot disks with an XP Professional Edition). Also, XP Professional Edition and XP Professional SP1 boot disks are different. Go to the Microsoft site and search for your edition and release at http://www.microsoft.com/downloads.

**Step 5** Although you can run the Recovery Console by booting directly to it from the Windows XP CD or Windows 2000 four-disk boot set, it's much more convenient to set it up as a startup option on your boot menu. In this step, you'll install the Windows XP Recovery Console as a boot option. You can do the same thing using the same steps for Windows 2000 (see Figure 8-14).

✔ **Hint**

To install the Recovery Console, you must have administrative rights on the computer.

a) Put your Windows XP (or Windows 2000) CD in the CD drive; if it auto starts, select Exit. You can also press and hold SHIFT until the CD stops loading.

b) Select Start | Run.

c) In the Open box, type **d:\i386\winnt32.exe /cmdcons** (where *d* is the drive letter for the CD drive).

d) A Windows Setup dialog box appears, which describes the Recovery Console option. The system prompts you to confirm installation. Click Yes to start the installation procedure.

e) When the installation is complete (Figure 8-15), restart the computer. You will see a Microsoft Windows Recovery Console entry on the boot menu.

It's wise to install the Recovery Console on important servers and on the critical workstations.

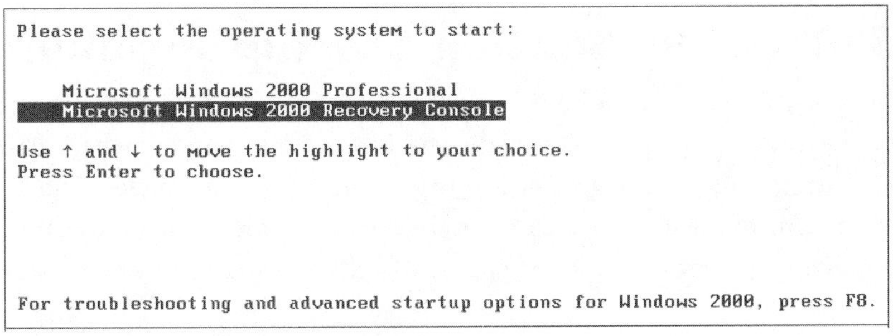

```
Please select the operating system to start:

    Microsoft Windows 2000 Professional
    Microsoft Windows 2000 Recovery Console

Use ↑ and ↓ to move the highlight to your choice.
Press Enter to choose.




For troubleshooting and advanced startup options for Windows 2000, press F8.
```

**FIGURE 8-14** Installing Windows 2000 Recovery Console

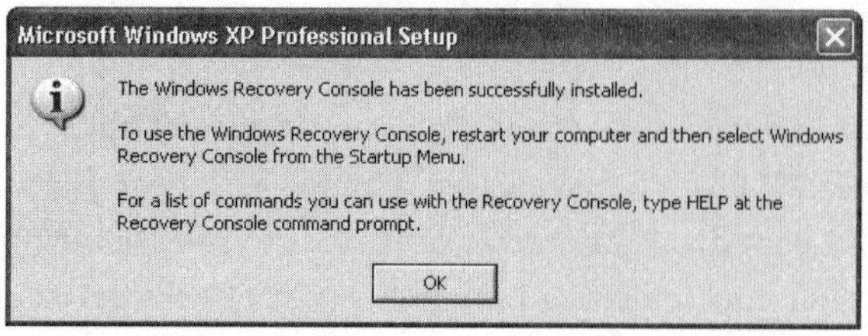

**FIGURE 8-15** Completing the Recovery Console installation

**Step 6** Reboot your system, and at the boot menu screen, select the Recovery Console. Watch for the boot menu; you have to be quick. Go directly to the command line prompt (you need the administrator's password).

To see a list of commands, type **help**. Type a command followed by **/?** to get an explanation of the command use.

These new commands are worth mentioning. Know what they do for the A+ exams:

**DISKPART**   The Windows 2000 equivalent to FDISK

**EXIT**   Exits the Recovery Console, and restarts your computer

**EXPAND**   Extracts copies of single files from the CAB files

**FIXBOOT**   Writes a new partition table

**FIXMBR**   Equivalent to FDISK /MBR

**HELP**   Displays a Help screen

The files that make up the Recovery Console reside on the system partition, making the Recovery Console useless for system partition crashes. If that's the case, you'll use the CD drive to access the Recovery Console. The Recovery Console shines in the business of manually restoring registries, stopping problem services, rebuilding partitions (other than the system partition), or using the EXPAND program to extract copies of corrupted files from a CD or floppy disk.

30 MINUTES

# Lab Exercise 8.05: Troubleshooting Startup Problems

When it comes to troubleshooting tools, Windows 2000 and Windows XP have inherited the best of both the Windows NT and 9x families. They have vintage tools such as the Last Known Good Configuration startup option for startup failures and the Task Manager for forcing errant programs to close. Both operating systems have the Recovery Console. Each has a completely revamped and improved Windows Help. Windows XP has a great tool, System Restore, which was actually introduced in Windows Me, but has been improved in Windows XP. I'll leave the finer details of these tools for you to explore through Windows Help, the main textbook, and previous labs. In this lab, I'll reintroduce you to a simple tool named the System Configuration utility.

## Learning Objectives

You'll be reintroduced to some troubleshooting tips using a vintage tool with Windows XP.

At the end of this lab, you'll be able to

- Use the System Configuration utility to perform diagnostic startups

## Lab Materials and Setup

The materials you need for this lab are

- Access to a Windows XP system

## Getting Down to Business

Many systems have way too many startup options enabled. This isn't only a source of boot problems, but it can slow down the boot process and hog RAM from programs that need it. When Windows XP experiences failures during startup, consider using the System Configuration utility to discover and fix the problem.

**Step 1** Go to Start | Run, type **msconfig**, and then press ENTER. The System Configuration Utility opens (see Figure 8-16).

Notice that on the General tab you can select Diagnostic Startup. This is useful if you have just added new hardware that's causing intermittent problems, because it enables you to boot with only basic devices.

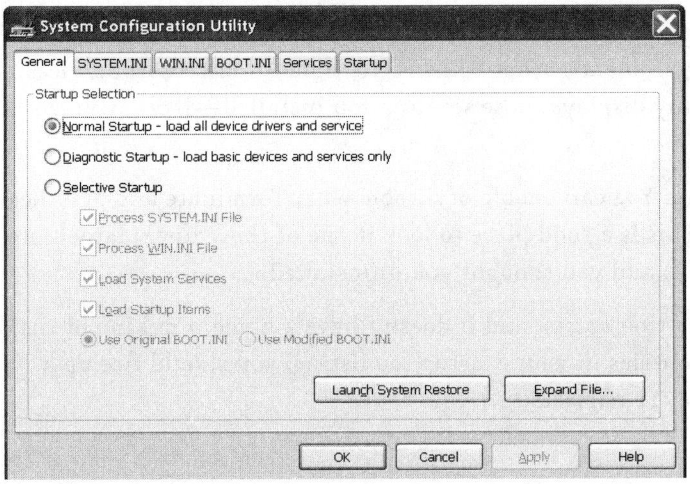

**FIGURE 8-16** Using the System Configuration Utility

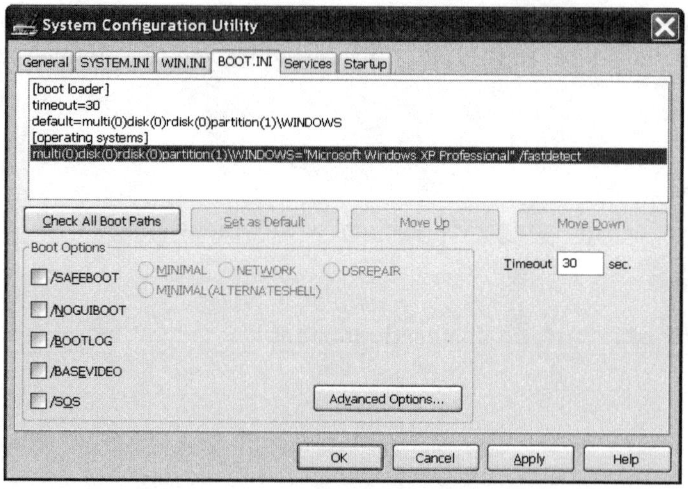

**FIGURE 8-17** Accessing the BOOT.INI tab

The Selective Startup is also nice; it lets you bypass some configuration files to see which one contains the errors that are causing problems.

Notice the SYSTEM.INI and WIN.INI tabs, which provide settings that enable you to change the load sequence of your drivers and edit the entries when you find an error.

**Step 2** The BOOT.INI tab is powerful (see Figure 8-17) and goes well beyond A+ exam requirements, but there are a couple options you should know about.

One important option for troubleshooting is to create a log of what transpired during the boot process. On the BOOT.INI tab, you can enable a BOOTLOG to be created each time the system boots.

If you're troubleshooting a problem and you need to start in the Safe Mode every time, instead of pressing F8, you can enable the /SAFEBOOT option.

**Step 3** One thing I find useful is under the Services tab. Microsoft has many services you can disable during boot if you believe they're causing problems. What I like is the Hide All Microsoft Services option. When you enable this option, it only displays those services you installed—like my video adapter (NVIDIA) driver in Figure 8-18.

**Step 4** The Startup tab is the most useful. You can enable or disable what Terminate and Stay Resident (TSR) programs you have installed. This is a good place to look if one of those unexplained programs is trying to load every time you boot, and you thought you uninstalled it.

Notice in Figure 8-19 I have a program that starts, and it doesn't have a name. I'm kind of suspicious of what it is. If you find suspicious entries in your Startup tab listing, you should fire up a browser and do some research to see if they're harmful.

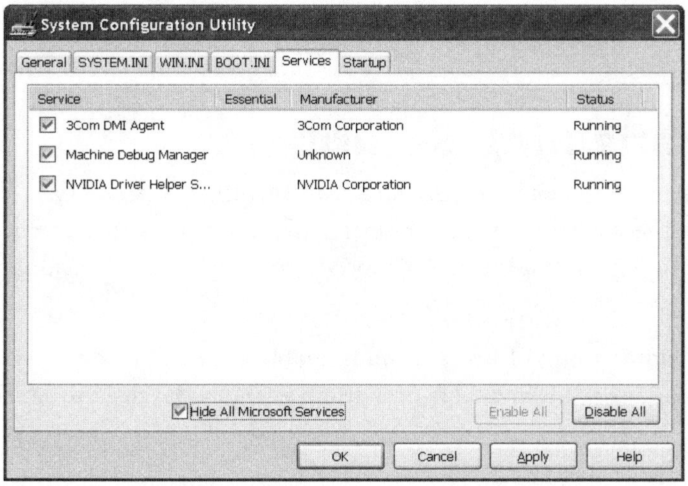

**Figure 8-18** Using the Services tab with Microsoft Services hidden

## ✔ Hint

You can also run the System Configuration utility while in Safe Mode. If you're having problems, you can boot to Safe Mode and use this utility to identify the source of the problem.

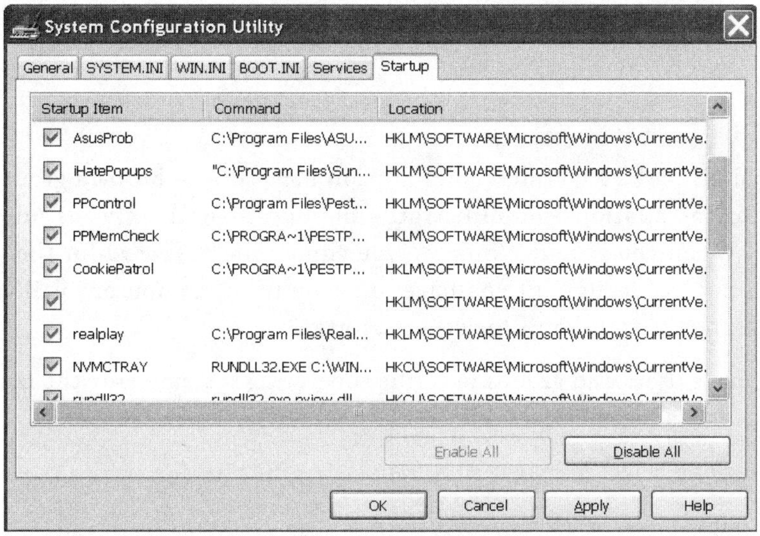

**Figure 8-19** Checking your startup programs

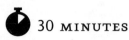 30 MINUTES

# Lab Exercise 8.06: Configuring Security

A part of optimizing either a PC or an entire network is setting and maintaining the security. The basic element of Windows security is the user account. Each user must present a valid username and the password of a local user account to log on to a Windows 2000 or Windows XP Professional computer.

Each user is also a member of one or more groups of users. Groups enable the system administrator to easily assign the same rights and permissions to all members of a group without the need to set those rights and permissions individually.

## Learning Objectives

I'll assume your study computer doesn't belong to a domain and show you how to create local accounts on your Windows 2000 and Windows XP computer.

At the end of this lab, you'll be able to

- Add user accounts

- Set passwords

## Lab Materials and Setup

The materials you need for this lab are

- Access to a Windows 2000 or XP system

## Getting Down to Business

Both Windows 2000 Professional and Windows XP Professional Edition have several built-in groups and two user accounts created during installation—Administrator and Guest—with only the Administrator account enabled by default. When you install Windows, you supply the password for the Administrator account. This is the only usable account you have to log on to the computer until you create a new local account or enable the Guest account for others to use.

**Step 1**   Network administrators manage users and groups for either operating system using the Local Users and Groups node in the Computer Management console:

   a)   Alternate-click My Computer and select Manage.

   b)   Expand Local Users and Groups in the left frame.

   c)   Open the Users folder to see the current user accounts.

   d)   Open the Groups folder to see the current group accounts.

✖ **Warning**

The Administrator account has total access to and control of the system. This means that a person using this account can snoop anywhere; change any system settings; copy, move, rename, or delete any files; and add or remove devices. Clearly, this must be a trusted account and not for everyone's use. Always select a complicated password for the Administrator account such as "G9_kl45bRy" so that no one will guess it. If you're the administrator, create another user account and make that account a limited user (Windows XP) or a power user (Windows NT/2000). Use the new account in your daily chores, using the Administrator account only in emergencies. *No one but the administrator should ever use the Administrator account.* Once the administrator's password is known, the entire system is compromised.

**Step 2** Using the Administrator account is just fine when you're doing administrative tasks, such as installing updates, adding printers, adding and removing programs and Windows components, and creating users and groups. However, even on your own computer, you should never log on with such a powerful account when you're doing ordinary tasks, such as writing and printing reports and browsing the Internet (certainly not!). It's the administrator's job to create additional accounts:

a)  Alternate-click Users and select New User.

b)  Enter a username provided by the instructor (for example, **Student 7**).

c)  Enter your name and optional description.

d)  For the password, type **password**.

e)  Don't change any other settings at this time.

f)  Click Create, then click Close.

You now have an account to use. Reboot your system and enter your new username and password. Notice that the first thing it displays is a message informing you that you must change your password at logon. Follow the instructions to change your password.

**Step 3** Now try making your new account a member of the Administrators group:

a)  Alternate-click My Computer and select Manage.

b)  Expand Local Users and Groups in the left frame.

c)  Open the Users folder, and double-click your new account.

d)  Select the Member Of tab, and then click Add to see Figure 8-20.

e)  Type **Administrators**, and click Add.

f)  Click OK.

g) At this point, it appears that it worked okay. A restricted user was able to add himself or herself to the Administrators group. But wait a minute, click Apply and notice the errors. Security will not allow a user to change their group affiliation.

h) Close the error messages, and return to the Desktop by closing all other open windows.

**Step 4** Log off the system and log back on as the administrator:

a) Alternate-click My Computer and select Manage.

b) Expand Local Users and Groups in the left frame.

c) Open the Users folder and double-click your new account.

d) Select the Member Of tab and then click Add.

e) Click the Advanced button to see Figure 8-21 and then click the Find Now button. Figure 8-22 shows the groups that appear.

f) Select Administrators from the list and click OK to return to the previous screen. Click OK again to add the user to that group. Notice that the group now shows up in the Member Of panel. Click OK once more to finish.

---

**✔ Hint**

For those of you using Windows XP, you'll find that there are a few more intermediate screens involved, but the concept is the same.

---

**Step 5** Now you'll see how easy it is for an administrator to change a user's password. Be sure you're logged on as the administrator. Simply select a user from the list, alternate-click, and select Set Password. Windows XP displays a warning message, but Windows 2000 doesn't even do that. Enter and confirm the new password in the Set Password box. Click OK to continue. That's all there is to it. Scary, huh?

There's more to security than just assigning a password. Security begins with turning on Users Must Enter a User Name and Password.

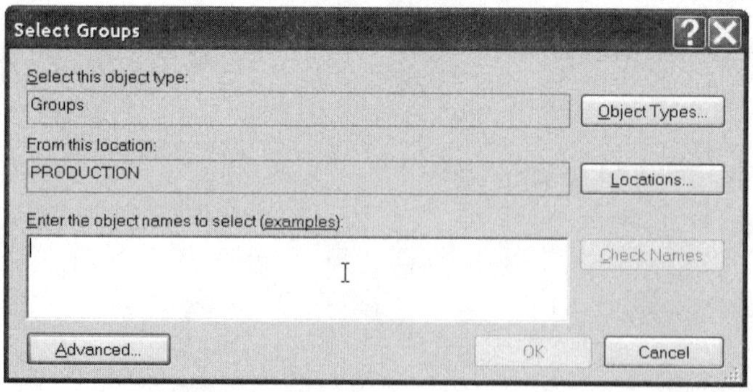

**Figure 8-20** Click the Advanced button to find a list of groups to pick from

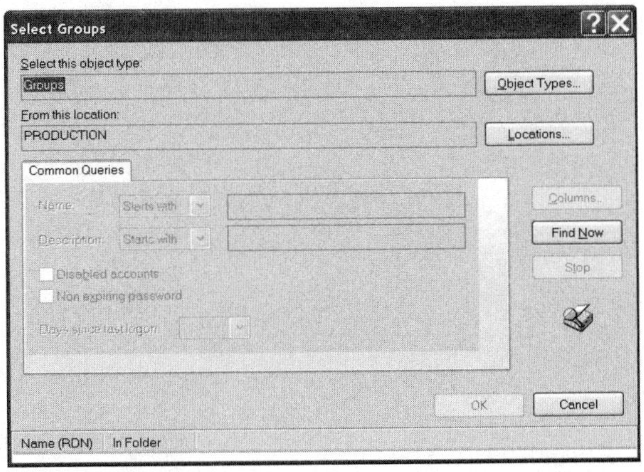

**FIGURE 8-21** Click Find Now to see a list of groups
to select from

Using a Windows 2000 system, go to the Control Panel and select Users and Passwords.

Be sure to enable the Users Must Enter a User Name and Password to Use This Computer setting
(see Figure 8-23).

✖ **Warning**

If this setting is turned off, anyone with physical access to your computer can turn it on and
use it without entering a username and password. It's important to enable this security setting.

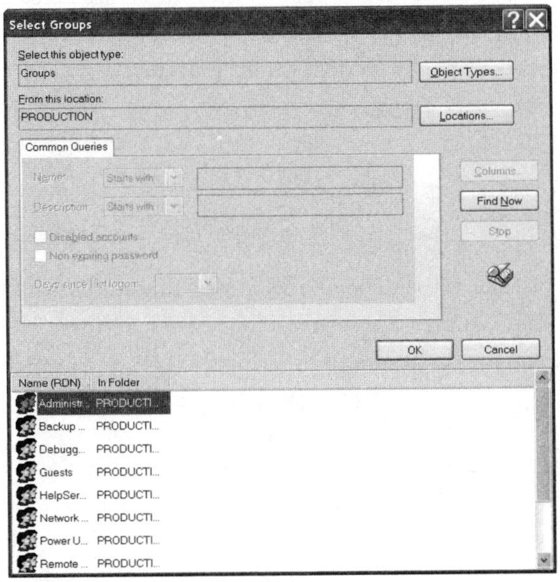

**FIGURE 8-22** Selecting Administrators from the
available groups

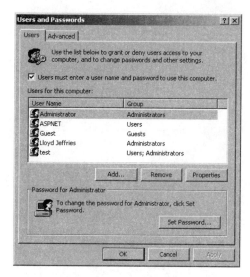

**FIGURE 8-23** Check the box next to "Users must enter a user name and password to use this computer."

Select the Advanced tab.

There's a second setting in Users and Passwords that's important to enable for the sake of security. If checked, it requires users to press CTRL-ALT-DELETE before logging on. This setting is a defense against certain viruses that try to capture your username and password.

---

✔ **Hint**

Windows XP also has settings to require username and password and require CTRL-ALT-DELETE before logging on. The settings are under the Advanced tab of the Users and Passwords dialog box. Note that these controls may not be available if your system is part of a domain on a network.

---

✔ **Hint**

Passwords are an important part of any security system. Most experts recommend using passwords that are at least eight characters long and that contain a mixture of numbers, letters (both uppercase and lowercase), and non-alphanumeric characters.

# Lab Analysis Test

1. What's the purpose of the MMC?

   _____

   _____

2. You've installed a new network card and sound card. Every time you boot, the system locks up, and you must boot into Safe Mode to get a GUI. What tool can you use to assist you in locating the source of the problem?

   _____

   _____

3. Edgar's system has crashed and won't boot. He's tried several times to access the files on his system using a Windows 98 SE boot disk, but each time it refuses to give him access. He has a Windows 2000 system. Why can't he access the files? How can he boot the system? What tool can he use after he boots?

   _____

   _____

4. Helen is the original and only user on the Windows 2000 system that she's been using for more than a year. Her company is going to a two-shift schedule, and Helen will be sharing her computer with another employee. She tried to add a new user to her Windows 2000 system, but got an "Access is denied" message. What could be the problem? What must she do to add the user?

   _____

   _____

5. William is going on vacation for two weeks. He's the administrator for ten PCs in the office, and he alone knows the Administrator password. Joe, a trusted employee, will be acting as administrator while William is gone. Should William give Joe the password? Why or why not? Does William have an alternative option?

   _____

   _____

# Key Term Quiz

Use the following vocabulary terms to complete the following sentences. Not all of the terms will be used.

Administrator account

Recovery Console

groups

MMC

MSCONFIG

passwords

Safe Mode

snap-ins

Event Viewer

1. The various tools in the MMC are known as _____.

2. The _____ can be added as a boot menu option.

3. The _____ is extremely powerful; it should be used sparingly and safeguarded closely.

4. The first line of security in Windows NT/2000/XP is using _____ and forced logons.

5. The best way to manage a large number of users is to put them into _____.

# Chapter 9

## Networking

### Lab Exercises

There's no doubt about it—a PC technician *will* have networking issues to work through at some point. Whether it's a three-computer, home-based local area network (LAN), a public WiFi access point, a large company with thousands of connected devices, or the Web itself, networks have become as common as PCs. This is why CompTIA now includes questions about the basic workings of networks on the A+ exam.

All too often, an A+ technician is called upon to be a network "guru." This happens frequently, especially in smaller companies that can't afford to hire multiple people to support both the network *and* the PCs.

In this chapter's labs, you'll imagine that you've been hired to work for a small company that has just (finally) decided to build a network in their office. You'll need to have a working understanding of network hardware and network operating system issues, as well as some good troubleshooting tools for when things don't work quite right.

 30 MINUTES

## Lab Exercise 9.01: Identifying Local Area Network Hardware

Your boss decides to finally network the eight computers in your office, and he wants your ideas about purchasing the right equipment. Your company is a small one, so the task is quite doable, but you need to make sure you know what you're talking about before you give your report.

### Learning Objectives

In this lab, you'll familiarize yourself with networking hardware.

At the end of this lab, you'll be able to

- Identify different kinds of network cabling
- Identify different network interface cards (NICs)
- Identify different types of network hubs
- Identify different wireless networking devices

## Lab Materials and Setup

The materials you need for this lab are

- Access to a PC running Windows 98/Me/2000/XP

- Access to a working local area network and the Internet (you may have demonstration devices provided by your instructor)

## Getting Down to Business

One of the best ways to find out what a network is made of is to physically look at all of its pieces. Even then, however, it may be necessary to access a manufacturer's web site to see, for instance, if the "hub" you're using is really a hub or maybe a switch.

**Step 1**   If you have access to a LAN (the classroom computer lab network, a friend's home network, or your company's network), spend some time exploring the physical hardware connections and devices.

---

### ✖ Warning

Don't disconnect anything and be careful while probing around. One small mistake, like removing a cable or turning off the wrong device, can disrupt the entire network. If you're using the classroom network, ask the instructor what you can and can't remove while you make closer inspections of the cables and devices.

---

### ✔ Cross-Reference

Be sure to check out Chapter 9 of *Mike Meyers' A+ Guide to Operating Systems* for help identifying network cables and connectors. It's a good idea to have the textbook handy while you progress through this lab.

---

What sort of cabling does the network use, or is it wireless? Is it twisted-pair cable or coaxial cable? Does it use "T" connectors? Are the cable ends BNC or RJ-45? Describe the physical layout of the LAN here.

_____

_____

_____

_____

**FIGURE 9-1** A network interface card (NIC)

What sort of NICs do the machines have? Describe the back of the card. Does it have a single connector or a combination of connectors (see Figure 9-1)? Does it have an antenna? Is there a link and/or activity LED? Which of the LEDs is on steady? Which is flashing? Describe the NIC here.

_____

_____

**Step 2** Hubs and switches are very much a part of every network.

Are the PCs connected with a single cable (crossover cable limited to two PCs), or are they connected to a hub (see Figure 9-2)? Is part of the network wireless? What is the model number of the network hub? Who manufactures the hub? How many devices can be attached? Record your findings here.

_____

_____

**FIGURE 9-2** A LAN hub with multiple cables/devices attached

Is the hub or switch a standard single speed (10BaseT, for instance) device, or can it handle multiple speeds (10/100/1000 Mbps)? Does it have wireless capabilities? If it isn't apparent or printed on the cabinet, ask the instructor or the network administrator.

_____

_____

**Step 3** Are you going to have a wireless network or wireless devices in your network? Do you plan on installing a wireless network sometime in the near future? Follow these steps:

a)  Go to http://www.linksys.com/products/; Linksys has an excellent selection of wireless products.

b)  Choose the Access Points, Routers & Gateways link, then choose WRT54G, and finally select Product Data Sheet.

    What's the WRT54G? Is it a router, switch, or wireless access point? Explain your answer.

_____

_____

c)  Look at the Wireless Network Adapters section of the Linksys site.

    Would you use the WMP54G or WMP11 NIC or both in your network with a WRT54G? Explain your answer.

_____

_____

✔ **Hint**

When researching wireless compatibility issues, always look at the product data or specification sheets of the devices to see if they'll work together.

 30 MINUTES

# Lab Exercise 9.02: Exploring Local Area Network Configuration Options

You've made your recommendation, and you've installed the network. The hardware side of installing a basic LAN is really simple these days, so you managed to get that put together in a flash. Now it's time to configure the PCs that connect to the network.

For the A+ exam and as a technician, you need to be able to set up, configure, and troubleshoot networks in Windows 98/Me/NT/2000/XP. From a network configuration standpoint, Windows Me and Windows NT mirror Windows 2000. This lab uses Windows XP to illustrate network configuration. There are notes about how other versions of Windows handle the same settings. If possible, you should practice the exercises using several different operating systems. The A+ exam will test your configuration knowledge for various versions of Windows, including the paths you use to locate configuration settings.

## Learning Objectives

In this lab, you'll explore the network configuration options in a Windows environment.

At the end of this lab, you'll be able to

- Configure network access using the networking applets

## Lab Materials and Setup

The materials you need for this lab are

- Access to a PC with Windows 98/Me/2000/XP installed

- Access to the LAN

---

✔ **Hint**

If possible, you should repeat the exercises in all three Windows environments. If you only have a single operating system, be sure you understand how to configure networks in the other operating system environments. It's also a good idea to have the drivers for your NICs handy just in case you need to reload any of them. Finally, you'll want to determine the relevant settings (in other words, the proper protocol, the name(s) of the workgroup(s) you'll be using, and so on); write them down, and keep them with you as you go from computer to computer.

## Getting Down to Business

For a computer to gain access or share resources on a network, it must have a NIC installed and certain basic information configured. Microsoft provides configuration wizards to set up your network with mostly default parameters and a lot of assumptions. In other words, you tell it the computer name, and it does the rest. Using the Microsoft wizards will allow you to set up a default configuration for quick access (good for at home), but this may not always work for a LAN in a business environment.

Whether you use the wizards or manually configure the system, the following steps must be accurately programmed into the software or you can't fully utilize the LAN. For the A+ exam, you need to know *where to locate* and *how to modify* the network configuration. Specifically, each computer that will be connected to the LAN must have the following:

- A NIC with correct drivers installed
- Client software, as this determines if it is a Microsoft or Novell Netware system
- Protocols (what language[s] you'll use on the network and the settings)
- Services, like File or/and Printer Sharing
- Computer name
- Workgroup name

**Step 1**  Go to Device Manager, and verify that the correct NIC drivers are installed. Reinstall the driver if necessary.

---

### ✔ Hint

This lab uses Windows XP and assumes you're running in Classic mode when viewing the Control Panel. You can switch from Category mode to Classic mode by clicking the entry at the top of the left column in the Control Panel. Throughout the exercises, you're told to "go to the Control Panel" or "go to Device Manager." If you have any questions about the path to use for various versions of Windows, refer to the path exercise in Lab Exercise 2.01.

---

In Device Manager, expand the Network Adapters. Alternate-click your network card, and select Properties. Click the Driver tab to see what driver is installed or to update the driver.

**Step 2**  In this step, you'll verify what network services are installed. In Windows XP, go to Control Panel | Network Connections. Alternate-click your Local Area Connection (if you have multiple network adapters in a single machine, there may be more than one connection), and select Properties. Select the General tab.

If you're using Windows 9x, go to Control Panel | Network and select the Configuration tab. In Windows 2000, go to the Control Panel, double-click Network and Dial-Up Connections and alternate-click your Local Area Connection.

You should find the following components listed in a selection window. Your system may have others as well.

**Client**   Client for Microsoft Networks (default**)**

**Protocol**   TCP/IP (default)

**Service**   File and Print Sharing for Microsoft Networks

 **Hint**

There's nothing wrong if you don't see any or all of these components listed or if you see more than the ones listed previously. It's just that the network configuration hasn't been completed on your system, or it's in a network supported by more than one server.

What client(s), other than the default, are listed in your system?

_____

What protocol(s), other than the default, are listed?

_____

What services, other than the default, are listed?

_____

**Step 3**   Now that you've found the network configuration screen, take a look at the various options:

**Install (Add in Windows 98)**   The Install button enables you to add network components. Clicking the Install button gives you three or four choices (depending on your system):

**Client**   Adds a client to the configuration (must have at least one).

**Adapter**   Installs your network adapter (this option is available in Windows 98, but not Windows 2000 or Windows XP).

**Protocol**   Microsoft TCP/IP is the default (the system must have a protocol to communicate).

**Service**   File and Print Sharing must be enabled for other computers on the network to access the one on which you're working.

**Remove/Uninstall**   The Remove button enables you to remove network components.

**Properties**   The Properties button displays a variety of dialog boxes based on the network component selected.

**File and Print Sharing (Windows 98/Me)**   The File and Print Sharing button opens a dialog box that offers two options for sharing: files and printers.

✔ **Hint**

Each of the previous options asks questions about what you want to change. If one or more of your required settings is missing, use this screen to add them. When you make changes, you may be asked to reboot the system.

**Step 4** Now that your system is configured for networking, you need to have an identity for it and join a workgroup to be recognized by the network and access network resources.

In Windows XP, go to the Control Panel, double-click System and select the Computer Name tab. Record your system settings here:

Computer name _____

Workgroup name _____

✔ **Hint**

In Windows 2000, the information is on the Network Identification tab. In Windows 98/Me, you must go to Control Panel | Network applet and then choose the Identification tab. Windows 98/Me also has an Access Control tab where you can set controls for access to shared resources.

**Step 5** Now that you've confirmed and recorded the networking components, your computer name, and your workgroup, the next step is to practice removing and reinstalling your network adapter.

✖ **Warning**

This step is optional and can cause you grief if you aren't prepared. Ask the instructor if it's okay for you to proceed with this step. If not (or if you think this may harm your configuration), skip this step.

Access Device Manager, and logically remove (uninstall) your network adapter. Yes, this will erase all your network settings. Did you take good notes earlier? Expand the network adapters heading, and alternate-click your specific adapter. Choose Remove or Uninstall.

✖ **Warning**

If your notes are incomplete, ask the instructor to fill in the correct settings you're missing.

Reboot your system, and the adapter will be detected (if it's Plug and Play) and installed. Access the Network Connections applet, and verify your network configuration using the information you recorded in steps 1, 2, and 4 previously. If your system doesn't load the drivers for the network card, you'll need the driver CD or disk to complete your settings.

Test your system by accessing the network. Can you browse the network now? Look in My Network Places (or Network Neighborhood if you're using Windows 98/Me). _____

 30 MINUTES

# Lab Exercise 9.03: Verifying TCP/IP Settings

Microsoft assigns TCP/IP settings automatically during the install process. This makes it easy to set up a small home or business network of PCs. All systems in the network will communicate with each other using these settings. The problem is that most businesses have their own set of TCP/IP settings that must be used for all new or repaired systems introduced into the network. Your responsibility as a PC technician is to verify the TCP/IP settings.

## Learning Objectives

In this exercise, you'll access and verify the TCP/IP settings for a given PC system.

At the end of this lab, you'll be able to

- Use a list of known good settings to configure the TCP/IP settings on a PC

## Lab Materials and Setup

The materials you need for this lab are

- A PC system that's *properly configured* for LAN access using Windows 98/Me/2000/XP

- A list of TCP/IP settings provided by the instructor

### ✔ Hint

This exercise is written for Windows XP with notes for Windows 98/Me/2000. You should be familiar with the process in all operating systems for the A+ exam.

## Getting Down to Business

No one is supposed to automatically know all of the TCP/IP settings for a network. For instance, when you're setting a small network up (one that connects to the Internet), you'll need to contact your Internet service provider (ISP) to set up your router's TCP/IP settings. So don't worry if you have no idea what settings to use. The trick is to learn how to get them.

**Step 1** TCP/IP requires each system to have two basic settings for accessing a LAN and two additional settings for accessing other LANs or the Internet. You can configure your system to automatically obtain the following settings when you log in, or you can specify them depending on the requirements of your network:

- IP address (unique to the PC)

- Subnet mask (identifies network information)

- Gateway (address of the router to the external realm)

- Domain Name Service (DNS)

**Step 2** First, you'll locate and verify your TCP/IP settings.

a) Go to Control Panel and double-click Network Connections. Alternate-click your local area connection, and select Properties. Highlight the Internet Protocol (TCP/IP) entry, and select Properties. When the Internet Protocol (TCP/IP) Properties dialog box appears, choose one of the following settings options (see Figure 9-3):

- If you want to use the Microsoft automatic settings or if the network has a DHCP server (ask the instructor), select the General tab and then select the Obtain IP Address Automatically and Obtain DNS Server Address Automatically radio buttons. Finish by clicking OK.

- If you have a list of settings to be entered or verified, follow the next few steps.

b) Select the Use the Following IP Address radio button.

c) Enter the IP, subnet mask, gateway, and DNS addresses.

d) Click OK to finish, and close all the windows.

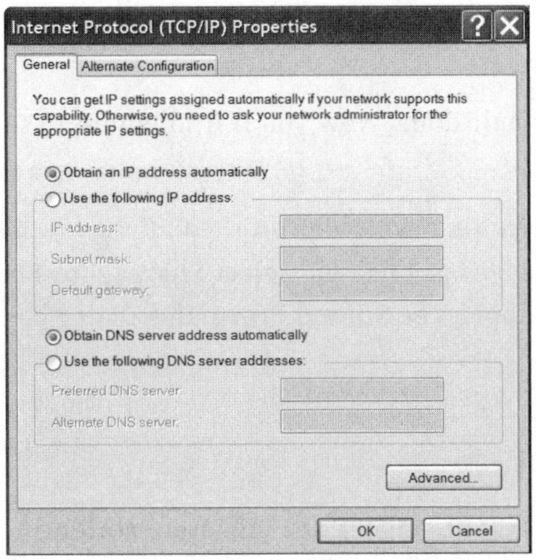

**FIGURE 9-3** Specifying TCP/IP settings in the TCP/IP Properties dialog box of a Windows XP system

 30 MINUTES

# Lab Exercise 9.04: Sharing Resources

With the network all set up properly, the next thing to do is decide how you want to share resources. You can share any folder or other resource. Floppy drives, CD drives, Zip drives, and hard drives can all be shared.

## Learning Objectives

In this lab, you'll set up file sharing for others to access information from their system.

At the end of this lab, you'll be able to

- Enable and configure shared directories and other resources

## Lab Materials and Setup

The materials you need for this lab are

- A PC system that's *properly configured* for LAN access using Windows 98/2000/XP

✔ **Hint**

The exercise is written for Windows XP with notes for how to share using Windows 98/2000. For the A+ exam, you should know how to share resources with any Windows operating system.

## Getting Down to Business

Whew! That last exercise was interesting, but the job is only half done. Now you'll find where to set up sharing for a particular resource.

**Step 1** Open My Computer, double-click the C: drive, and create a new folder on the C: drive. Name it "Shared." Alternate-click the Shared folder icon to see the folder options, and select Sharing (or Sharing and Security, depending on your operating system). This will open the Shared Properties dialog box (see Figure 9-4).

✔ **Hint**

If the Sharing tab isn't there, it's probably because you forgot to enable the File and Printer Sharing option in the Networking applet. Go back and do that.

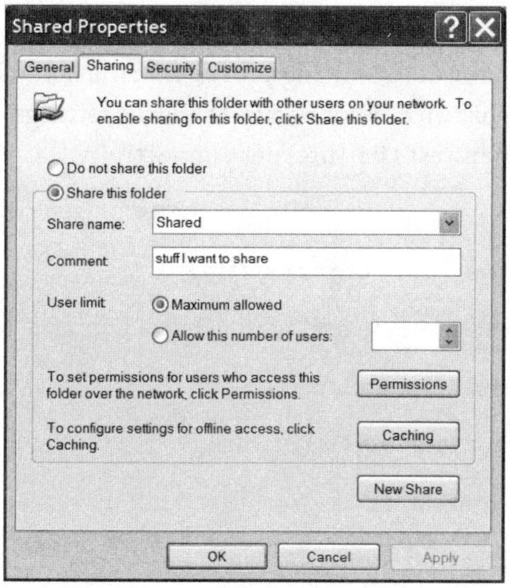

**FIGURE 9-4** Sharing tab of the Shared Properties dialog box in Windows XP

---

✔ **Hint**

If you're running Windows XP Home Edition or Windows XP Professional Edition in a workgroup environment, the Sharing dialog box is much simpler. It contains Share/Do Not Share buttons and a space to provide a share name.

---

**Step 2** Try sharing and unsharing the folder. Note that the share name and permissions are grayed out when you select Do Not Share This Folder. Share the folder again, change the share name, and look at the various levels of permissions: Full Control, Change, and Read.

**Step 3** When you're done, click OK to close the dialog box.

🕑 30 MINUTES

# Lab Exercise 9.05: Testing Your LAN Connections

There are tools available that will help you test and troubleshoot your new network. The textbook covers using these tools in detail. Some of these tools are beneficial to you now as an A+ Certified technician and are covered on the A+ exam. This lab exercise lets you practice several key network troubleshooting tools on various operating systems.

## Learning Objectives

In this exercise, you'll be introduced to troubleshooting tools for determining proper installation of the network components. These tools are covered in order of importance. First verify the local settings before trying to access other systems on the same LAN and then test the Internet connectivity.

At the end of this lab, you'll be able to

- Use the WINIPCFG/IPCONFIG commands to determine local network settings

- Use the NET CONFIG command to check the local system name and who is logged on as a user

- Use the PING command to test the local TCP/IP software and adapter

- Use the NET VIEW command to check for other computers on the network

- Use the PING command to test connecting to other computers

- Use the NSLOOKUP command to translate IP addresses and domain names

- Use the TRACERT command to check the path to other computers

## Lab Materials and Setup

The materials you need for this lab are

- A PC system that's *properly configured* for network access using Windows 98/2000/XP

- Access to the Internet

✔ **Hint**

The commands vary slightly depending on the operating system you use. You should practice with all three operating systems if possible. Test the LAN first by accessing another computer on the network using Network Neighborhood.

## Getting Down to Business

A PC technician should be familiar with several networking tools, both for his or her own good and because they're covered on the A+ exam. You'll begin by looking at WINIPCFG and IPCONFIG.

**Step 1**   You'll now use the WINIPCFG and IPCONFIG commands to determine local network settings. Checking the automatic TCP/IP settings given to you by a DHCP server and verifying your manual settings is easy:

   a)   Begin by accessing the command line prompt. For Windows 98, select Start | Run, type **command**, and press ENTER. For Windows 2000 or XP, select Start | Run, type **cmd**, and press ENTER (see Figure 9-5).

b) Enter the appropriate configure command, depending on your operating system. For Windows 98, type **winipcfg /all** and press ENTER. An IP Configuration applet will open (see Figure 9-6).

c) Select the More Info button to enlarge the window with more details.

d) In the drop-down menu at the top, select your adapter card and look at all the settings. The entries are the ones automatically assigned by the DHCP server or the ones you entered manually (see Figure 9-7).

Record your settings here:

IP address _____

Subnet mask _____

Default gateway _____

DNS _____

e) For Windows 2000/XP, type the **ipconfig /all** command at the command prompt and press ENTER. A text display will become visible on the screen.

Does the display contain the settings that were automatically assigned by the DHCP server or the ones you entered manually (see Figure 9-8)? _____

f) Record your settings here:

IP address _____

Subnet mask _____

Default gateway _____

DNS _____

---

✔ **Hint**

If you have a system in a peer-to-peer network (no servers) and there are no routers installed, you won't see information about gateways and DNS. What may appear are WINS settings. More of this is covered in a Network+ course.

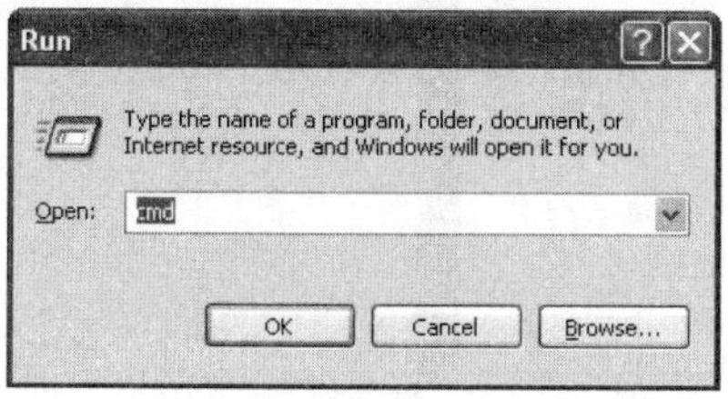

---

**FIGURE 9-5** Entering the CMD command

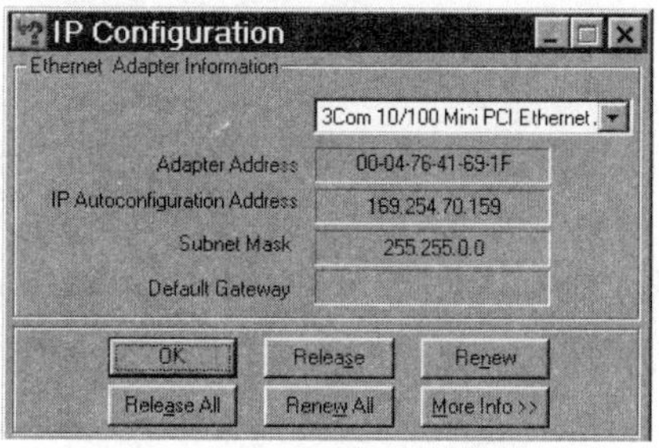

**FIGURE 9-6** The Windows 98 IP Configuration window

IP Configuration
Host Information
Host Name
laptop11.totalhome
DNS Servers
192.168.4.155
Node Type
Broadcast
NetBIOS Scope Id
IP Routing Enabled
WINS Proxy Enabled
NetBIOS Resolution Uses DNS
Ethernet Adapter Information
3Com 10/100 Mini PCI Ethernet
Adapter Address
00-04-76-41-69-1F
IP Address
192.168.4.7
Subnet Mask
255.255.255.0
Default Gateway
192.168.4.151
DHCP Server
192.168.4.155
Primary WINS Server
Secondary WINS Server
Lease Obtained
08 08 03 12:05:27 PM
Lease Expires
08 16 03 12:05:27 PM
OK
Release
Renew
Release All
Renew All

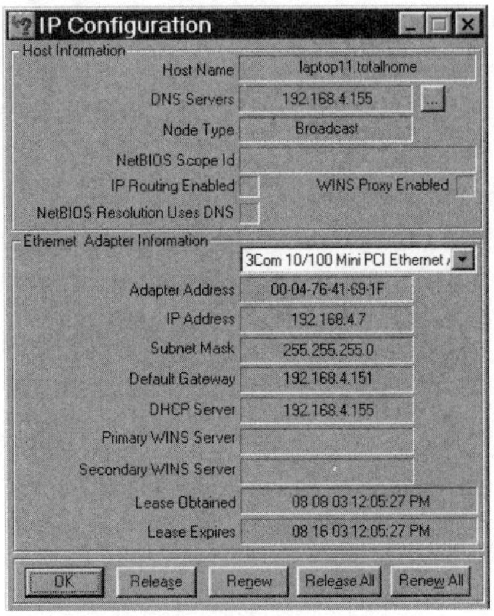

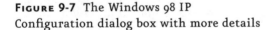

**FIGURE 9-7** The Windows 98 IP Configuration dialog box with more details

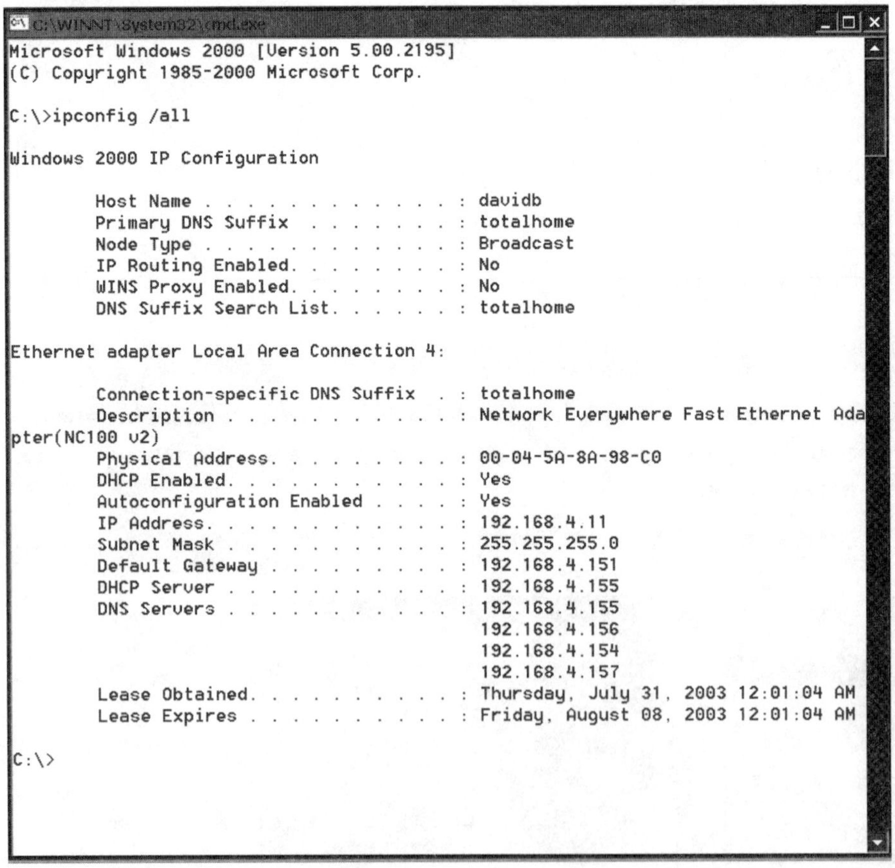

C:\WINNT\System32\cmd.exe
Microsoft Windows 2000 [Version 5.00.2195]
(C) Copyright 1985-2000 Microsoft Corp.
C:\>ipconfig /all
Windows 2000 IP Configuration
Host Name . . . . . . . . . . . . : davidb
Primary DNS Suffix . . . . . . . : totalhome
Node Type . . . . . . . . . . . . : Broadcast
IP Routing Enabled. . . . . . . . : No
WINS Proxy Enabled. . . . . . . . : No
DNS Suffix Search List. . . . . . : totalhome
Ethernet adapter Local Area Connection 4:
Connection-specific DNS Suffix . : totalhome
Description . . . . . . . . . . . : Network Everywhere Fast Ethernet Ada
pter(NC100 v2)
Physical Address. . . . . . . . . : 00-04-5A-8A-98-C0
DHCP Enabled. . . . . . . . . . . : Yes
Autoconfiguration Enabled . . . . : Yes
IP Address. . . . . . . . . . . . : 192.168.4.11
Subnet Mask . . . . . . . . . . . : 255.255.255.0
Default Gateway . . . . . . . . . : 192.168.4.151
DHCP Server . . . . . . . . . . . : 192.168.4.155
DNS Servers . . . . . . . . . . . : 192.168.4.155
192.168.4.156
192.168.4.154
192.168.4.157
Lease Obtained. . . . . . . . . . : Thursday, July 31, 2003 12:01:04 AM
Lease Expires . . . . . . . . . . : Friday, August 08, 2003 12:01:04 AM
C:\>

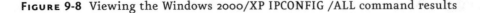

**FIGURE 9-8** Viewing the Windows 2000/XP IPCONFIG /ALL command results

g) Leave the command prompt window open; you'll use it throughout the rest of this exercise.

**Step 2** You'll now use the NET CONFIG command to check the local system name and to see who is logged on as a user. Confirming the computer name and who is currently logged on is another way of using the command line. Windows 98 and Windows 2000/XP are slightly different, but the concept is the same.

In Windows 98, type the **net config workstation** command at the command prompt and press ENTER. You'll see how the identification is set up for your local PC. There's a lot of information here, but you're only interested in a couple of items (see Figure 9-9).

How are these listed for your system?

Computer name _____

User name _____

Workgroup _____

Root directory _____

In Windows 2000/XP, type the **net config workstation** command at the command prompt and press ENTER. You'll see how the identification is set up for your local PC. There's a lot of information listed, but once again you're only interested in a couple of items.

How are these listed?

Computer name _____

User name _____

Workstation domain (workgroup) _____

Software version _____

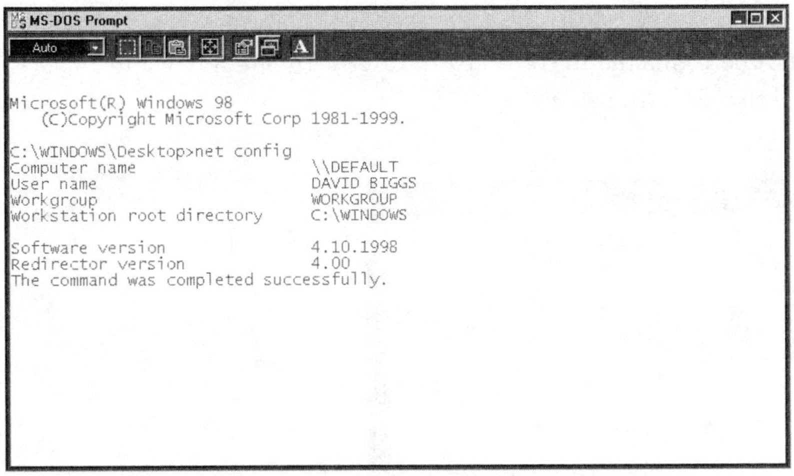

**FIGURE 9-9** Using the NET CONFIG command in Windows 98

**Step 3**    You'll now use the PING command to test the local TCP/IP software and adapter.

At the command line prompt, type **ping 127.0.0.1** (including the periods) and press ENTER. This will test the TCP/IP software and the internal part of the local network card. Look at Figure 9-10 to see a successful test. If you don't see the test results, there are serious problems with the software. Reinstall your network drivers, and reconfigure the TCP/IP settings.

**Step 4**    You'll now use the NET VIEW command to check for other computers on the network.

Can you see anyone else on the network that will prove your network card can transmit and receive data?

At the command line prompt, type **net view** and press ENTER. You'll see what other computers are on the network by a listing of their computer names (see Figure 9-11).

**Step 5**    Now you'll use the PING command to test your ability to connect to other computers on the network.

Okay, so now you can actually get the IP address and names of other systems on the local area network, but can you actually communicate with them?

At the command line prompt, type **ping** *computer name*, where *computer name* is another PC on the network you found in step 4, and press ENTER. The results will look the same as when you used PING to see your own computer but with the other computer's IP address (see Figure 9-12). Be sure to put a space between the PING command and the computer name. If you get errors, use the NET VIEW command again to be certain of the computer name's spelling.

---

✔ **Hint**

If the DNS is down, you can adjust by pinging the other computer's IP address instead of its name.

---

**Step 6**    You'll now use the NSLOOKUP command to translate an Internet domain name to an IP address or an IP address to an Internet domain name.

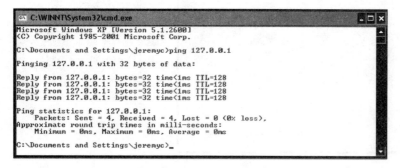

**FIGURE 9-10**  A successful PING test

```
C:\WINNT\System32\cmd.exe                                        _ □ x
Microsoft Windows XP [Version 5.1.2600]
(C) Copyright 1985-2001 Microsoft Corp.

C:\Documents and Settings\jeremyc>net view
Server Name            Remark
-------------------------------------------------------------------------------
\\BRANDYT
\\CARY
\\CARYXP                Cary's XP System
\\CINDY
\\DAVIDB
\\DUDLEYDELL            Dudley's Dell
\\JANELLE               Janelle
\\JEREMYC
\\KATHY
\\MARTIN
\\MELISSA
\\MIKEOFFICE
\\ROGER-OLD             roger
\\SCOTTXP
\\SHIPPING
\\TOTALFS1
\\TOTALHOMEDC1
\\TOTALHOMEDC2
The command completed successfully.

C:\Documents and Settings\jeremyc>_
```

**FIGURE 9-11** Using the NET VIEW command

This command works in Windows 2000/XP but isn't available with Windows 98. This is a good command for finding out the IP addresses of web sites. Why do I want this, you ask? Well, when you use a URL in your browser, it has to be translated somewhere to an IP address. This slows down your access time. If you know the IP address and type that into the address of your Internet browser, the site will pop up faster. Follow these steps:

a) Type **nslookup microsoft.com**, and then press ENTER.

What's the IP address(s) of http://www.microsoft.com? _____

Try http://www.totalsem.com. What's the IP address(s)? _____

b) Now enter the IP address you got when you did a lookup for http://www.microsoft.com. If you get a different result, it could be that a web site is being hosted by someone other than the original domain you looked up.

```
C:\WINNT\System32\cmd.exe                                        _ □ x
C:\>ping mikeoffice

Pinging mikeoffice.totalhome [192.168.4.2] with 32 bytes of data:

Reply from 192.168.4.2: bytes=32 time<10ms TTL=128
Reply from 192.168.4.2: bytes=32 time<10ms TTL=128
Reply from 192.168.4.2: bytes=32 time<10ms TTL=128
Reply from 192.168.4.2: bytes=32 time<10ms TTL=128

Ping statistics for 192.168.4.2:
    Packets: Sent = 4, Received = 4, Lost = 0 (0% loss),
Approximate round trip times in milli-seconds:
    Minimum = 0ms, Maximum = 0ms, Average = 0ms

C:\>
```

**FIGURE 9-12** Using PING to view a computer by its name

**Step 7**  You'll now use the TRACERT command to check the path to other computers or web sites on the Internet.

This command will show you where the bottlenecks are in the Internet. The TRACERT command will list the time it takes to get from your PC to the web site or other system you're accessing. Follow these steps:

a)  Type **tracert maxtor.com**, and then press ENTER.

Was it successful? _____

How many hops did it take? _____

What's the IP address of the first hop? _____

b)  Use the NSLOOKUP command with the IP address of the first hop to see where your first server is located. For example, type **nslookup 207.46.130.108**, and then press ENTER.

Go ahead—have fun with this! Part of the learning process with PCs is to dive in and tackle a subject that you're not completely familiar with. As long as you remember to write down any information you want to change before you change it, you can enjoy exploring the amazing world of computers and still have a recovery point.

# Lab Analysis Test

1.  A user complains that after you installed the new NIC in her system, she can see everyone on the network but can't access the Internet. What did you forget to do?

_____

_____

2.  What command would you use to test the NIC's internal TCP/IP capabilities?

_____

_____

3.  Teresa's boss bought a wireless network adapter for her laptop. It works great in the office. What does she need for it work with her PC at home?

_____

_____

4.  Where is the Network Connections applet located in Windows XP?

_____

_____

5. Kal has replaced his older ISA NIC with a new wireless NIC. The office wireless network is set up and works fine for everyone else. Now he can't see anyone on the network or access the Internet. What possibilities should he check and in what order?

_____

_____

_____

# Key Term Quiz

Use the following vocabulary terms to complete the following sentences. Not all of the terms will be used.

Device Manager

hub

Network applet

NIC

PING

RJ-45

router

switch

UTP

wireless

1. You use an access point when you network _____ devices.

2. You make changes to the network configuration in Windows 98 through the _____.

3. A _____ can effectively place a device on its own collision domain, thereby increasing network bandwidth.

4. Twisted-pair network cabling uses a(n) _____ connector.

5. To check the version of the NIC driver, go to the _____.

# Chapter 10

## Internet

### Lab Exercises

The Internet is a complex system of communication that allows computers, in-business networks, mobile computers, and home PCs to share information worldwide. Today we even have cell phones, personal digital assistants (PDAs), and other personal devices that can connect to the Internet for accessing e-mail, downloading MP3s, and doing other tasks.

Connecting to the Internet requires three pieces in place and functioning: a modem, a wire, and an Internet service provider (ISP). The modem can be a 56 kilobits per second (Kbps) dialup modem or a high-speed or broadband modem. The wire can be a phone line, a coaxial cable, a digital subscriber line (DSL) or Integrated Services Digital Network (ISDN) line, or even a dedicated T1 or T3 connection. The ISP provides access to the worldwide network that makes up the Internet.

Because nearly everyone wants to "get on" the Internet, troubleshooting Internet connectivity is a PC technician's bread and butter. The A+ certification exams recognize this and test you on the nitty-gritty details of installing and configuring a dialup analog modem used to connect to an ISP through a phone line.

This chapter's labs start by going through the properties for an installed and properly configured modem and then take you through the steps needed to perform such installations.

30 MINUTES

# Lab Exercise 10.01: Identifying Modem Properties

A new client has signed up with your firm and needs to have proper Internet connectivity at their new satellite office. Your first job is to assess what modems they currently have and make a recommendation for upgrades if necessary.

## Learning Objectives

This lab tests basic assessment skills. Every technician should be able to go into a situation and quickly understand the state of the hardware in question—in this case, an analog modem. Plus, you should feel comfortable telling your clients about any problems with the hardware because of damage or aging technology.

At the end of this lab, you'll be able to

- Verify a modem is installed

- Check the properties of an installed modem

- Perform an Internet search for replacement parts

## Lab Materials and Setup

The materials you need for this lab are

- A working computer running Windows 98/Me/2000/XP, with a modem installed

- Internet connectivity or access to a local computer store that sells modems (to do your research)

## Getting Down to Business

You'll be digging around the inside of a PC in this lab, so grab your anti-static wristband and get started!

**Step 1**   Look on at the back of your computer for the modem connection.

Most modems come as expansion cards plugged into a PCI slot on the motherboard, but some motherboards may have built-in modems. Figure 10-1 shows a common PCI modem. Notice the two RJ-11 plugs. If your modem is built into the motherboard, look at the back of your system for the RJ-11 plug(s) near the serial and parallel ports.

Is your modem a PCI card, or is it built in? _____

**Step 2**   Once you've determined that the PC has a modem installed or built in, you need to go to Device Manager to check its basic hardware properties. In other words, open Device Manager to make sure the modem has drivers loaded and isn't in conflict with another device.

**Figure 10-1** Viewing an internal PCI modem

**Step 3**    After you cover the basics in Device Manager, open the Phone and Modem Options applet in the Control Panel. Note that Windows NT/9x/Me call it the Modems applet.

Windows NT/9x/Me will display a Modems Properties dialog box. Look on the General tab to see a list of the modem(s) your system believes are installed and the associated COM ports. Windows 2000/XP displays a Phone and Modem Options dialog box; you must click the Modems tab to see the list of installed modems and associated COM ports (see Figure 10-2).

What's the name of the modem installed in your system? _____

**Step 4**    In the Phone and Modem Options dialog box, highlight the modem and select the Properties button to get the particulars of your modem. Explore all the tabs and buttons while at the Properties screen, and answer as many of the following questions as you can. All the answers are available in Windows, so if you need help locating them, be sure to ask the instructor for assistance.

What communications port is being used? _____

What's the maximum speed? _____

Is the speaker volume on or off? _____

Is the receive buffer set to High or Low? _____

Is the transmit buffer set to High or Low? _____

What type of flow control is used? _____

**Step 5**    Fire up a web browser on a PC connected to the Internet, and go to http://www.directron.com to do some research on the current state of modem hardware. If you don't have a working Internet connection at this point, then put on your field trip hat and head to the computer store.

What types of modems do you find? How do the external modems connect to the PC?

_____

What V standard(s) do they support? _____

What sorts of extra features do you find that make one or another product stand out?

_____

**FIGURE 10-2** Checking the installed modem in Windows XP

30 MINUTES

# Lab Exercise 10.02: Installing a Modem

Although the client has some modems installed, most use older technology and have connection speeds of 28 Kbps or 33 Kbps. They're in desperate need of an upgrade. The client opts for internal PCI modems, and you get to install them.

## Learning Objectives

Installing a modem requires four major actions. First, you physically install the device. Second, you assign it unused system resources, either manually or by using the Plug and Play (PnP) feature of Windows. Third, either you or the system (using PnP) must install the proper drivers for the card. Fourth, you configure the proper settings required by the ISP.

At the end of this lab, you'll be able to

- Install a modem

- Install or update your modem drivers

---

✔ **Cross-Reference**

Refer to the "Modems" section of Chapter 10 of *Mike Meyers' A+ Guide to Operating Systems* for more information on modems.

---

## Lab Materials and Setup

The materials you need for this lab are

- A PC system with no modem installed

- A PCI modem card

- Access to the proper driver software (either built-in Windows drivers or a separate CD)

- A copy of the Windows CD (may be needed, depending on the system)

## Getting Down to Business

Break out your trusty screwdriver and anti-static wrist strap. It's time to install a modem!

**Step 1** Make sure the PC is off and unplugged. Take proper ESD precautions, and remove the cover of the PC. Choose any free PCI slot to install the modem. Remove the back plate if one exists.

**Step 2** Plug the modem card into the PCI slot (see Figure 10-3). Physically inserting the modem into the PC is the easiest part of the task. Take care to avoid touching the pins or any of the chips on the modem. Once the card is inserted, secure it by putting the proper screw through the metal tab of the card and screwing it to the frame. Put the cover back on your computer, and restart your computer.

**Figure 10-3** Inserting a PCI modem

**FIGURE 10-4** Using the Found New Hardware Wizard

---

✔ **Hint**

You'll best understand step 3 if you're running Windows 9x, Me, or 2000.

---

**Step 3**   Now that you have physically installed the modem, the next step is to load the drivers. When you restart your computer, if you're running Windows 9x, Me, or 2000, the operating system will recognize that you've added new hardware and launch the Found New Hardware Wizard. Windows XP is far advanced; when you install a PnP device, the drivers are most likely already part of the operating system, so they'll be installed automatically. This all occurs with no user intervention. The operating system reports success installing the new device with a small balloon from the system tray.

The following is the Found New Hardware Wizard driver installation process in Windows 2000:

a)   As Windows boots, it displays the Found New Hardware Wizard screen (see Figure 10-4).

b)   Click Next to continue. Select the option that directs Windows to search for a suitable driver for the new device (see Figure 10-5). If the driver is on a floppy disk or CD, select that as the search location, insert the media for the driver before continuing, and then click Next.

---

✔ **Hint**

Every Windows operating system has the most popular modem drivers built in at the time of release, but your driver may not be one of them. For example, if the modem you're installing was manufactured after the release of software you're using, the drivers may not be part of the operating system and will need to be put in manually.

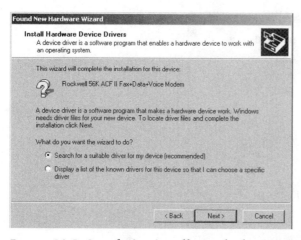

**FIGURE 10-5** Completing installation by locating a suitable device driver

---

✔ **Hint**

A popular trick is to copy the drivers from the CD onto the PC's hard drive and then install them from there. That way, if you ever need the drivers again, you won't need to rummage around for the driver CD. You need to know exactly where you store the drivers, though, because you'll be asked to locate them during the install process. You could create a Drivers folder at the root of the C: drive to serve as a central repository for drivers. Remember, drivers are constantly being updated by manufacturers. Check the manufacturer's web site before using the driver CD.

---

c) The wizard will search the drivers built into Windows and then the location you specified for the file(s) and will (you hope) report that it found the appropriate driver. Click Next. If prompted, you may also need to insert your Windows CD. When the wizard is finished, it'll prompt you a final time. Click the Finish button, and reboot your system. The new modem and drivers are now properly installed.

If Windows doesn't detect the driver right away, you'll need to do a little extra work. Modem manufacturers bundle drivers for multiple operating systems on the driver CD, so you often need to navigate to the appropriate folder for your operating system before Windows will find the driver. In other words, look for a Win2k folder when installing modem drivers on a Windows 2000 machine. Other manufacturers package the drive into an installation routine. Check the CD for a SETUP.EXE file, and run it if you find it.

**Step 4** Now that the drivers are installed, you should confirm the modem properties and verify what drivers are installed, depending on the operating system you're running:

**Windows 9x/Me** Select Start | Settings | Control Panel and double-click Modems. This will open to the General tab. Select Properties to view general information. Select the Diagnostics tab, highlight the port assigned to your modem, and click Driver.

**Windows 2000**    Select Start | Settings | Control Panel and double-click Phone and Modem Options. Click the Modems tab, select your modem, and click Properties. This will give you all the modem properties except the driver. To confirm the driver installation, go to Control Panel, double-click System, select the Hardware tab, and click Device Manager. In the list of hardware, expand the modems, right-click your specific modem, and select Properties. From this window, select the Driver tab.

**Windows XP**    In Classic view, select Start | Settings | Control Panel and double-click Phone and Modem Options. If you're in Category view, select Start | Control Panel and then click Phone and Modem Options in the left column. Click the Modems tab, select your modem, and click Properties. In Windows XP, you can confirm all the general modem information as well as the driver information in this window.

Record all the information provided about the driver you installed.

_____

_____

 30 MINUTES

# Lab Exercise 10.03: Configuring Dialup

Installing the modem card and the software drivers completes only the first part of configuring your system for dialup networking. You also need to set up the dialup networking in Windows to connect to your ISP properly. To configure dialup networking, you'll need some basic information from your ISP. Be sure you have this information before you begin this exercise.

## Learning Objectives

You'll look at the Network and Internet Connections applet in Windows XP.

At the end of this lab, you'll be able to

- Configure a new dialup connection

### ✔ Hint

For the most part, going through the full configuration of dialup networking is beyond the scope of this book, but you should at least know where to go to follow instructions from your ISP; that's the purpose of this exercise.

## Lab Materials and Setup

The materials you need for this lab are

- A working computer running Windows XP

- A modem installed and verified per Lab Exercises 10.01 and 10.02

- Configuration information from the ISP or instructor

## Getting Down to Business

The ISP provides a dialup telephone number, your username, and an initial password. In addition, the ISP will inform you of any special configuration options you need to specify in the software setup.

---

✔ **Hint**

In Windows 9x, you set up dialup connections by opening My Computer and Dial-Up Networking. Click Make a New Connection to launch the wizard. In Windows 2000, go to Control Panel and open Network and Dial-Up Connections. Choose Make New Connection to launch the wizard.

---

**Step 1** To begin configuring a dialup connection, open the Control Panel. Click Network and Internet Connections. From the Pick a Task options, select Set Up or Change Your Internet Connection (see Figure 10-6).

---

✔ **Hint**

To be sure you see the same illustrations as in this exercise, look under the heading Control Panel and be sure you've chosen the Category view, not the Classic view.

---

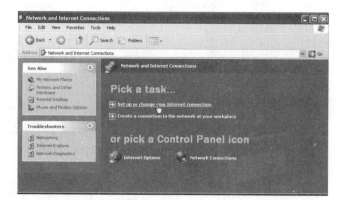

**FIGURE 10-6** Selecting the Set Up or Change Your Internet Connection option

**FIGURE 10-7** Accessing the Connections tab in the Internet Properties dialog box

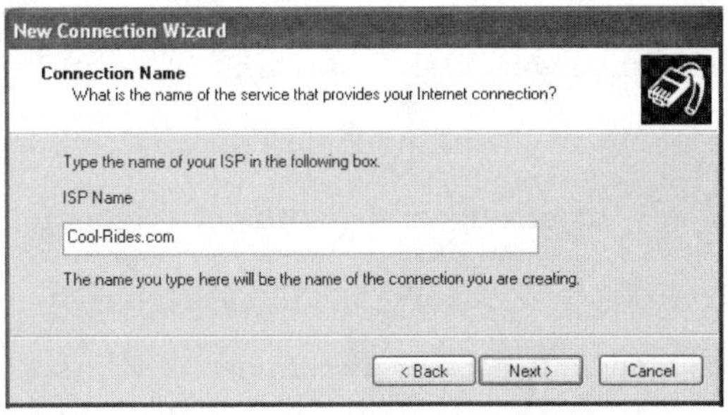

**FIGURE 10-8** Using the New Connection Wizard

**Step 2** Now that the Internet Properties dialog box is open (see Figure 10-7), select the Setup button to continue. The New Connection Wizard will open for you to input the information from your ISP. Simply work your way through the screens as follows:

a) Select Connect to the Internet, and click Next.

b) Select Set Up My Connection Manually, and click Next.

c) Select Connect Using a Dial-Up Modem, and click Next.

At this point, you need the information provided by your ISP or instructor to configure your connection properly. Enter the ISP name (see Figure 10-8). Continue through the wizard, entering the phone number to dial into the ISP and the username and password for your account.

When you finish the configuration, you'll see get a new entry in the Connect To menu on the Start menu. Figure 10-9 shows my computer's option to connect to a fictitious ISP, Cool-Rides.com.

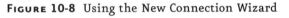

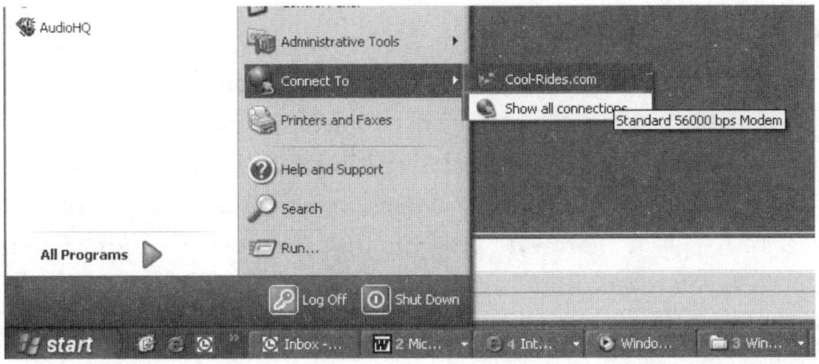

**FIGURE 10-9** Viewing connections options on the Start menu

30 MINUTES

# Lab Exercise 10.04: Dealing with Internet Problems

After getting your client's satellite office up and running on the Internet, the inevitable tech-support call came through to your desk. They can't connect. You need to figure out why.

When a previously working dialup network has a problem, it's usually one of three reasons:

- There's something wrong with the telephone line.

- The ISP might be experiencing problems.

- The modem is dead or disconnected (if it's an external model). Dead modems usually appear after major electrical storms.

In each case, the technician needs to test each part of the system to identify and correct the problem if possible. If the problem is at the ISP, all you can do is report the problem and wait.

## Learning Objectives

Windows XP comes with an excellent built-in modem-testing utility. Combine that with common sense troubleshooting, and you can solve most connection problems.

At the end of this lab, you'll be able to

- Use observation skills to troubleshoot an improperly installed modem

- Use the modem-testing utility built into Windows XP

## Lab Materials and Setup

The materials you need for this lab are

- A working computer running Windows XP with a modem installed

## Getting Down to Business

You can troubleshoot many modem problems with a quick trip inside Windows, but occasionally you need specialized tools. The most important is probably a cheap telephone that you can plug in to test a phone line. If you do a lot of modem work, then having a known good Universal Serial Bus (USB) external modem in your toolbox helps greatly. Finally, if you service pre–Windows XP systems, you should get a copy of Modem Doctor (search the Internet for this program), a great shareware program that analyzes analog modem hardware rigorously. Even without all three tools, you can do a lot, so you'll now go through the process.

**Step 1**    Check the telephone line first. Is everything plugged in properly? Plug a phone into the jack to check for a dial tone. (This may not be practical in a classroom.)

**Step 2**  Check for a poor cable connection to an external modem. Also check the power to an external modem plugged into a serial port.

**Step 3**  If the phone line checks out fine and the modem is plugged in properly, then it's time to contact the ISP technical help line (or instructor) to

- Find out whether the ISP is having difficulties
- Have a support person walk you through your settings

**Step 4**  After you've gone through the obvious possibilities and everything checks out, then it's time to dig into your modem for damage. This is especially true after an electrical storm if the modem was left plugged into a telephone jack. Telephone cables carry electricity, and a near strike by lightning can send a blast up the phone line, toasting any connected modems.

Windows XP comes with an excellent built-in modem-testing utility. Open the Phone and Modem Options applet in the Control Panel. If you're still viewing the Control Panel in Category view, the Phone and Modem Options is in the area on the left under See Also (see Figure 10-6). Select the Modems tab, and click the Properties button. This opens the Modem Properties dialog box.

Select the Diagnostics tab, and you'll see the Query Modem button. Click it! If a string of commands rolls through the little window, that's a good sign. Windows ran through some tests, and the modem responded properly. The modem query results may be incomprehensible to you, but the modem and the operating system understand each other.

---

✔ **Hint**

If you want to delve more deeply into the modem commands, check out the excellent resources at http://www.modemhelp.org, specifically on Init (initialization) strings.

---

# Lab Analysis Test

1.  John wants to install a PCI modem. What resource availability should he check for?

   _____

   _____

2.  Kal installed a modem and ran all the tests. Everything seems okay, but it still won't get a dial tone when trying to dial the ISP. What could be the problem?

   _____

   _____

3. What three things do you need from the ISP to connect to the Internet?

   _____

   _____

4. Teresa installed a modem in her Windows 98 system but can't see it in the Device Manager to test. She has rebooted several times, but it still won't show up. Why?

   _____

   _____

5. What are the three steps to installing dialup networking?

   _____

   _____

# Key Term Quiz

Use the following vocabulary terms to complete the following sentences. Not all of the terms will be used.

   analog

   demodulate

   dialup

   digital

   drivers

   ISP

   modulate

   RJ-11

   telephone

   PnP

1. A modem will _____ an analog signal so it can be used by the computer.

2. Incorrect _____ will keep a modem from functioning properly.

3. If the modem isn't detected by _____, run the Add New Hardware Wizard.

4. No dial tone can be caused by some thing as simple as a broken _____ cable.

5. All access to the Internet via a modem is controlled by the _____.

# Glossary

## Numerals

**10BaseT**  An Ethernet LAN designed to run on UTP cabling. 10BaseT runs at 10 megabits per second. The maximum length for the cabling between the NIC and the hub (or switch, repeater, etc.) is 100 meters. It uses baseband signaling. No industry standard spelling exists, so sometimes written 10BASE-T or 10Base-T.

**100BaseT**  A generic term for any Ethernet cabling system that is designed to run at 100 megabits per second on UTP cabling. It uses baseband signaling. No industry standard spelling exists, so it's sometimes written 100BASE-T or 100Base-T.

**286 protected mode**  286 protected mode was introduced with the 80286 processor. It enables an operating system (written for this mode) to access up to 16 megabytes (MB) of physical RAM, but it does not enable the operating system to create virtual machines.

**386 protected mode**  386 protected mode enabled an OS to use up to 4 gigabytes (GB) of physical RAM. This mode also allows the use of virtual machines in which older programs can be run.

**40-pin ribbon cable**  This type of cable is used to attached EIDE devices (such as hard disk drives) or ATAPI devices (such as CD-ROMs) to a system.

**802.11b**  A wireless networking standard that operates in 2.4-GHz band with a theoretical maximum throughput of 11 Mbps.

**802.11g**  The latest-and-greatest version of 802.11, it has data transfer speeds equivalent to 802.11a, up to 54 Mbps, with the wider 300-foot range of 802.11b, and it is backward-compatible with 802.11b.

**8.3 naming system**  The filename system used by DOS and early versions of Windows, where the filename could be no longer than eight characters, and the extension three characters, and they were separated by a period (dot). Pronounced "eight dot three."

## A

**Access speed**  The amount of time needed for the DRAM to supply the Northbridge with any requested data.

**Active Matrix**  Also called **TFT (Thin Film Transistor)**. A type of liquid crystal display that replaced the passive matrix technology used in most portable computer displays.

**Active partition**  One of the four primary partitions on a hard drive can be designated as the *active* partition, meaning the partition the master boot record scans for a boot sector and operating system files.

**Address bus**  The wires leading from the CPU to the memory controller chip (chipset) that enable the CPU to address RAM. Also used by the CPU for I/O addressing. An internal electronic channel from the microprocessor to Random Access Memory, along which the addresses of memory storage locations are transmitted. Like a post office box, each memory location has a distinct number or address; the address bus provides the means by which the microprocessor can access every location in memory.

**Administrative tools** A new applet in the Windows 2000 and XP Control Panel that includes a number of pre-made consoles, most notably Computer Management, Event Viewer, Performance, and Services.

**Administrator account** A user account, created when the OS is first installed, that is allowed complete, unfettered access to the system without restriction. Think of this account as the "god" account.

**Advanced Startup Options menu** A menu that can be reached during the boot process that offers advanced OS startup options, such as boot in Safe Mode or boot into Last Known Good Configuration.

**API (Application Programming Interface)** A software definition that describes operating system calls for application software; conventions defining how a service is invoked.

**Archive attribute** An attribute of a file that shows whether the file has been backed up since the last change. Each time a file is opened, changed, or saved, the archive bit is turned on. Some types of backups will turn off this archive bit to indicate that a good backup of the file exists on tape.

**ASCII (American Standard Code for Information Interchange)** The industry-standard 8-bit characters used to define text characters, consisting of 96 upper- and lowercase letters, plus 32 non-printing control characters, each of which is numbered. These numbers were designed to achieve uniformity among different computer devices for printing and the exchange of simple text documents.

**ATTRIB.EXE** A command used to view the specific properties of a file; can also be used to modify or remove file properties, such as Read-Only, System, or Archive.

**Autodetection** The process through which new disks are automatically recognized by the BIOS.

**Automated System Recovery (ASR)** A utility, included with Windows XP, which allows a user to create a complete system backup.

**Automatic Skip Driver (ASD)** A utility for preventing "bad" drivers from running the next time you boot your computer. This utility examines startup log files and removes problematic drivers from boot process.

**AUTORUN.INF** A file included on some CD-ROMs that automatically launches a program or installation routine when the CD-ROM is inserted into a CD-ROM drive.

# B

**Backside bus** The set of wires that connect the CPU to Level 2 cache. First appearing in the Pentium Pro, most modern CPUs have a special backside bus. Some buses, such as that in the later Celeron processors (300A and beyond), run at the full speed of the CPU, whereas others run at a fraction. Earlier Pentium IIs, for example, had backside buses running at half the speed of the processor. *See also* Frontside bus and External data bus.

**Backup and Restore Wizard** A utility contained within Windows that allows a user to create system backups and set system restore points.

**Bandwidth**   A piece of the spectrum occupied by some form of signal, such as television, voice, fax data, etc. Signals require a certain size and location of bandwidth in order to be transmitted. The higher the bandwidth, the faster the signal transmission, allowing for a more complex signal such as audio or video. Because bandwidth is a limited space, when one user is occupying it, others must wait their turn. Bandwidth is also the capacity of a network to transmit a given amount of data during a given period.

**Basic disk**   A hard disk drive partitioned in the "classic" way with a master boot record (MBR) and partition table. *See also* Dynamic disk.

**Basic Input/Output Services**   *See* BIOS.

**Baud**   One analog cycle on a telephone line. In the early days of telephone data transmission, the baud rate was often analogous to bits-per-second. Due to advanced modulation of baud cycles as well as data compression, this is no longer true.

**Beep codes**   A series of audible tones produced by a motherboard during the POST. These tones identify whether the POST has completed successfully or whether some piece of system hardware is not working properly. Consult the manual for your particular motherboard for a specific list of beep codes.

**Binary numbers**   A number system with a base of 2, unlike the number systems most of us use which have bases of 10 (decimal numbers), 12 (measurement in feet and inches), and 60 (time). Binary numbers are preferred for computers for precision and economy. An electronic circuit that can detect the difference between two states (on-off, 0-1) is easier and more inexpensive to build than one that could detect the differences among ten states (0–9).

**BIOS (Basic Input/Output Services)**   Classically, the software routines burned onto the System ROM of a PC. More commonly seen as any software that directly controls a particular piece of hardware. A set of programs encoded in Read-Only Memory (ROM) on computers. These programs handle startup operations and low-level control of hardware such as disk drives, the keyboard, and monitor.

**Bit (binary digit)**   A bit is a single binary digit. Any device that can be in an on or off state.

**Bit depth**   The number of colors a video card is capable of producing. Common bit depths are 16-bit and 32-bit, representing 65,536 colors and 16.7 million colors respectively.

**Boot**   To initiate an automatic routine that clears the memory, loads the operating system, and prepares the computer for use. The term is derived from "pull yourself up by your bootstraps." PCs must do that because RAM doesn't retain program instructions when power is turned off. A *cold boot* occurs when the PC is physically switched on. A *warm boot* loads a fresh OS without turning off the computer, lessening the strain on the electronic circuitry. To do a *warm* boot, press the CTRL-ALT-DELETE keys at the same time twice in rapid succession (the three-fingered salute).

**Bootable disk**   A disk that contains a functional operating system; can also be a floppy disk or CD-ROM.

**BOOT.INI**   A text file used during the boot process that provides a list of all OSs currently installed and available for NTLDR. Also tells where each OS is located on the system.

**BOOTLOG.TXT**   A text file where information concerning the boot process is logged; useful when troubleshooting system boot errors and problems.

**Boot menu**   If a designated key (often F8) is pressed as Windows loads, the Windows boot menu loads. The Windows boot menu provides a method for technicians to perform a number of boot methods "on the fly" in different troubleshooting scenarios. Not all systems show the same boot options, but these commonly include Safe mode, Safe mode with network support, Step-by-step confirmation, Command prompt only, and Safe Mode command prompt only.

**Boot sector**   The first sector on an IBM-PC hard drive or floppy disk, track 0. The boot-up software in ROM tells the computer to load whatever program is found there. If a system disk is read, the program in the boot record directs the computer to the root directory to load the operating system.

**Bootstrap loader**   Lines of code in a system's BIOS that scan for an operating system; looks specifically for a valid boot sector and when one is found, control is handed over to boot sector and bootstrap loader removes itself from memory.

**BPS (bits per second)**   Measurement of how fast data is moved from one place to another. A 56K modem can move 56,000 bits per second.

**Browser**   A program specifically designed to retrieve, interpret, and display web pages.

**Bus**   A series of wires connecting two or more separate electronic devices that enable those devices to communicate.

**Bus topology**   A configuration wherein all computers connect to the network via a central bus cable.

**Byte**   Eight contiguous bits, the fundamental data unit of personal computers. Storing the equivalent of one character, the byte is also the basic unit of measurement for computer storage. Bytes are counted in powers of two.

## C

**CAB files**   Short for "cabinet files." These files are compressed and most commonly used during OS installation to store many smaller files, such as device drivers.

**Cache**   A special area of RAM that stores the data most frequently accessed from the hard drive. Cache memory can optimize the use of your systems.

**Cache memory**   A special section of fast memory chips set aside to store the information most frequently accessed from RAM.

**Caching**   The act of holding data in cache memory for faster access and use.

**Cathode ray tube (CRT)**   The tube of a monitor in which rays of electrons are beamed onto a phosphorescent screen to produce images. Also a shorthand way to describe a monitor that uses CRT rather than LCD technology.

**CD-R (Compact Disk Recordable)**   A type of CD technology that accepts a single "burn" but cannot be erased after that one burn.

**CD-ROM (Compact Disk Read-Only Memory)**   A read-only compact storage disk for audio or video data. Recordable devices, such as CD-Rs, are updated versions of the older CD-ROM players. CD-ROMs are read using *CD-ROM drives*.

**CD-RW (Compact Disk Read/Write)**   A type of CD technology that accepts multiple reads/writes like a hard drive.

**Central Processing Unit**   *See* CPU.

**Chipset**   Electronic chips that handle all of the low-level functions of a PC, which in the original PC were handled by close to 30 different chips. Chipsets usually consist of one, two, or three separate chips embedded into a motherboard to handle all of these functions.

**Clean installation**   An operating system installed on a fresh drive, following a reformat of that drive. A clean install is often the only way to correct a problem with a system when many of the crucial operating system files have become corrupted.

**Client**   A computer program that uses the services of another computer program. Software that extracts information from a server; your auto-dial phone is a client, and the phone company is its server. Also a machine that accesses shared resources on a server.

**Clock**   An electronic circuit utilizing a quartz crystal that generates evenly spaced pulses at speeds of millions of cycles per second. The pulses are used to synchronize the flow of information through the computer's internal communication channels. Some computers also contain a circuit that tracks hours, minutes, and seconds.

**Clock cycle**   A single charge to the clock wire of a CPU.

**Clock multiplying CPU**   A CPU that takes the incoming clock signal and multiples it inside the CPU to let the internal circuitry of the CPU run faster.

**Clock speed**   The speed at which a CPU executes instructions, measured in MHz or GHz. In modern CPUs, the internal speed is general a multiple of the external speed. *See also* Clock multiplying CPU.

**Cluster**   The basic unit of storage on a floppy or hard disk. Two or more sectors are contained in a cluster. When DOS/Windows 9x stores a file on disk, it writes those files into dozens or even hundreds of contiguous clusters. If there aren't enough contiguous open clusters available, the operating system finds the next open cluster and writes there, continuing this process until the entire file is saved. The FAT tracks how the files are distributed among the clusters on the disk.

**CMOS (Complimentary Metal-Oxide Semiconductor)**   Originally, the type of non-volatile RAM that held information about the most basic parts of your PC such as hard drives, floppies, and amount of DRAM. Today, actual CMOS chips have been replaced by Flash-type non-volatile RAM. The information is the same, however, and is still called CMOS—even though it is now almost always stored on Flash RAM.

**Coaxial cable**   Cabling in which an internal conductor is surrounded by another, outer conductor, thus sharing the same axis.

**COMMAND.COM**   In DOS, a file that contains the command processor. This must be present on the startup disk for DOS to run. COMMAND.COM is usually located in the root directory of your hard drive.

**Command line interface**   A user interface for a non-graphical OS. The user interacts with the OS, somewhat in the manner of an online chat, by typing commands at a command prompt; any response from the system is displayed as text also.

**Command prompt**   A set of characters generated by a non-graphical OS to indicate it is ready to receive a user command. *See* DOS prompt.

**CONFIG.SYS**   An ASCII text file in the root directory that contains configuration commands. CONFIG.SYS enables the system to be set up to configure high, expanded, and extended memories by the loading of HIMEM.SYS and EMM386.EXE drivers, as well as drivers for non-standard peripheral components.

**Control Panel**   Part of the Windows operating system that handles most of the maintenance, upgrade, and configuration tasks. The Control Panel contains a collection of applets that enable a user to manage and modify the settings pertaining to most parts of the system. The Display, Add/Remove Programs, and System applets are the ones most used by PC techs.

**Counter**   Used to track data about a particular object when using the Performance console.

**CPU (Central Processing Unit)**   The "brain" of the computer. The microprocessor that handles the primary calculations for the computer. They are known by names such as Pentium 4 and Athlon.

**Cursor**   A graphical pointer that moves across the screen in reaction to the user's movement of a pointing device such as a mouse.

## D

**Data structure**   A term that is used interchangeably with the term "file systems." *See also* File system.

**Defragmentation (DEFRAG)**   A procedure in which all the files on a hard disk are rewritten on disk so that all parts of each file reside in contiguous clusters. The result is an improvement of up to 75 percent of the disk's speed during retrieval operations.

**Detlog.txt**   A log file created during the initial operating system installation that tracks the detection, query, and installation of all devices.

**Device driver**   A subprogram to control communications between the computer and peripherals.

**Device Manager**   A utility that allows techs to examine and configure all the hardware and drivers in a Windows PC.

**Differential backup**   Similar to an incremental backup. Backs up the files that have been changed since the last backup. This type of backup does not change the state of the archive bit.

**Digitally signed driver**   All drivers designed specifically for Windows 2000 and Windows XP are digitally signed, meaning they are tested to work stably with these operating systems.

**DIR command**   A command used in the command line interface that displays the entire contents of the current working directory.

**Directory**   Also called a folder in Windows. Part of an operating system's data storage hierarchy, a directory works like a virtual file folder for storing files or other folders. Directories stored inside other directories are referred to as subdirectories.

**DirectX**   A series of standards promulgated by Microsoft that enables applications running on Windows platforms to control hardware directly.

**Disk cache**   A piece of DRAM, often integrated into a disk drive, that is used to store frequently accessed data in order to speed up access times.

**Disk cleanup**   A series of utilities, built into Windows, that can help a user clean up their disks by removing temporary internet files, deleting unused program files, and more.

**Disk drive**   Storage drive on a PC that uses disks or platters to store information. Examples include hard drives, floppy drives, CD drives, and DVD drives.

**Disk management**   A snap-in available with the Microsoft Management Console that allows a user to configure the various disks installed in a system; available from the Administrative Tools area of the Control Panel.

**Display adapter**   *See* Video card.

**DOS prompt**   A symbol, usually a letter representing the disk drive followed by the greater-than sign (>), which tells the user that the operating system is ready to receive a command. Windows 9x and 2000 systems use the term *command prompt* rather than DOS prompt.

**DOS Protected Mode Interface (DPMI)**   A DOS-like environment found in Windows 9x/Me consisting of three main files: IO.SYS, MSDOS.SYS, and COMMAND.COM. Unlike DOS, the DPMI has support for FAT32 and long filenames.

**Dot pitch**   A value relating to CRTs, showing the diagonal distance between phosphors measured in millimeters.

**Double Data Rate SDRAM (DDR SDRAM)**   A type of DRAM that makes two processes for every clock cycle. *See also* DRAM.

**DRAM (Dynamic Random Access Memory or Dynamic RAM)**   The memory used to store data in most personal computers. DRAM stores each bit in a "cell" composed of a transistor and a capacitor. Because the capacitor in a DRAM cell can only hold a charge for a few milliseconds, DRAM must be continually refreshed, or rewritten, to retain its data.

**DSL (Digital Subscriber Line)**   A high-speed Internet connection technology that uses a regular telephone line for connectivity. DSL comes in several varieties, including Asynchronous (ADSL) and Synchronous (SDSL), and many speeds. Typical home-user DSL connections are ADSL with a download speed of up to 1.5 Mbps and an upload speed of 384 Kbps.

**Dual Inline Memory Module (DIMM)**   A type of DRAM packaging, similar to SIMMs with the distinction that each side of each tab inserted into the system performs a separate function. Comes in a compact 72-pin SO DIMM format, and full-size 144- and 168-pin formats. This 64-bit memory module is currently the standard memory package on modern computers. Types of DIMMs include SDRAM and DDR SDRAM.

**DVD (Digital Versatile Disk)**   A CD media format that provides for 4–17 GB of video or data storage.

**DVD Multi**   A description given to DVD drives that are capable of reading all six DVD formats.

**DVD+RW**   A type of rewriteable DVD media.

**DVD-ROM**    The DVD-ROM is the DVD equivalent of the standard CD-ROM.

**DVD-RW**    A type of rewriteable DVD media.

**DVD-Video**    A DVD format used exclusively to store digital video; capable of storing more than two hours of high-quality video on a single DVD.

**Dynamic disk**    A special feature of Windows 2000 and Windows XP that allows a user to span a single volume across two or more drives. Dynamic disks do not have partitions; they have volumes. Dynamic disks can be striped, mirrored, and striped or mirrored with parity.

## E

**EAX**    3-D sound technology developed by Creative Labs, but now supported by most soundcards.

**EDB (external data bus)**    The primary data highway of all computers. Everything in your computer is tied either directly or indirectly to the external data bus. *See also* Frontside bus and Backside bus.

**Emergency Repair Disk (ERD)**    This disk saves critical boot files and partition information and is our main tool for fixing boot problems in Windows 2000.

**Encrypting file system (EFS)**    The encryption tool found in NTFS 5.

**End User License Agreement (EULA)**    An agreement that accompanies a piece of software that the user must agree to in order to use the software. This agreement outlines the terms of use for software and also lists any actions on the part of the user that violate the agreement.

**Error correction code (ECC) DRAM**    A type of RAM that uses special chips to detect and fix memory errors. This type of RAM is commonly used in high-end servers where data integrity is crucial.

**Ethernet**    Name coined by Xerox for the first standard of network cabling and protocols. Ethernet is based on a bus topology.

**Event Viewer**    A utility made available as an MMC snap-in that allows a user to monitor various system events, including network bandwidth usage and CPU utilization.

**EXPAND**    A CAB file utility program included with Windows 2000. Usage of EXPAND is similar to usage of EXTRACT. *See also* EXTRACT.

**Expansion bus**    Set of wires going to the CPU, governed by the expansion bus crystal, directly connected to expansion slots of varying types (ISA, PCI, AGP, etc.). Depending on the type of slots, the expansion bus runs at a percentage of the main system speed (8.33–66 MHz).

**Expansion bus crystal**    A crystal, originally designed by IBM, which controls the speed of the expansion bus.

**Expansion slots**    1. Connectors on a motherboard that allow a user to add optional components to a system. *See also* AGP (Accelerated Graphics Port) and PCI (Peripheral Component Interconnect). 2. A receptacle connected to the computer's expansion bus, designed to accept adapters.

**Extended partition**    A type of hard disk partition. Extended partitions are not bootable and you may only have one extended partition per disk. The purpose of an extended partition is to divide a large disk into smaller partitions, each with a separate drive letter.

**Extension**   The three letters that follow a filename; an extension identifies the type of file. Common file extensions are .ZIP, .EXE, and .DOC. *See* 8.3 naming system.

**External data bus (EDB)**   The primary data highway of all computers. Everything in your computer is tied either directly or indirectly to the external data bus. *See also* Frontside bus and Backside bus.

**EXTRACT**   A program native to Windows 9x/Me that can be used to extract data from compressed CAB files. *See also* EXPAND.

# F

**FAT (File Allocation Table)**   A hidden table of every cluster on a hard disk. The FAT records how files are stored in distinct clusters. The address of the first cluster of the file is stored in the directory file. In the FAT entry for the first cluster is the address of the second cluster used to store that file. In the entry for the second cluster for that file is the address for the third cluster, and so on until the final cluster, which gets a special "end of file" code. This table is the only way DOS knows where to access files. There are two FATs, mirror images of each other, in case one is destroyed or damaged.

**FAT16**   File allocation table that uses 16 bits for addressing clusters. Commonly used with DOS and Windows 95 systems.

**FAT32**   File allocation table that uses 32 bits for addressing clusters. Commonly used with Windows 98 and Windows ME systems. Some Windows 2000 Professional systems also use FAT32, although most use the more robust NTFS.

**FDISK**   A disk partitioning utility included with Windows 9x/Me.

**File**   A collection of any form of data that is stored beyond the time of execution of a single job. A file may contain program instructions or data, which may be numerical, textual, or graphical information.

**File allocation unit**   Another term for cluster. *See also* cluster.

**File Allocation Table**   *See* FAT.

**File format**   The way information is encoded in a file. Two primary types are binary (pictures) and ASCII (text), but within those there are many formats, such as BMP and GIF for pictures; commonly represented by a suffix at the end of the filename, for example, .txt for a text file, or .exe for an executable).

**File system**   A scheme that directs how an OS stores and retrieves data on and off a drive; FAT32 and NTFS are both file systems.

**File Transfer Protocol**   *See* FTP.

**Filename**   A name assigned to a file when the file is first written on a disk. Every file on a disk within the same folder must have a unique name. Since Windows 95, you may use up to 32 characters for filenames, and filenames can contain any character (including spaces), except the following: \ / : * ? " < > |.

**Firmware**   Embedded programs or code that is stored on a ROM chip. Firmware is generally OS-independent, thus allowing devices to operate in a wide variety of circumstances without direct OS support.

**Flash ROM**   A type of ROM technology that can be electrically reprogrammed while still in the PC. Flash is overwhelmingly the most common storage medium of BIOS in PCs today, as it can be upgraded without even having to open the computer on most systems.

**Formatting**   The process of magnetically mapping a disk to provide a structure for storing data; can be done to any type of disk, including a floppy disk, hard disk, or other type of removable disk.

**Fragmentation**   Occurs when files and directories get jumbled on a fixed disks and are no longer contiguous. Fragmentation can significantly slow down hard disk drive access times and can be repaired by using the DEFRAG utility that is included with each version of Windows. *See also* Defragmentation (DEFRAG), File fragmentation.

**Frontside bus**   Name for the wires that connect the CPU to the main system RAM. Generally running at speeds of 66–133 MHz. Distinct from the Expansion bus and the Backside bus, though it shares wires with the former.

**FTP (File Transfer Protocol)**   A set of rules that allows two computers to talk to one another as a file transfer is carried out. This is the protocol used when you transfer a file from one computer to another across the Internet.

## G

**General Protection Fault (GPF)**   A Windows error that often causes a PC to lock up. Most commonly caused by two programs accessing the same resources. Also, General Protection Fault is a great geek-oriented comic strip you can find online at www.gpf-comics.com.

**Gigabyte**   1,024 megabytes.

**Graphical device interface (GDI)**   The portion of the Windows OS that supports graphical elements such as scroll bars, menus, icons, and the like.

**Graphical user interface (GUI)**   *See* GUI.

**Guest account**   One of the default accounts on a Windows NT/2000/XP system that gives users limited access to the resources of a PC. Disabled by default in all three operating systems.

**GUI (graphical user interface)**   An interface is the method by which a computer and a user interact. Early interfaces were text-based; that is, the user "talked" to the computer by typing and the computer responded with text on a CRT. A GUI (pronounced "gooey"), on the other hand, enables the user to interact with the computer graphically, by manipulating icons that represent programs or documents with a mouse or other pointing device.

## H

**Hard disk**   *See* Hard drive.

**Hard drive**   A data-recording system using solid disks of magnetic material turning at high speeds to store and retrieve programs and data in a computer. Also called a *hard disk*.

**Hardware** Physical computer equipment such as electrical, electronic, magnetic, and mechanical devices. Anything in the computer world that you can hold in your hand. A floppy drive is hardware; Microsoft Word is not.

**Hardware Abstraction Layer (HAL)** A part of the Windows OS that separates system-specific device drivers from the rest of the NT system.

**Hardware Compatibility List (HCL)** A list that is maintained by Microsoft that lists all the hardware that is supported by an operating system. This list is helpful to use when upgrading a system; with a quick glance, you can make sure that support is available for all the devices in a system before you begin the upgrade.

**Hardware protocol** A hardware protocol defines many aspects of a network, from the packet type to the cabling and connectors used.

**Hibernation** A power management setting where all data from RAM is written to the hard drive before going to sleep. Upon waking up, all information is retrieved from the hard disk drive and returned to RAM.

**Hidden attribute** A file attribute that, when used, does not allow a file to be seen when using the DIR command.

**Hierarchical directory tree** The method by which Windows organizes files into a series of folders, called directories, under the root directory. *See also* Root directory.

**High-level formatting** A type of format that sets up a file system on a drive.

**Horizontal refresh rate (HRR)** The amount of time it takes for a CRT to draw one horizontal line of pixels on a display.

**HotSync (Synchronization)** A term used to describe the synchronizing of files between a PDA and a desktop computer. HotSync is the name of the synchronization program that is used by PalmOS-based PDAs.

**HTTP (HyperText Transfer Protocol)** Extremely fast protocol used for network file transfers in the WWW environment.

**HTTP Secure (HTTPS)** A secure form of HTTP, used commonly for Internet business transactions or any time where a secure connection is required. *See also* HTTP.

**Hub** An electronic device that sits at the center of a star topology network and provides a common point for the connection of network devices. In a 10BaseT Ethernet network, the hub contains the electronic equivalent of a properly terminated bus cable; in a Token Ring network, the hub contains the electronic equivalent of a ring.

**HyperText Transfer Protocol** *See* HTTP

**I**

**Icon** A small image or graphic, most commonly found on a system's desktop, which launches a program when selected.

**IDE (Intelligent [or Integrated] Drive Electronics)**   A PC specification for small to medium sized hard drives in which the controlling electronics for the drive are part of the drive itself, speeding up transfer rates and leaving only a simple adapter (or "paddle"). IDE only supported two drives per system of no more than 504 megabytes each, and has been completely supplanted by Enhanced IDE. EIDE supports four drives of over 8 GB each and more than doubles the transfer rate. The more common name for ATA drives. (*See* ATA.)

**IEEE 1284**   A standard governing parallel communication. *See also* IEEE.

**Image file**   A bit-by-bit image of the data to be burned on the CD or DVD—from one file to an entire disc—stored as a single file on a hard drive. Image files are particularly handy when copying from CD to CD or DVD to DVD.

**Image installation**   An operating system installation that uses a complete image of a hard disk drive as an installation media. This is a helpful technique to use when installing an operation system on a large number of identical PCs.

**Incremental Backup**   A type of backup that backs up all files that have their archive bits turned on, meaning that they have been changed since the last backup. This type of backup turns the archive bits off after the files have been backed up.

**INI files**   Text files with the extension .INI used by Windows to initialize just about everything from device drivers to applications to Windows itself.

**INF file**   A Windows driver file.

**Input**   *See* I/O.

**Installable File System (IFS)**   Part of the Windows GUI, the installable file system (IFS) provides support for hard, CD-ROM, and network drives. The IFS also provides the support for long filenames. DPMI, as well as the GUI, require the IFS.

**Integrated Drive Electronics**   *See* IDE.

**Integrated Services Digital Network**   *See* ISDN.

**Internet Access Message Protocol (IMAP)**   A method of accessing e-mail kept on a remote and possibly shared mail server. It enables an e-mail program to access remote message stores as if they were stored locally on that system.

**Internet Connection Firewall (ICF)**   A software firewall built into Windows XP that protects your system from unauthorized access from the Internet.

**Internet Connection Sharing (ICS)**   A method for allowing a single network connection to be shared among several machines. ICS was first introduced with Windows 98.

**Internet service provider**   *See* ISP.

**Interrupt**   A suspension of a process, such as the execution of a computer program, caused by an event external to the computer and performed in such a way that the process can be resumed. Events of this kind include sensors monitoring laboratory equipment or a user pressing an interrupt key.

**Interrupt request (IRQ)**   IRQs are hardware lines over which devices can send interrupt signals to the microprocessor. When you add a new device to a PC, you sometimes need to set its IRQ number. This specifies which interrupt line the device may use. IRQ conflicts used to be a common problem when adding expansion boards, but the Plug-and-Play specification has removed this headache in most cases.

**I/O (input/output)**   A general term for reading and writing data to a computer. The term "input" includes data from a keyboard, pointing device (such as a mouse), or loading a file from a disk. "Output" includes writing information to a disk, viewing it on a CRT, or printing it to a printer.

**I/O addressing**   The process of using the address bus to talk to system devices.

**I/O Process**   *See* I/O (input/output).

**IO.SYS**   One of the three main files that compose the DPMI (the other two are MSDOS.SYS and COMMAND.COM). One of its functions is to start the boot menu if it detects that the F8 key has been pressed during the Windows boot process.

**IP address**   Also called Internet Address. The numeric address of a computer connected to the Internet. The IP address is made up of octets of 8-bit binary numbers that are translated into their shorthand numeric values. The IP address can be broken down into a network ID and a host ID.

**ISDN (Integrated Services Digital Network)**   The CCITT (Comité Consutatif Internationale de Télégraphie et Téléphonie) standard that defines a digital method for communications to replace the current analog telephone system. ISDN is superior to telephone lines because it supports up to 128 Kbps transfer rate for sending information from computer to computer. It also allows data and voice to share a common phone line.

**ISP (Internet service provider)**   A company that provides access to the Internet, usually for money.

# K

**Kernel (KRNL386.EXE)**   The kernel is the core portion of the program that resides in memory and performs the most essential operating system tasks. KRNL386.EXE is the filename of the Windows kernel.

**Keyboard**   An input device. There are two common types of keyboards—those that use a mini-DIN (PS/2) connection and those that use a USB connection.

**Kilohertz (KHz)**   A unit of measure that equals a frequency of one thousand cycles per second.

**Knowledge Base**   A large collection of documents and FAQs that is maintained by Microsoft. Found on Microsoft's web site, the Knowledge Base is an excellent place to search for assistance on most operating system problems.

# L

**Last Known Good Configuration**   An option on the Advanced Startup Options menu that allows your system to revert to a previous configuration in order to troubleshoot and repair any major system problems.

**LCD (Liquid Crystal Display)**   A type of display commonly used on portable PCs. Display technology that relies on polarized light passing through a liquid medium rather than on electron beams striking a phosphorescent surface.

**Legacy device**   Any device that is not Plug-and-Play compatible.

**Limited account**   A type of user account that has limited access to a system. Accounts of this type cannot alter system files, cannot install new programs, and cannot edit settings using the Control Panel.

# M

**MAC (Media Access Control) address**   Unique 48-bit address assigned to each network card. IEEE assigns blocks of possible addresses to various NIC manufacturers to help ensure that the address is always unique. The Data Link layer of the OSI model uses MAC addresses for locating machines.

**Master Boot Record (MBR)**   A tiny bit of code that takes control of the boot process from the system BIOS.

**Master File Table (MFT)**   An enhanced file allocation table used by NTFS. *See also* FAT (File Allocation Table).

**Megabyte**   One megabyte is 1,048,576 ($2^{20}$) bytes. Sometimes shortened to **Meg**, as in "a 286 has an address space of 16 Megs."

**Memory**   A device or medium for temporary storage of programs and data during program execution. The term is synonymous with storage, although it is most frequently used for referring to the internal storage of a computer that can be directly addressed by operating instructions. A computer's temporary storage capacity is measured in kilobytes (KB) or megabytes (MB) of RAM (random-access memory). Long-term data storage on disks is also measured in kilobytes, megabytes, gigabytes, and terabytes.

**Memory management**   The process of coordinating and controlling the use of memory in a computer system. In particular, the use of virtual memory to augment the address space available to software programs.

**Microcomputer**   A computer system in which the central processing unit is built as a single tiny semiconductor chip or as a small number of chips.

**Microprocessor**   See CPU.

**Microsoft CD-ROM Extensions (MSCDEX)**   This program takes the device name set up in the CD-ROM's device driver line in CONFIG.SYS and assigns it a drive letter, thus allowing for CD-ROM support in DOS.

**Microsoft Management Console (MMC)**   A new means of managing a system, introduced by Microsoft with Windows 2000. The MMC allows an Administrator to customize his management tools by allowing him to pick and choose from a list of "snap-ins." Some snap-ins that are available are the Device Manager, Users and Groups, and Computer Management.

**Microsoft Product Activation (MPA)**   Introduced by Microsoft with the release on Windows XP, Microsoft Product Activation is to prevent unauthorized use of Microsoft's software by requiring a user to "activate" the software.

**Mini power connector**    A type of connector used to provide power to floppy disk drives.

**Mirrored volume**    A volume that is mirrored on another volume. *See also* Mirroring.

**Mirroring**    Also called **Drive mirroring**. Reading and writing data at the same time to two drives for fault tolerance purposes. Considered RAID level 1.

**Modem (MOdulator/DEModulator)**    A device that converts a digital bit stream into an analog signal (modulation) and converts incoming analog signals back into digital signals (demodulation). The analog communications channel is typically a telephone line and the analog signals are typically sounds.

**Molex connector**    A type of computer power connector. CD-ROM drives, hard disk drives, and case fans all use this type of connector. A Molex connector is keyed to prevent it from being inserted into a power port improperly.

**Monitor**    The computer's display screen device. Traditionally a cathode ray tube (CRT) display similar to a television, but now also including displays using liquid crystal display (LCD) technology.

**Motherboard**    A flat piece of circuit board that resides inside your computer case. The motherboard has a number of connectors on it; you can use these connectors to attach a variety of devices to your system, including hard disk drives, CD-ROM drives, floppy disk drives, and sound cards.

**Mount point**    A drive that functions like a folder mounted into another drive.

**Mouse**    An input device that allows a user to manipulate a cursor on the screen in order to select and manipulate icons, windows, and other elements of the GUI.

**MP3**    Short for MPEG, Layer 3. MP3 is a type of compression used specifically for turning high-quality digital audio files into much smaller, yet similar sounding, files.

**MSCONFIG**    A utility found in Windows that allows a user to configure a system's boot files and critical system files.

**MS-DOS (Microsoft Disk Operating System)**    The first operating system released by Microsoft.

**MSDOS.SYS**    One of the three main files that compose the DPMI (the other two are IO.SYS and COMMAND.COM). The original Windows 3.x functions of MSDOS.SYS have been folded into IO.SYS. MSDOS.SYS has been turned into a hidden, read-only text file in the root directory of the boot drive. MSDOS.SYS is used as a startup options file.

**Multiboot installation**    A type of OS installation where multiple operating systems are installed on a single machine.

**My Computer**    An applet that allows a user to access a complete listing of all fixed and removable drives contained within a system. Each version of Windows adds more functions to My Computer. With Windows XP, for example, My Computer offers quick access to the Control Panel, Add/Remove Programs, the System Information utility, and more.

**My Documents**    Introduced with Windows 98, the My Documents folder provides a convenient place for a user to store his or her documents, log files, and any other type of files. Windows NT/2000/XP systems provide a separate My Documents folder for each user while Windows 9x/Me systems do not.

# N

**Network**   A collection of two or more computers interconnected by telephone lines, coaxial cables, satellite links, radio, and/or some other communication technique. A computer "network" is a group of computers that are connected together and that communicate with one another for a common purpose.

**Network Operating System (NOS)**   An NOS is an operating system that provides basic file and supervisory services over a network. While each computer attached to the network will have its own OS, the NOS describes which actions are allowed by each user and coordinates distribution of networked files to the user who requests them.

**NIC (Network Interface Card)**   An expansion card that enables a PC to physically link to a network.

**Non-system disk or disk error**   An error that occurs during the boot process. Common causes for this error are leaving a non-bootable floppy disk in the floppy disk drive while the computer is booting.

**Non-volatile**   A type of memory that retains data even if power is removed.

**Northbridge**   The Northbridge is the chip or chips that connect a CPU to memory, the PCI bus, Level 2 cache and AGP activities. The Northbridge chips communicate with the CPU through the FSB.

**NT File System (NTFS)**   A file system for hard drives that enables object-level security, long filename support, compression, and encryption. NTFS 4 debuted with Windows NT 4.0. Windows 2000 comes with the updated NTFS 5.

**NT kernel (NTOSKRNL.EXE)**   One of the core files of the Windows NT OS.

**NTLDR**   A Windows NT/2000/XP boot file. Launched by the MBR or MFT, NTLDR (pronounced *NT loader*) looks at the BOOT.INI configuration file for any installed operating systems to begin the process of booting Windows.

**NTFS Permissions**   A set of restrictions that determine the amount of access given to a particular user on a system using NTFS.

**NTFS 4**   A robust and secure file system that was introduced by Microsoft with Windows NT 4. NTFS provides an amazing array of configuration options for user access and security. Users can be granted access to data on a file by file basis.

**NTFS 5**   An improvement of NTFS that was released with Windows 2000. *See also* NTFS.

# O

**Object**   A system component that is given a set of characteristics and can be managed by the operating system as a single entity.

**Ohm(s)**   Electronic measurement of a cable's impedance.

**Open source**   A certification standard of the Open Source Initiative (OSI) through which a program's source code (the original language in which a program is written) is made available free of charge to the general public.

**Operating system (OS)**    A series of programs and code that create an interface so that a user can interact with a system's hardware.

**Option ROM**    BIOS programs stored in a ROM attached to an external controller card.

**Output**    Anything that comes out of a computer, including information on a display screen, a printer, or other

# P

**P1 connector**    A type of connector used to provide power to ATX motherboards.

**P4 12V connector**    A type of connector used to provide additional 12v power to motherboards that support Pentium IV processors.

**Packets**    Small data units sent across a network.

**Parallel ATA (PATA)**    A disk drive implementation that integrates the controller on the disk drive itself. *See also* ATA (AT Attachment).

**Parity**    A method of error detection where a small group of bits being transferred are compared to a single "parity" bit that is set to make the total bits odd or even. The receiving device reads the parity bit and determines if the data is valid based on the oddness or evenness of the parity bit.

**Partition**    A section of the storage area of a hard disk. A partition is created during initial preparation of the hard disk, before the disk is formatted.

**Partition table**    A table located in the boot sector of a hard drive that lists every partition on the disk that contains a valid operating system.

**Password Reset Disk**    A special type of floppy disk that can allow a user to recover a lost password without losing access to any encrypted, or password-protected, data.

**Patch**    A small piece of software released by a software manufacturer that is used to correct a flaw or problem with a particular piece of software.

**Path**    The route the operating system must follow to find an executable program stored in a subdirectory.

**PCI (Peripheral Component Interconnect)**    A design architecture for the sockets on the computer motherboard that enable system components to be added to the computer. PCI is a "local bus" standard, meaning that devices added to a computer through this port will use the processor at the motherboard's full speed (up to 33 MHz), rather than at the slower 8 MHz speed of the regular bus. In addition to moving data at a faster rate, PCI moves data 32 or 64 bits at a time, rather than the 8 or 16 bits that the older ISA buses supported.

**PCMCIA (Personal Computer Memory Card International Association)**    Also called **PC Card**. A consortium of computer manufacturers who devised the standard for credit card-sized adapter cards that add functionality in many notebook computers, PDAs, and other computer devices. The simpler term "PC Card" has become more common in referring to these cards.

**PDA (Personal Digital Assistant)**   A handheld computer that blurs the line between the calculator and computer. Earlier PDAs were calculators that enabled the user to program in such information as addresses and appointments. Newer machines, such as the Palm Pilot, are fully programmable computers. Most PDAs use a pen/stylus for input rather than a keyboard. A few of the larger PDAs have a tiny keyboard in addition to the stylus.

**Pin 1**   A designator used to ensure proper alignment of floppy disk drive and hard disk drive connectors.

**Pin Grid Array (PGA)**   A popular CPU package where a CPU is packaged in a ceramic material and a large number of pins extend from the bottom of the package in a regular pattern or array.

**Ping (Packet Internet Groper)**   Slang term for a small network message (ICMP ECHO) sent by a computer to check for the presence and aliveness of another. Also used to verify the presence of another system.

**Pipeline**   A processing methodology where multiple calculations take place simultaneously by being broken into a series of steps. Often used in CPUs and video processors.

**Pixel (picture element)**   In computer graphics, the smallest element of a display space that can be independently assigned color or intensity.

**Plug and Play**   Also called **PnP**. A combination of smart PCs, smart devices, and smart operating systems that automatically configure all the necessary system resources and ports when you install a new peripheral device.

**Point-to-Point Protocol**   *See* PPP.

**POP3 (Post Office Protocol version 3)**   Also called **Point Of Presence**. Refers to the way e-mail software such as Eudora gets mail from a mail server. When you obtain a SLIP, PPP, or shell account you almost always get a POP account with it; and it is this POP account that you tell your e-mail software to use to get your mail.

**Port**   That portion of a computer through which a peripheral device may communicate. Often identified with the various plug-in jacks on the back of your computer. On a network hub, it is the connector that receives the wire link from a node.

**Post Office Protocol version 3**   *See* POP3.

**PostScript**   A language defined by Adobe Systems, Inc. for describing how to create an image on a page. The description is independent of the resolution of the device that will actually create the image. It includes a technology for defining the shape of a font and creating a raster image at many different resolutions and sizes.

**Power supply**   A device that provides the electrical power for a PC. A power supply converts the 110-volt AC power into usable types of DC electricity in a PC.

**Power-On Self Test (POST)**   A basic diagnostic routine completed by a system at the beginning of the boot process. The POST checks to make sure that a display adapter is installed, that a system's memory is installed, and then searches for an operating system before handing over control of the machine to an operating system, if one is found.

**PPP (Point-to-Point Protocol)**   A protocol that enables a computer to connect to the Internet through a dial-in connection and enjoy most of the benefits of a direct connection. PPP is considered to be superior to SLIP because of its error detection and data compression features, which SLIP lacks, and the ability to use dynamic IP addresses.

**Print resolution**   The number of pixels per inch of a print image.

**Printer**   An output device that can print text or illustrations on paper.

**Prompt**   A character or message provided by an operating system or program to indicate that it is ready to accept input.

**Proxy server**   A device that fetches Internet resources for a client without exposing that client directly to the Internet. Most proxy servers accept requests for HTTP, FTP, POP3, and SMTP resources. The proxy server will often cache, or store, a copy of the requested resource for later use. A common security feature in the corporate world.

# Q

**Quick Launch menu**   A toolbar that used to launch commonly used programs with a single click.

# R

**RAID (Redundant Array of Independent** or **Inexpensive Devices** or **Disks)**   A way of creating a fault-tolerant storage system. There are six levels. Level 0 uses byte-level striping and provides no fault tolerance. Level 1 uses mirroring or duplexing. Level 2 uses bit-level striping. Level 3 stores error-correcting information (such as parity) on a separate disk, and uses data striping on the remaining drives. Level 4 is level 3 with block-level striping. Level 5 uses block level and parity data striping.

**RAID-5 volume**   A striped set with parity. *See also* RAID (Redundant Array of Independent or Inexpensive Devices or Disks).

**RAM (Random Access Memory)**   Memory that can be accessed at random, that is, in which any memory address can be written to or read from without touching the preceding address. This term is often used to mean a computer's main memory.

**Read-only attribute**   A file attribute that does not allow a file to be altered or modified. This is helpful when protecting system files that should not be edited.

**Recovery console**   A DOS-like interface that can be used to repair a Windows 2000 or Windows XP system that is suffering from massive OS corruption or other problems.

**Recycle Bin**   When files are "deleted" from a modern Windows system, they are moved to the Recycle Bin. To permanently remove files from a system, they must be removed from the Recycle Bin.

**Redundant Array of Independent Disks**   *See* RAID.

**REGEDIT.EXE**   A program used to edit the Windows registry.

**REGEDT32.EXE**   A program used to edit the Windows registry. REGEDT32.EXE is available in Windows 2000 and XP only.

**Registers**    Tiny temporary storage areas inside the CPU, used by the microprocessor to process complex commands. Modern registers come in 64- and 128-bit sizes.

**Registry**    A complex binary file used to store configuration data about a particular system. To edit the Registry, a user can use the applets found in the Control Panel or REGEDIT.EXE or REGEDT32.EXE.

**Remote Installation Services (RIS)**    A tool introduced with Windows 2000 that can be used to initiate either a scripted installation or an installation of an image of an operating system on to a PC.

**Resolution**    A measurement for CRTs and printers expressed in horizontal and vertical dots or pixels. Higher resolutions provide sharper details and thus display better-looking images.

**Restore point**    A system snapshot created by the System Restore utility that is used to restore a malfunctioning system. *See also* System Restore.

**RJ (Registered Jack)**    UTP cable connectors, used for both telephone and network connections. **RJ-11** is a connector for four-wire UTP; usually found in telephone connections. **RJ-45** is a connector for eight-wire UTP; usually found in network connections and used for 10BaseT and 100BaseT networking.

**ROM (Read-Only Memory)**    The generic term for non-volatile memory that can be read from but not written to. This means that code and data stored in ROM cannot be corrupted by accidental erasure. Additionally, ROM retains its data when power is removed, which makes it the perfect medium for storing BIOS data or information such as scientific constants.

**Root directory**    The directory that contains all other directories.

**Run dialog box**    Accessed by clicking on the Start menu and selecting Run from the options, the Run dialog box enables you to type the name of programs that Windows will then load. The Run dialog box saves you from searching for the program icon, as long as you know the actual file name. Also useful for getting to a command prompt by typing **command** or **cmd** (Windows NT/2000/XP only) in the dialog box.

## S

**SATA bridge**    In order to use a PATA hard disk drive with a SATA controller, you must use a SATA bridge—a device that plugs into the 40-pin connector on the drive and has its own separate power connector.

**ScanDisk**    A utility included with Windows designed to detect and repair bad sectors on a hard disk.

**SCSI (Small Computer System Interface)**    A powerful and flexible peripheral interface popularized on the Macintosh and used to connect hard drives, CD-ROM drives, tape drives, scanners, and other devices to PCs of all kinds. Because SCSI is less efficient at handling small drives than IDE, it did not become popular on IBM-compatible computers until price reductions made these large drives affordable. Normal SCSI enables up to seven devices to be connected through a single bus connection, whereas Wide SCSI can handle 15 devices attached to a single controller.

**Serial ATA (SATA)**    A hard drive technology that offers many advantages over PATA (Parallel ATA) technology, including thinner cabling, keyed connectors, and hot swapability.

**Serial-Attached SCSI (SAS)**    A serial version of SCSI. The industry's response to Serial ATA, SAS is a point-to-point interface that uses a reduced-size data cable and has reduced power consumption demands.

**Service pack**    A collection of software patches released at one time by a software manufacturer.

**Setuplog.txt**    A log file that tracks the complete installation process, logging the success or failure of file copying, Registry updates, and reboots.

**Simple Mail Transport Protocol**    *See* SMTP.

**Simple volume**    A type of volume created when setting up dynamic disks. A simple volume acts like a primary partition on a dynamic disk.

**Small Outline DIMM (SO DIMM)**    A type of memory used in portable PCs because of its small size. SO DIMMs commonly have 72-, 144-, or 200-pins.

**SMM (System Management Mode)**    A special CPU mode that enables the CPU to reduce power consumption via the selective shutdown of peripherals.

**SMTP (Simple Mail Transport Protocol)**    The main protocol used to send electronic mail on the Internet.

**Snap-in**    A small utility that can be used with the Microsoft Management Console.

**Socket**    A combination of a port number and an IP address that uniquely identifies a connection. Also a mounting area for an electronic chip.

**Socket services**    Device drivers that support the PC Card socket, enabling the system to detect when a PC Card has been inserted or removed, and providing the necessary I/O to the device.

**Soft-off by PWRBTN**    A value found in the BIOS of most ATX motherboards. This value controls the length of time that the power button must be depressed in order for an ATX computer to turn off. If the on/off switch is set for a four-second delay, you must hold down the switch for four seconds before the computer cuts off.

**Soft power**    A characteristic of ATX motherboards. They can use software to turn the PC on and off. The physical manifestation of soft power is the power switch. Instead of the thick power cord used in AT systems, an ATX power switch is little more than a pair of small wires leading to the motherboard.

**Sound card**    An expansion card that can produce audible tones when connected to a set of speakers.

**Sounds and audio devices**    A Control Panel applet used to configure audio hardware and software in Windows XP.

**Southbridge**    The Southbridge is part of a motherboard chipset. It handles all the inputs and outputs to the many devices in the PC.

**Spanned volume**    A volume that uses space on multiple dynamic disks.

**SRAM (Static RAM)**    A type of RAM that uses a flip-flop type circuit rather than the typical transistor/capacitor of DRAM to hold a bit of information. SRAM does not need to be refreshed and is faster than regular DRAM. Used primarily for cache.

**Start menu**   A menu that can be accessed by clicking the Start button on the Windows taskbar. This menu enables you to see all programs loaded on the system and to start them.

**Startup disk**   A bootable floppy disk that contains just enough files to perform basic troubleshooting from an A:\ prompt.

**STP (Shielded Twisted Pair)**   A popular cabling for networks composed of pairs of wires twisted around each other at specific intervals. The twists serve to reduce interference (also called *crosstalk*). The more twists, the less interference. The cable has metallic shielding to protect the wires from external interference. Token Ring networks are the only common network technology that uses STP, although Token Ring more often now uses UTP.

**Stripe set**   Two or more drives in a group that are used for a striped volume.

**Subdirectory**   A directory that resides inside of another directory.

**Subnet mask**   The value used in TCP/IP settings to divide the IP address of a host into its component parts: network ID and host ID.

**Super video graphics array (SVGA)**   Any display mode that goes beyond VGA (640 × 480 at 16 colors) in either resolution or color depth can be labeled as SVGA, or Super VGA.

**Swap file**   A name for the large file used by virtual memory.

**Switch**   In the context of a command line interface, extra letters and numbers added at the end of a command to modify its operation.

**Symmetric multiprocessing (SMP)**   The processing of programs by multiple linked CPUs sharing common memory and managed by a single operating system.

**Synchronous DRAM (SDRAM)**   A type of DRAM that is synchronous, or tied to the system clock. This type of RAM is used in all modern systems.

**System attribute**   A file attribute used to designate important system files, like CONFIG.SYS or WIN.INI.

**System BIOS**   The primary set of BIOS stored on an EPROM or Flash chip on the motherboard. Defines the BIOS for all the assumed hardware on the motherboard, such as keyboard controller, floppy drive, basic video, RAM, etc.

**System monitor**   A utility that can be used to evaluate and monitor system resources, like CPU usage and memory usage.

**System resources**   System resources are I/O addresses, IRQs, DMA channels, and memory addresses.

**System Restore**   A utility in Windows Me that enables you to return your PC to a recent working configuration when something goes wrong. System Restore returns your computer's system settings to the way they were the last time you remember your system working correctly—all without affecting your personal files or e-mail.

**System Tools menu**   A menu that can be accessed by selecting Start | Accessories | System Tools. In this menu, you can access tools like System Information and Disk Defragmenter.

**System tray**   Located by default at the lower right edge of the Windows 98/Me/2000/XP taskbar, the system tray contains icons representing background processes and contains the system clock.

**SYSTEM.INI**   An early Windows 3.*x* configuration file used to load device drivers. Windows 9*x*/Me systems require this file or they will not boot. Windows 2000 and XP systems do not require this file, but often have a copy in order to maintain backward compatibility with older Windows applications.

# T

**Task Manager**   The Task Manager shows all running programs, including hidden ones. You access the Task Manager by pressing CTRL-ALT-DEL. You can use it to shut down an unresponsive application that refuses to close normally.

**Taskbar**   Located by default at the bottom of the Desktop, the Taskbar contains the Start button, the System Tray, the Quick Launch bar, and buttons for running applications.

**TCP/IP (Transmission Control Protocol/Internet Protocol)**   A set of communication protocols developed by the U.S. Department of Defense that enables dissimilar computers to share information over a network.

**TCP/IP services**   A set of special sharing functions unique to TCP/IP. The most famous is Hypertext Transfer Protocol (HTTP), the language of the World Wide Web. Telnet and Ping are two other widely used TCP/IP services.

**Telnet**   A program that enables users on the Internet to log in to remote systems from their own host system.

**Termination**   The use of terminating resistors to prevent packet reflection on a network cable.

**Text mode**   During a Windows installation, the period when the computer displays simple textual information on a plain background, before switching to full graphical screens. During this part of the installation, the system inspects the hardware, displays the EULA for you to accept, enables you to partition the hard drive, and copies files to the hard drive, including a base set of files for running the graphical portion of the OS.

**Thin film transistor (TFT)**   A type of LCD screen. *See also* Active Matrix.

**Token Ring**   A LAN and protocol in which nodes are connected together in a ring; a special packet called a *token* passed from node to node around the ring controls communication. A node can send data only when it receives the token and the token is not in use. This avoids the collision problems endemic to Ethernet networks.

# U

**UART (Universal Asynchronous Receiver/Transmitter)**   A UART is a device that turns serial data into parallel data. The cornerstone of serial ports and modems.

**Upgrade Advisor**   The Upgrade Advisor is the first process that runs on the XP installation CD. It examines your hardware and installed software (in the case of an upgrade) and provides a list of devices and software that are known to have issues with XP. It can also be run separately from the Windows XP installation, from the Windows XP CD.

**Upgrade installation**   An installation of Windows on top of an earlier installed version, thus inheriting all previous hardware and software settings.

**UPS (uninterruptible power supply)**   A device that supplies continuous clean power to a computer system the whole time the computer is on. Protects against power outages and sags. The term UPS is often used mistakenly when people mean SPS (Stand-by Power Supply).

**USB (universal serial bus)**   A 12 Mbps serial interconnect for keyboards, printers, joysticks, and many other devices. Enables hot-swapping and daisy chaining devices.

**User (USER.EXE)**   One of the three core files that handle the main GUI functions of Windows 9x/Me (the other two are KRNL386.EXE and GDI.EXE). User (USER.EXE) handles specifics about things like individual user preferences.

**User Account**   A container that identifies a user to an application, operating system, or network, including name, password, user name, groups to which the user belongs, and other information based on the user and the OS or NOS being used. Usually defines the rights and roles a user plays on a system.

**User interface**   A visual representation of the computer on the monitor that makes sense to the people using the computer, through which the user can interact with the computer.

**UTP (Unshielded Twisted Pair)**   A popular type of cabling for telephone and networks, composed of pairs of wires twisted around each other at specific intervals. The twists serve to reduce interference (also called *crosstalk*). The more twists, the less interference. The cable has *no* metallic shielding to protect the wires from external interference, unlike its cousin, STP. 10BaseT uses UTP, as do many other networking technologies. UTP is available in a variety of grades, called *categories*, as defined here:

| | |
|---|---|
| **Category 1 UTP** | Regular analog phone lines—not used for data communications. |
| **Category 2 UTP** | Supports speeds up to 4 megabits per second. |
| **Category 3 UTP** | Supports speeds up to 16 megabits per second. Minimum cabling for 10BaseT. |
| **Category 4 UTP** | Supports speeds up to 20 megabits per second. |
| **Category 5 UTP** | Supports speeds up to 100 megabits per second. Minimum cabling for 100BaseT. |
| **Category 5e UTP** | Supports speeds up to 1 gigabit per second. |
| **Category 6 UTP** | Supports speeds up to 10 gigabits per second. |

# V

**V standards**   Standards established by CCITT for modem manufacturers to follow (voluntarily) to ensure compatible speeds, compression, and error correction.

**VGA (Video Graphics Array)**   The standard for the video graphics adapter that was built into IBM's PS/2 computer. It supports 16 colors in a 640 × 480 pixel video display, and quickly replaced the older CGA (Color Graphics Adapter) and EGA (Extended Graphics Adapter) standards.

**Video card**   An expansion card that works with the CPU to produce the images that are displayed on your computer's display.

**Virtual**   Pertaining to a device or facility that does not physically exist, yet behaves as if it does. For example, a system with 4 MB of virtual memory may have only 1 MB of physical memory plus additional (slower and cheaper) auxiliary memory. Yet programs written as if 4 MB of physical memory were available will run correctly.

**Virtual Device Driver (VxD)**   A special type of driver file used to support older Windows programs. Windows protection errors take place when VxDs fail to load or unload. This usually occurs when a device somehow gets a device driver in both CONFIG.SYS and SYSTEM.INI or the Registry.

**Virtual memory**   A section of a system's hard drive that is set aside to be used when physical memory is unavailable or completely in use.

**Virtual memory manager (VMM)**   Part of the Windows 9x/Me GUI architecture, VMM supports memory usage at both the DPMI and GUI levels. When the GUI is loaded, VMM takes advantage of the power of 386 protected mode to create virtual machines, one for Windows 9x/Me and one for each DOS program running in Windows 9x/Me.

**Virus**   A program that can make a copy of itself without you necessarily being aware of it; some viruses can destroy or damage files, and generally the best protection is always to maintain backups of your files.

**Virus Definition**   These files are also called signature files depending on the virus protection software in use. These files enable the virus protection software to recognize the viruses on your system and clean them. These files should be updated often.

**Volts (V)**   The pressure of the electrons passing through a wire is called voltage and is measured in units called volts (V).

**Volume**   A physical unit of a storage medium, such as tape reel or disk pack that is capable of having data recorded on it and subsequently read. Also refers to a contiguous collection of cylinders or blocks on a disk that is treated as a separate unit.

**Volume boot sector**   The first sector of the first cylinder of each partition also has a boot sector called the volume boot sector, which stores information important to its partition, such as the location of the operating system boot files.

# W

**Wattage (watts or W)**   The amount of amps and volts needed by a particular device to function is expressed as how much wattage (watts or W) that device needs.

**Wildcard**   A character used during a search to represent search criteria. For instance, searching for "*.doc" will return a list of all files with a .doc extension, regardless of the filename. "*" is the wildcard in that search.

**Windows Catalog**    Microsoft provides a list of applications and hardware compatible with Windows called the Windows Catalog. Theoretically, the Windows Catalog is for all versions of Windows, but it primarily applies to Windows XP. You can access the Windows Catalog directly at www.microsoft.com/windows/catalog.

**WIN.INI**    The AUTOEXEC.BAT of Windows 3.x, it defined all the personalizations of Windows, such as fonts, screen savers, and display colors, and it defined how resources interacted with applications.

**World Wide Web**    *See* WWW.

**Worm**    A worm is a very special form of virus. Unlike other viruses, a worm does not infect other files on the computer. Instead, it replicates by making copies of itself on other systems on a network by taking advantage of security weaknesses in networking protocols.

**WWW (World Wide Web)**    A system of Internet servers that support documents formatted in HTML and related protocols. The Web can be accessed using Gopher, FTP, HTTP, telnet, Usenet, WAIS, and other tools.

# Z

**ZIF (Zero Insertion Force) Socket**    A socket for CPUs that enables insertion of a chip without much pressure. Intel promoted the ZIF socket with its overdrive upgrades. The chip is dropped into the socket's holes and a small lever is flipped to lock them in. Somewhat replaced in modern motherboards by Slot 1 and Slot A architecture, but still in style in Super Socket 7, Socket A, and Socket 370 motherboards.

# Index

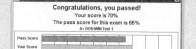

# INTERNATIONAL CONTACT INFORMATION

**AUSTRALIA**
McGraw-Hill Book Company
Australia Pty. Ltd.
TEL +61-2-9900-1800
FAX +61-2-9878-8881
http://www.mcgraw-hill.com.au
books-it_sydney@mcgraw-hill.com

**CANADA**
McGraw-Hill Ryerson Ltd.
TEL +905-430-5000
FAX +905-430-5020
http://www.mcgraw-hill.ca

**GREECE, MIDDLE EAST, & AFRICA**
**(Excluding South Africa)**
McGraw-Hill Hellas
TEL +30-210-6560-990
TEL +30-210-6560-993
TEL +30-210-6560-994
FAX +30-210-6545-525

**MEXICO (Also serving Latin America)**
McGraw-Hill Interamericana Editores
S.A. de C.V.
TEL +525-1500-5108
FAX +525-117-1589
http://www.mcgraw-hill.com.mx
carlos_ruiz@mcgraw-hill.com

**SINGAPORE (Serving Asia)**
McGraw-Hill Book Company
TEL +65-6863-1580
FAX +65-6862-3354
http://www.mcgraw-hill.com.sg
mghasia@mcgraw-hill.com

**SOUTH AFRICA**
McGraw-Hill South Africa
TEL +27-11-622-7512
FAX +27-11-622-9045
robyn_swanepoel@mcgraw-hill.com

**SPAIN**
McGraw-Hill/
Interamericana de España, S.A.U.
TEL +34-91-180-3000
FAX +34-91-372-8513
http://www.mcgraw-hill.es
professional@mcgraw-hill.es

**UNITED KINGDOM, NORTHERN,**
**EASTERN, & CENTRAL EUROPE**
McGraw-Hill Education Europe
TEL +44-1-628-502500
FAX +44-1-628-770224
http://www.mcgraw-hill.co.uk
emea_queries@mcgraw-hill.com

**ALL OTHER INQUIRIES Contact:**
McGraw-Hill/Osborne
TEL +1-510-420-7700
FAX +1-510-420-7703
http://www.osborne.com
omg_international@mcgraw-hill.com